The Presenting Past
An introduction to practical psychodynamic counselling

THE PRESENTING PAST

An introduction to practical-
psycho dynamic counselling

Michael Jacobs

Department of Adult Education, University of Leicester

Open University Press
Milton Keynes · Philadelphia

Open University Press
Celtic Court
22 Ballmoor
Buckingham
MK18 1XW

and
1900 Frost Road, Suite 101
Bristol, PA19007, USA

First published 1985
Reprinted 1988, 1989, 1990, 1991

British Library Cataloguing in Publication Data

Jacobs, Michael, *1941–*
    The presenting past : an introduction to
    practical psychodynamic counselling.
    1. Psychotherapy
    I. Title
    616.89'14   RC480

    ISBN 0 335 09815 0

Typeset by Burns & Smith Ltd, Derby

Printed and bound by
Butler & Tanner Ltd, Frome and London.

'It's in vain, Trot, to recall the past, unless
it works some influence upon the present.'

Charles Dickens   *David Copperfield*

Time present and time past
Are both perhaps present in time future,
And time future contained in time past

T. S. Eliot 'Burnt Norton', in *Four Quartets*

CONTENTS

. . . AND VARIATIONS

PREFACE

Without two groups of people this book would not have been possible. The first consists of those clients with whom I have worked over 12 years, who have provided confirmation (at times) and the necessity of refinement (at other times) of analytic theory. Should any of them, despite my disguises, recognize themselves, or parts of themselves which today are hopefully less troublesome than once they were, let me reassure them that their identity remains known only to me. And I can only thank them for all they have taught and given me.

The second group consists of the students at Vaughan College Leicester, who by their questions, their confusions, and their wish for material to be relevant to their helping work, have forced me to clarify what I mean when I use terms used in analytic theory. So often in teaching it is the teacher who learns most. Apart from the lecture material which my colleague Alan Lilley and I have given, our classes have studied Lowe's *Growth of Personality* and Rayner's *Human Development*. The influence of both will be obvious (and I hope acknowledged) in various places in the text. Since Eric Rayner was at one time my own therapist, his influence will no doubt be more extensive than even I have realized. Yet Lowe lacks illustrations of counselling situations, and Rayner's ideas, although thought-provoking, are frequently so terse that their relevance to counselling can easily be missed. I hope I have been able to provide a ready-reference for counsellors which draws together, and supplements, longer and more detailed texts recommended in counselling training, and that in doing so I may help establish the relevance of analytic theory for those who are tempted to rely on the here-and-now alone.

Others, past and present, have been important in my own development: different generations of my own family have helped mould me, and present friends, especially Denis Rice, and Simon and Mary Phipps, have positively encouraged my teaching and writing. All these people illustrate for me the significance of my theme, and my hope is that they will share in anything of merit found in these pages.

Michael Jacobs
Leicester 1985

KEY

'Psychodynamic' refers in this context to the theories of Freud and post-Freudians, that there is a lively relationship between different aspects of the personality, formed through past and present relationships between the growing individual and significant others, and thereafter consciously and unconsciously influencing relationships with the 'internal world' of the mind, and with the external world of persons and objects.

All writers referred to in the main text are listed in the bibliography. Where more than one work by the same author is listed, the date of publication is included in the main text (e.g. Winnicott 1965).

All references in square brackets [   ] are to other sections of the main text which are considered of direct relevance to the stage under discussion.

With constant references to the first three stages of development, abbreviations for these stages are used throughout. It will become obvious that I do not limit development to pleasurable physical zones (oral, anal and genital), preferring with the post-Freudians to stress the importance of relationship styles at each stage. If I appear to have retained Freudian stages in the abbreviations, in fact I intend:

O.S.　to stand for Oral/Dependency/Trust Stage;

A.S.　to stand for Anal/Authority/Autonomy Stage;

G.S.　to stand for Genital (Sexual)/Oedipal/Rivalry/Social Stage.

I intend no sexist implication in referring to boys and girls, men and women as 'he', although where gender differences are important I have used 'he' and 'she'. I recognize that any writer is limited in insight by virtue of her or his own gender, but use 'he' and 'she' interchangeably of the counsellor, hoping that such apparent textual inconsistency at least obviates conscious sexism.

Erikson's 'Eight Ages of Man' (adapted)

Age	Oral	Muscular-anal	Locomotor-genital	Latency	Adolescence	Early adulthood	Adulthood	Maturity
Basic Virtues	Drive/ Hope	Self-control Willpower	Direction Purpose	Method Competence	Devotion Fidelity	Affiliation Love	Production Care	Renunciation Wisdom
Relevance for Society	Faith 'Religion'	Law and justice	Importance of role	Technolog- ical ethos	Ideology Aristocracy	'Utopia of genitality'	Productivity Creativity	Followership Leadership
	Basic trust vs mistrust	Autonomy vs shame, doubt	Initiative vs guilt	Industry vs inferiority	Identity vs role confusion	Intimacy vs isolation	Generativity vs stagnation	Integrity vs despair

Sexual identity

Autonomy from parents, economic independence

Ideas, beliefs sense of meaning

PRELUDE

· 1 ·

INTRODUCTION

In recent years, 'listening' has become fashionable, and 'counselling' has acquired a popular appeal. Many helpers, paid or voluntary, are learning the technical skills of the professional therapist or counsellor, and there is no doubt that some are able to apply those skills to good effect. They enable their 'clients' to speak more freely and openly about themselves and their concerns. Their training has taught them about the value of silent attention, of responding sensitively, and, above all, of accepting the other.

Good listening and responding are essential. I have written elsewhere of techniques which can enhance natural empathy and awareness (Jacobs 1982; 1985). This present work assumes prior training in the various ways of enabling clients to express themselves. At the same time, I am aware that there is more to counselling than technical expertise, and becoming an accepting person. The counsellor (a term I use of paid and unpaid, full-time and part-time counsellors, together with those who use counselling as part of their work) also wishes to understand the significance of the client's words and feelings. I suggested in my first book that the question 'why?' is not generally a helpful one to ask. If people knew the answers to such questions as 'why do I feel this way?' or 'why do these things always happen to me?', they would probably have less need of the skilled helper. Yet the questions are not invalid: counselling often involves more than helping people to unburden themselves. It may also help them to understand their situation, setting present troubles in a wider context, and sometimes preparing them to meet future recurrences of similar feelings. Answers to the question 'why?' are found through counselling, though seldom in the first meeting.

Such answers are not possible without some knowledge of the personal history of the client in particular, and of human development and relationships in general. Some of this knowledge is already in the life experience of the counsellor. As a fellow human being, she knows something about work, love and play, knows what it is to be irritable, jealous, tired or fed up; she probably knows directly, or through her relationships with others, some of the life 'crises' through which most people pass. She understands that being upset following a loss is natural, that to feel anxious when faced with illness is a normal reaction. She is able to draw upon the accumulated experience of her own life and of the lives of others known in friendship, family and in helping work. She may draw upon the human drama which forms the substance of novels, plays and films. In all these ways she acquires knowledge to help the client accept what is happening, and to understand it more fully. Life experience cannot be overvalued. I remember a client telling me that she wanted to help others but that she only had a degree in English, and not in psychology. I replied that the degree which she had, together with the experience she had been through, were just as valuable, if not more so for the work that she had in mind, as much of the psychology taught in our universities.

I do not deny the value of some approaches in psychology. Developmental psychology — the study of the growth of the person from birth to death — has obvious relevance. When faced with such a universal experience as bereavement, many studies of the process of grief certainly enrich the counsellor's expertise. Knowing that in bereavement a person often passes through a number of stages [Bereavement, p. 199] the counsellor is more able to understand the grieving client. Should such a person say, a few days after a traumatic loss, 'I can't believe it. I should be feeling so much more upset than I am', the counsellor can give the reassurance that this is normal. Knowing that one is 'normal' often makes pain a little easier to bear. Similarly, should a person have been unable to grieve (the adolescent, for example, who has to remain strong to support the remaining parent), but two years later shows every sign of being depressed, a counsellor can explore the suppression of grief and test out the possibility that present feelings are related to those earlier unexpressed feelings.

The example is obvious, and counsellors no doubt already use such book-knowledge as well as their own life experiences. There is, however, a large area of one approach to developmental psychology of which some counsellors are less aware; or, if they know it, do not know how to apply it in the actual counselling session. Early development in particular is in danger of simply remaining academic knowledge. It is not surprising that this should be so. Although we frequently have vivid (if partial) memories of later childhood and adolescence, early experience is less easy to remember. Even if some events are vividly recalled, their significance to us, and their impact on our subsequent development is less clear. Yet, if in our counselling there is the implicit assumption that the present can influence and change the future (or at least the impact of the future), it is equally possible that the past will likewise be influencing the present for good or ill. Knowledge of the past, and the skill to apply that knowledge, are therefore important tools for the counsellor to possess. Many clients already have an awareness of the influence of the past. For some it is the immediate past which helps them understand their present mood. In others there is a readiness to look even further back — I do not mean in a facetious way, such as 'I'm only this way because I was dropped on my head as a baby' – in a serious endeavour to connect and make sense of life experience at different stages. For example:

> Alice spoke of her husband's unhappiness in his job, and the resentment he seemed to have of her own job. Her job was new and satisfying to her, bringing a sense of independence. She seemed to understand her husband's difficulties, saying that he had always been very close to his mother. Her work threatened to come between the two of them. This led Alice on to talk about her own parents, and her difficulty separating herself in adolescence from the façade of 'doing things together' which the family put up. She found herself talking about her father's dissatisfaction with his job at that time, and suddenly recognized parallels between past and present situations. She had become aware of another element in the current situation which was troubling her.

Experience suggests, and I hope the brief examples in this book will confirm it, that knowledge of the client's past enables the client or the counsellor to make links to the present position. The view of development taken here is that unfinished business and unresolved issues from the past can have a damaging effect on living in the present, just as by contrast satisfactory resolution in the present facilitates negotiation of the future. Counselling is one way of opening up the past in a safe environment so that it can be faced, renegotiated and in some respects even relived 'but with a new ending' (Alexander et al. 1946).

Counsellors accumulate information about the client's past from the stories which the client tells, and from the questions which they can ask him. But the past is also to be seen actively working in the present. My aim is to outline facets of every stage of development, together with the ways in which the past can be seen working, reflected in the present. To do this I use throughout the twin hypotheses of psychoanalytic therapy: firstly, that the difficulties which the client brings to counselling represent a repetition, sometimes in a different form, of former conflicts, which analysts call 'the return of the repressed'; secondly, that in the relationship style(s) which the client adopts towards the counsellor there are signs of past relationships, which analysts call 'transference'.

To do this in a practical way (this is, I hope, a book to be used, and not just to be read) a simple model helps — a 'map' of personal development which guides us through the successive stages, one which isolates the tasks that begin to be mastered at each age (trust, autonomy, coping with rivalry, etc.), and which identifies the major emotions that people contend with in and between themselves (love, anger, jealousy, etc.). The model which I find most useful is Erikson's *Eight Ages of Man* (Erikson 1965) [see the chart, p. xiii]. I have adapted it to underline (as Erikson's own work does) the significance of adolescence. This model is not an absolute plan, nor a Platonic Ideal against which to measure all human development; neither can it cover every eventuality in counselling. It is more like a model used in the design of a large-scale project, a way of testing out what the client brings, to see if it fits. It provides a number of convenient pegs with which to map out an individual's development. It is a framework into which it is possible to integrate — at different points — the work and insights of many other analysts as well as Erikson. Those who know them will recognize aspects of Sigmund Freud, Anna Freud, Melanie Klein, Fairbairn, Winnicott, Guntrip and others. (For further study of the models used by these analysts see Guntrip 1961.) I am obviously indebted to these major figures, yet in disclaiming much originality on my own part I am reminded of some words from Winnicott (1965b): 'It is more difficult for an analyst to be original than for anyone else, because everything we say truly has been taught us yesterday (i.e. by patients).' The most original material in these pages will also be that which has come from clients, which I use as examples and concrete illustration. It is, as every major analyst testifies, from our clients that we learn most. The skilled counsellor constantly draws upon his experience of clients' lives and stories, as in supervision he draws upon the supervisor's wealth of experience. Theory only serves us well if it serves the client, and it is primarily clients who make theory, and not theory that makes therapy.

The examples used in this book may give the impression that the interpretations are obvious, and brought instant insight. In fact, because they are essentially illustrations of the themes, they do not reflect within them the time taken to listen, to formulate, and to test out understanding which is inevitably necessary; nor do they reflect the time that it often takes for new insights to be worked through by the client, sometimes week after week, before they begin to take effect. Counselling is seldom as slick as these condensed examples would appear to suggest.

The section 'Themes' concentrates upon the early stages of infancy and childhood. These are not only basic for all later development (whether successfully or unsuccessfully negotiated), but are also those areas of knowledge less practically applied by counsellors. The Erikson model is progressive. It can be compared to a tower of children's wooden building bricks. As long as each brick is placed squarely upon the one below, and the first one has a firm foundation, the tower grows in a stable way. Using Erikson's terms, where sufficient trust is achieved in the first stage, built upon the foundation of the relationship with mother, it forms a strong base upon which to build autonomy in the second stage. Upon autonomy is built the capacity for initiative, and so on. Staying with this image, if the bricks are not set squarely upon each other, the tower grows but with inbuilt weaknesses. There comes a point at which the stress of external circumstances, or internal pressures, causes the structure to collapse — however squarely the upper bricks have been placed on top of the one which is not well aligned. When such a tower falls, it normally falls only as far as the badly placed brick. It seldom takes the lower, stable bricks with it. So it is in a human crisis. Where the weight of later stresses in adult life, external or internal, impose impossible strain, collapse or breakdown frequently goes back as far as that stage at which issues were not satisfactorily resolved. This is known technically as 'regression' (movement back), and was compared by Freud to an army needing to retreat to its first secure base. Pursuing the image once there we can rebuild, regroup or renegotiate earlier issues which were not favourably dealt with in earlier times. Counselling is one way of enabling this process to take place.

Such a model of progressive stages has its weaknesses. For instance, it appears to imply that once a stage has been negotiated satisfactorily the basic strengths are acquired once and for all. This is plainly not so. Trust, the issue in the first stage, is built up throughout life, and changes its characteristics at different stages. The blind trust of the baby is not suitable in the second stage, where increased mobility means learning *not* to trust dangerous situations and objects — fires, stairs, etc. Parents of the second-stage child need to learn a new kind of trust which is careful but not over-cautious. The strengths which form the major part of each stage continue to develop throughout life, in the new circumstances constantly presented to each individual. Erikson himself recognized this, and stated in a footnote (1965, p. 265): 'The assumption that at each stage a goodness is achieved which is impervious to new inner conflicts and to changing conditions is, I believe, a projection on child development of that success ideology which can so dangerously pervade our private and public daydreams.'

This weakness can be overcome if we see our 'tower' more as a spiral staircase, so introducing a cyclical element into that of progression. It also increases the stresses in the structure, but that is also true to life. Issues in early life are reintroduced in the normal process of living, particularly in those crises of adult life through which nearly every person has to pass. Erikson already allows for such a cyclical element in his famous remark about the final stage: 'Where adults have integrity enough not to fear death their children will not fear life' (1965, p.261). It is also evident in adolescence, where others before me have shown how issues from early childhood are thrown into the melting pot, although I have drawn out the significance of this for the stages of adult life in a way which I think is new.

It is not only in adolescence that this happens. In the section 'Variations' we shall see the themes reworked at every stage. My concern in those shorter chapters is to refer back to the earlier stages rather than dwell on the current issues, since current concerns are known well enough to counsellors from their own experience. In addition to the cross-referencing in the text, summaries of the major points from the early stages will be found in the Appendix, to facilitate location of the material either spoken by the client, or perceived in the client's problems or in the client's relationship with the counsellor.

How theory can be used in practice

As I suggest in the next chapter, there is some danger in possessing theoretical knowledge alone, because it can be applied indiscriminately. One of the misconceptions about psychoanalysis is that all analysts make standard interpretations of the images and symbols used by their patients. It is true that at times it seems that Freud equates all dream symbols with representations of the sexual organs; and Melanie Klein in some of her case histories appears to make what can only be called leading interpretations. Yet such examples do not give a fair picture. In reply to such criticisms, Freud himself writes: 'Whatever in the doctor's conjectures is inaccurate drops out in the course of the analysis; it has to be withdrawn and replaced by something more correct' (Freud 1963, p.505). Furthermore, there would have been no development of analytic theory in directions which are far from Freud's initial hypotheses were it not for analysts listening more comprehensively to their patients. Analytic literature contains frequent references to present uncertainty and tenuous understanding, which qualify what might otherwise appear to be definitive statements. Because analysts tend to write for other analysts, they usually frame what they have to say in learned jargon, and they often fail to give us a true picture of the give-and-take of the consulting room. Despite going on to write a highly technical book on groups, the French analyst Anzieu underlines in his opening pages that 'in everyday practice . . . [the analyst] expresses himself as much as possible in everyday language' (1984, p.4). That language, of course, should be the client's own language.

If one danger of book knowledge lies in wild interpretation, the reader may also wonder how to relate theory both to what the client says, and to the relationship experienced by client and counsellor. Since clients in counselling do not always speak of the past, and few speak of the long-distant past, how can knowledge of psychodynamic development be applied in everyday practice? How might the reader *use* this book in the 'here-and-now'?

In the first place, the Appendix has a more important function than its name would appear to suggest. It is more than an optional extra. It is intended to summarize the substance of the text. In it the reader will find listed many of the difficulties that clients describe, as well as pointers to the type of relationship the client openly seeks from the counsellor or which the counsellor more intuitively feels to be present. These two sections in each of the three thematic stages contain signs, hints and even obvious indications of themes related to the past coming to light in the present. They also comprise two points of what is known as 'the triangle of insight'.

The triangle of insight describes a type of interpretation open to the counsellor, which links the client's past with the client's relationships to others currently, both outside and inside the counselling room. Making links between a client's current relationships and the relationship with the counsellor is not at all uncommon in much counselling practice. A Rogerian counsellor, for instance, will think nothing of taking up a remark such as 'I run out of things to say to people' with the reflection, and what I would call interpretation: 'And you're looking rather uncomfortable here, as if that's happening with me too.' (I think there is a similar interchange in the film made by Rogers, *Three Approaches to Psychotherapy (II)* — *Kathy. Part 1*. This is available for hire from AVA Unit, BAC, 37a Sheep Street, Rugby CV21 3BX.)

The psychodynamic school of counselling also uses this technique, linking two points of the triangle — out there and in here. Yet it goes further and uses the third point, 'back there' — the past. This can only be done when the client has already described memories of past events or past relationships. This third point can be linked to 'out there' or 'in here' or to both. Here are some examples:

> 'You say you become very anxious when things in your room are out of place: that reminds me of you saying that your mother was always anxious about tidiness at home.'
>
> 'You say your mother was always anxious that everything should be kept tidy at home. I wonder whether you wish I could order everything for you here, because you appear anxious that I can't give you a neat answer.'

The complete triangle would conflate both these remarks; other examples of three-sided links are:

> 'You were very open two weeks ago when you said you had a crush on me, but today you are wanting to give up counselling. I wonder if there's any connection between your worry about feelings here, and what you've said about relating to other men; you say you run if they get too close. Perhaps that is also like your close relationship to your father in childhood, but which became distant at puberty. Perhaps you worry whether sexual feelings can be kept under control?'
>
> 'You seem to want to argue quite strongly with things that I say: of course I may be wrong, but I feel you're doing to me what you've done with other men who have some authority over you. Now I know you say your father has always been a very weak man, but you've also said you could cheerfully hit him.'

The objection can be raised that such links to the past appear to be superfluous: what do they add to the current link that is likely to change the client's situation or behaviour? We do have to be careful not to parade gratuitous intellectual information simply to make a neat interpretation, or to show prowess. However, good, pertinent intellectual knowledge can also have an emotional impact, as when scientific facts lead to wonder, or explanations to a sense of personal satisfaction, of loose ends being tied. Understanding can even carry with it a sense of relief. In fact understanding is one of the elements of a psychodynamic view of personality. Alongside the more usual desires that are described in analytic literature, the group analyst W.R. Bion posits another one: the desire to *know*. Such a phrase is a considerable advance on the somewhat restricted Freudian expression 'infantile sexual curiosity', and is a refinement of what Melanie Klein calls the 'epistemophilic drive' (see Anzieu 1984). If there is indeed in human beings a desire to know and understand, then that understanding must surely extend to knowing themselves, and what has made them as they are.

The wish to understand is sometimes only achieved through and after a period of painful insight. Many prefer the more immediate pleasure of alternative comforts, or of shutting the mind, as a defence against such pain. It is therefore quite possible that the counsellor who only sees his role as one of providing positive regard, warmth and support, colludes with that defence. Encouraging the wish to understand, often through the pain of insight, is an important aim in counselling, which this book endeavours to address.

Such depth of understanding does not come from clever interpretations. Linking in the past will only produce relief and response when it is relevant to a client's current experience, outside the counselling room, or present within it. Nor is it likely that such understanding *of itself* will alter behaviour or attitudes. The relationship between the counsellor and the client can provide a way of re-experiencing old patterns; not just by substituting good parenting for what was *felt* as bad, nor just by providing favourable conditions in which a person may grow. The counsellor also mirrors what was felt to be less than ideal parenting: like the absent or preoccupied mother she is not always there, and is not constantly on tap; like the parent who inadvertently fails to give reassurance, he does not give orders and instructions; like the controlling parent he sets limits (times of sessions) and rules (e.g. no acting out here) either explicitly or implicitly; like the 'oedipal' parent she is not available as a partner with whom the client can make a permanent relationship. Many counsellors are unaware of the way in which *negative* experiences from the past are also re-lived in the relationship betwen themselves and their clients, and so do not make as constructive a re-learning from them as they might otherwise do.

All this may lead to the impression that renegotiating the past through re-living aspects of it in the present, in order to adapt better in the future, necessitates knowing the details of a client's personal history. That helps of course, but in counselling a history is not always sought as it is in a psychiatric interview or a clinical psychologist's assessment. Knowing what *generally* applies in human development can often be used without necessarily having confirmatory evidence from a particular client of past events. The present frequently provides clues which enable the present to be understood, in the light of the imagery which is associated with earlier development. An example will illustrate the point:

Melanie presents two problems when she first visits the counsellor. The first is that she is binge-eating, and making herself ill. The second is that her husband has left her, but she cannot get from him any confirmation of his intentions: he is unwilling to pronounce the relationship finished, but he will not return to her permanently.

Melanie says little about her childhood and adolescence — certainly not enough to help the past to be linked to the present. What she does describe, very fully, is her present behaviour and feeling, and what she says enables the counsellor to make what are initially tentative links to the oral stage — as we might expect from a symptom connected with eating. He begins to use the language of the oral stage to see if this throws light upon her present condition. She tells him, for instance, how she desperately wants her husband to return so that she can have a baby to give her love to; but it would be sufficient for him to return long enough for her to become pregnant; she does not wish to have a baby to tie him to her. She describes their relationship when they were together, as one where she mothered him so much, doing everything for him, that he began to feel hemmed in and dependent.

So the counsellor wonders (aloud) whether she needs to give love so much because she in fact *needs* love so much: she projects the unloved self into her husband, or the wished-for baby. She is empty inside, and she tries to fill this void by eating, now that her husband is away, and when she has no baby to feed and look after. Melanie reacts to this interpretation with real understanding; and the understanding appears to be translated into changed behaviour, because from that time onwards she develops the imagery herself, and tells how she is beginning to make more appropriate demands upon her husband: she asks him where she stands, they start to sort out money problems, and they both begin to accept responsibility for some of the domestic issues. Melanie starts to make legitimate demands for herself, rather than to act out demands through oblique, obscure, unsatisfying and potentially damaging means. Her eating steadily comes under control, and she talks of beginning to feel a sense of self once more; it is as yet a shadowy self, but she feels she has more substance. Whereas before, she now says, she lived from point to point through each day — breakfast to lunch, lunch to tea, supper to bed (note the three- to four-hour span so reminiscent of early feeding patterns) — she is now able to look and plan further ahead. Whereas before her arms and legs seemed all over the place and not to belong to her (what an image of the baby's flailing limbs!) she is beginning to come together.

Within the counselling relationship the counsellor recognizes similar signs of her demanding nature: she talks very freely, but at such speed and length that it is often impossible for him to get a word in edgeways, and it is difficult to bring the session to a close. We might think that because he has to say very little the session is a relatively easy one; but he wishes he could say a little more than he does, and actually feels quite drained at the end of each of their meetings. He considers it inappropriate in what is only a short series of meetings to use this counter-transference feeling: if he feels drained it appears to be that Melanie is feeding off his presence and his time, but is building herself up in a way which no amount of physical eating could achieve.

In this example the oral stage provided a way of understanding a considerable amount about this client's dynamics. The counsellor did not know, and may never know, whether Melanie was, or felt, starved of love during her infancy, and it did not matter, except as an academic point, whether she was or not. What helped the counsellor, and consequently the client, was the understanding that came from his knowledge of the issues around feeding, emptiness, making demands, boundaries, etc. He was able to reflect back to her aspects of how she might feel, which she could accept, and which provided her with a different way of looking at herself, on a deeper level than the surface problems which up to that time had predominated. Had there been any knowledge of her past, especially her infancy, which confirmed his impressions, he might have added some tentative explanation to his description of her present responses to significant others.

It so happens that in this example, the oral imagery is more obvious than the imagery from other stages, although it would be possible to speak in A.S. terms. [See the key on p. xii for abbreviations.] Melanie liked to organize her husband, while he was a more disorganized person who needed to break free from her oppressive control. She liked to keep people happy by saying what she felt they wanted to hear, and so was unable to be assertive and autonomous. She dressed very neatly, even when she would have otherwise preferred to wear casual clothes, as if she had to look perfect for any casual visitor who might come unannounced. Her rapid delivery in the counselling session might have been a way of keeping the counsellor in his place, controlling how much he was permitted to say. There was some confirmatory evidence of A.S. material from her descriptions of her parents. Her mother was very controlled about showing feelings, particularly those she felt others might criticize, and her father appeared to have been strict with the children. While the A.S. imagery is there, the predominating O.S. imagery appears to indicate that Melanie had regressed from being controlled and controlling when she was with her husband, to an earlier stage, out of control and unable to make appropriate demands when he left her.

There is even less that points to the G.S., although Melanie's husband left her initially for another woman. While this is clearly a three-person situation, typical of problems related to that stage, it stands alone, and G.S. imagery has little practical use in this case, at least to the point the counselling reached. In other clients, A.S. or G.S. material is more obvious than O.S. imagery, and in many there is a combination of two or three of the stages which will be described in the 'Themes' of this book. The counsellor will avoid confusion in his own mind, and for the client, if he listens carefully for the predominating theme in each session, and addresses his remarks and interpretations to one level at a time.

The 'Themes' which follow thus present the raw material from which formulations might be made, together with illustrations of childhood developmental stages as seen in adult clients. To complete the Appendix there are sections on the counsellor's task, related to each stage, and suggestions of what makes for satisfactory and mature develop-ment — the aim of counselling. Terms like 'maturity' and 'satisfactory' are of course relative. They are definitions which are bound by time and culture, and even by the value system of one particular sub-culture, or one person, the author, within it. I do not expect every reader to agree with all that is contained there. Each counsellor has a value system, even if some pretend otherwise. The reader will wish to refine and amend the map in the light of his or her own experience and philosophy. It is the principle that remains the same, that to have a map, and to know one's way through psychodynamic development, is an important tool for both the counsellor, and for the client. I argue in the next chapter that each client must be treated as a unique individual, and clearly each counsellor needs to develop an individual view of what constitutes maturity. Psychodynamic theory helps the development and clarification of such a view, and can indeed be translated into the everyday practice of the counsellor.

References

Alexander F. and French T.M. (1946) *Psychoanalytic Therapy*, Ronald Press, New York.

Anzieu D. (1984) *The Group and the Unconscious*, Routledge & Kegan Paul, London.

Erikson E. (1965) *Childhood and Society*, Penguin, Harmondsworth.

Freud S. (1963) *Introductory Lectures on Psychoanalysis*, Hogarth Press, London.

Guntrip H. (1961) *Personality Structure and Human Interaction*, Hogarth Press, London.

Jacobs M. (1982) *Still Small Voice*, S.P.C.K., London.

Jacobs M. (1985) *Swift to Hear*, S.P.C.K., London.

Winnicott D.W. (1965b) *The Maturational Processes and the Facilitating Environment*, Hogarth Press, London.

· 2 ·

THE NATURE AND APPLICATION OF THEORY

A young woman was referred by her doctor for counselling because she was sleeping badly. Over recent weeks Brenda had had a series of dreams of a most macabre nature which terrified her so much she was afraid to go to sleep. The counsellor asked her to describe them, and she told of one which stood out as particularly horrific. She had dreamed that her grandmother was hanging on to the mummified corpse of an old aunt, who had died three years previously. In the dream Brenda had gone upstairs to say goodnight to her grandmother, and she had to take the body out from under the bed, and to lay it alongside her grandmother.

The other dreams were also about people who were dead. The counsellor observed that the worst dream seemed to centre on an image of the difficulties of letting go of someone who had died. He pointed out to Brenda that she had said in passing that her own mother found it difficult to let her go and become independent. Perhaps Brenda shared some of these anxieties? His observation seemed to bring relief to Brenda, not least because it made some sense of the dream, and when she left the first session she was less fearful of another nightmare; indeed she was interested in what subsequent dreams might themselves reveal. The following week Brenda described a dream she had had on the night after the first session. She had dreamed of a schoolfriend dying, but of writing a letter to her telling her not to be afraid. It was felt to be a healing dream, and she had found herself able to sleep better now that she had realized that dreams were not necessarily literal statements, but symbolic of current feelings.

Why should this dream have been about Brenda and her mother? We cannot be sure that it was, since there is no objective way of interpreting its meaning. We can say that the counsellor was aware of the dream images falling into place as the client talked more openly. We can also say that his interpretation helped her to get in touch with feelings which were less obvious to her conscious self than they seemed to the counsellor. He had been able to draw on his knowledge of what some young people feel at the stage of breaking away from an anxious parent.

If later stages of life receive ample confirmation from observation and experience, the same cannot be said so convincingly of the earliest years, of which we have little or no memory. Even the observation of little children brings us no closer to their thoughts or less obvious feelings, because they have few, if any, words with which to express them. Adults also experience the difficulty of describing subtleties of feeling if their command of language is poor. When working through the section 'Themes' the reader will legitimately ask on what evidence analysts can make the statements they do, when there is only adult language to describe children's phantasies and emotions.

Indeed it has even been questioned whether psychotherapy, and by implication counselling, is an art or a science. People tell stories about their lives; they describe their thoughts and feelings; they communicate experiences. Yet this is not the raw material of scientific theory. There is certainly much that is akin to art in counselling — art meaning more than a skill or set of skills. In other contexts the stories told could form the basis of a novel, a poem or drama. D.M. Thomas (1981) in the preface to *The White Hotel*, goes so far as to say of Freud's writings that they are 'masterly works of literature, apart from anything else'. His own fictitious case-history, ascribed to Freud in the novel, is itself a masterly pastiche of psychoanalytic writing, which reflects with great accuracy Freud's own fascinating explanation of dream imagery and of free association. Furthermore, it illustrates how coterminous are the boundaries of the art and the science of psychoanalysis. Thomas goes on in his preface to describe Freud as

> the discoverer of the great and beautiful modern myth of psychoanalysis. By myth I mean a poetic, dramatic expression of a hidden truth: and in placing this emphasis I do not intend to put into question the scientific validity of psychoanalysis.

Myth seeks to express truth, even if it is not a scientific explanation. The images portrayed in the arts and language, which is the vehicle of communication in the literary arts, as well as the means of interpreting visual arts and music, all attempt to give substance to truth, even if it is of a

different order from scientific hypothesis. Language and imagery also lie at
the centre of most counselling methods. As the counsellor listens to the
language and imagery by which people tell their personal stories, she is
often able to identify allusions and connections within the material. Each
person has a unique story to tell, with both idiosyncratic and shared images
with which to illustrate it. The counsellor does more than help the client to
speak the story. She also helps the client to clarify the images. For the
counsellor it is not unlike reading a poem or a novel, and then asking what
the author is trying to convey of the way he sees the world, or this
dilemma, or that relationship, or what the author is trying to express of his
own mind, thoughts and emotions. The similarity between such literary
criticism and psychoanalysis is no doubt one of the reasons why the early
analysts found it difficult to resist analyzing the life and work of artists and
writers, and the great religious myths — a feature of Freud's work, but *par
excellence* seen in Jung's fascination with the art, artefacts and myths of
our own and of other cultures.

Both art and the extensive use of language are unique to our own
species, and yet still remain at times crude and approximate means with
which to express the inexpressible. How can we communicate infancy, for
instance, when there are no words for babies to attach to their experience?
We have adult words only, rough tools with which to describe or explain
the thoughts and feelings of infants. Images, often based upon the most
obvious levels of experience (the physical), have to suffice. The reader
may want to question those images, perhaps at times substituting others;
but remember that language is symbolic, and should not be taken too
literally. Metaphor and simile are a common feature of everyday speech,
but neither is intended to be taken literally. Metaphor and simile are also
ever present in counselling: 'it feels like . . .', 'it is as if . . .'. Part of the art of
counselling consists of the ability to build upon such images, to take up the
client's phrases, to speak their language. For example, the client says, 'It
feels as if I'm drifting through life.' The counsellor replies, having heard
much more than this, 'Drifting . . . but drifting on an undercurrent of what
others have always told you to be doing'.

Many of us are fascinated by symbols and images, and even enjoy
playing with words. Perhaps that in itself indicates how they stand for
feelings and thoughts which run deep within us, helping us to make sense
of our experience. Each person has his or her own imagery, as each has a
unique experience of growing and living; but certain symbols seem to have
universal appeal: light and dark, the circle, the pillar, the mountain, etc.

Since many of these universal images are borrowed from the natural world it would suggest the importance of the external environment, traces of those times, not so long ago, when the species was often at the mercy of elemental forces. Psychoanalysts go further and suggest that such powerful images also describe our internal world, that they are attempts to express what is going on within us. Rayner argues that many of the metaphors and symbols are not chance imagery, but linked to childhood phantasy. He gives examples of such phantasy in everyday speech, such as oral stage phrases like: 'I've bitten off more than I can chew', 'She's a sweet girl', and 'The team was hungry for goals' (1978, p. 37).

It is therefore clear that in counselling, in assisting people to express themselves, and in helping to interpret what is expressed, there is much to be said for the phrase 'the art of psychotherapy', which is the title of one of Anthony Storr's books (1979). By contrast D. H. Malan (1979) calls one of his *Individual Psychotherapy and the Science of Psychodynamics*. He is not alone in calling psychotherapy a science. How far is such a claim justifiable? Behavioural therapists certainly question the scientific basis of psychodynamic therapy.

The term 'science' conveys different images to different people. Those who are not scientists often endow those who are with more omniscience than scientists would claim. The latter know how fickle scientific explanation can prove to be. Use a word like 'science', and many think only of inviolable laws by which organic and inorganic matter behaves. There is something reassuring about being told that a theory is scientifically demonstrable, even when we are insufficiently knowledgeable to understand the proof ourselves. Yet scientific information ranges from constants like the speed of light, indisputably accepted as 186 282.4 (+ 0.2) miles per second, to information about human beings where the constants are few and the number of variables huge. If we doubt whether it is valid to call psychotherapy a science, we may need to start by questioning our definition of science. One simple definition states that science consists of: observation; the ordering of observations; suggesting an explanation for what is observed; providing information to make such observations capable of repetition and yielding the same results.

Art also starts with observation. It also goes on to order those observations, within the frame of a picture, or in musical or literary form. It is only at that point that art and science begin to diverge. Art tends to *interpret* what is observed, but seldom seeks to *explain* it. If it is to be original, art is not capable of repetition, except by mere copying. Each work of art is unique, with part of its appeal lying in its originality. Even music, which is repeated in performance, is interpreted differently each time, the musician adding his own artistic vision to that of the composer.

The arts and the sciences therefore start from the same position, but separate out in different directions, and so express a different kind of truth. Freud, in common with many educated people of his generation, was educated in both disciplines. The scientist in him seems at times to want to universalize from the particular, which has made it doubly difficult for some to accept his work — the other difficulty being that his theories about the unconscious are, almost by definition, not easily demonstrable. (Hypnosis, even if questionable as a practice, does in fact demonstrate at least two distinct levels of mental activity.) Freud earnestly desired psychoanalysis to be accepted as a science, and his own scientific education is the background against which his early models of the mind need to be understood. Explanations have changed in Freudian writing, just as science from his day to this has undergone radical changes, although many of Freud's *observations* remain valid material with which to construct refined theories. Any scientific discipline which fails to develop soon acquires the characteristics of the myth. So too post-Freudian thought and practice both continue to develop.

The life sciences contain more variables than the material sciences. Psychological and sociological research therefore has limitations, arising from applying research on a small sample to the whole population. This can be seen, for instance, in opinion polls. It is possible to say that given a certain sample of the population on a given date so many thought this and so many thought that, and so many were undecided or refused to reply. We are also informed of the margin of error. The information gathered and analyzed is hedged in qualification, yet it tells us something. It acts as a guide. Likewise we take the information provided by psychologists with some caution. We have to be careful lest information from people of one class, in one culture, at one point in history is taken as universal. Conversion hysteria (paralysis of a limb, or impediment of one of the senses due to psychological conflict) may have been a common enough problem among middle-class women in late nineteenth-century Vienna, and it seems plausible that it was an expression of sexual anxiety. But it is not so common today. The equivalent presenting problem among young middle-class women in Britain today might be anorexia nervosa, in which sexual anxieties also play a part. But other variables are also present: issues of dependency, of control, issues of rivalry, as well as the influence of cultural norms about 'attractiveness'. It can be seen that a person's problems may be located in any part of our scheme. All the information in a book such as this has limitations, but is nonetheless a guide.

As Rayner observes, the helper who is 'case-loaded' pays a price, since

> his ideas are only tested informally through his experience, reading and conversation with others. [His ideas] do not meet the criterion of formal testability in an experimental design which is espoused by the research psychologist (1978, p. 16).

Yet people do have certain common experiences. At the simplest level, all are born, need nurturing for a considerable time, develop physically at roughly the same pace, have certain basic needs, and all age and die. In our own culture the majority of people are brought up by one or two parents, and undergo common experiences dictated by society — such as education to mid-adolescence. They live in a culture which has explicit and implicit values. Yet there are many different responses to these conditions. Each person grows in a unique way.

It is therefore not easy to hold together the approach of the scientist, who attempts to categorize experience and observations, with that of the artist, who wishes to express an individual reaction to common experience. Those who work with 'the living human document', a phrase used in American Clinical Pastoral Education, are aware of a dilemma. It is possible, and sometimes most useful, to categorize the experiences and symptoms of emotional and mental distress, in much the same way as physical illness is described. It is important for a general practitioner to make an accurate diagnosis before prescribing a drug to ensure that it has the desired effects and that it is given in the right dosage. Even helpers who are not medically trained need sufficient skills to be able to assess where a client might need psychiatric or medical help, which they themselves are unable to offer. Diagnosis requires a structure, and a language which will assist communication between the helping professions; a specialized language is part and parcel of every serious discipline.

As an example, the American Diagnostic and Statistical Manual includes the following clinical definition of schizophrenia: a person should show certain symptoms before being diagnosed schizophrenic — delusions of control; somatic or grandiose religious delusions; persecutory or jealous delusions; hearing voices; incoherence, loose association, poverty of speech or illogical speech. Where any of these conditions have been present for at least six months, appeared before the age of forty-five and are not organically based, the diagnosis applies!

So says one specific sub-culture within the American culture, but such signs are interpreted differently in other sections of that culture and in other societies. There appear to be cases where political dissidents have been diagnosed as schizophrenic, while in more primitive societies some of these signs, such as the hearing of voices, are interpreted as a sign of holiness and wisdom. We may therefore validly ask whether Joan of Arc was a saint, a witch, a political dissident or a schizophrenic. Diagnostic structures have their limitations. On the other hand it would be foolish for the counsellor not to have knowledge of extreme mental disorder and of the signs which could indicate a condition which he is not equipped to handle. While there is always danger in labelling, since some people can become metaphorically, if not literally, imprisoned by a label, the ability to structure our assessment of clients assists the counsellor to be alert to those who need specialist help.

Although serious disturbance is mentioned in the chapters which follow, in order to promote such an awareness, the major concern is to provide useful information for working with less seriously ill, but equally unhappy, people. Links and possibilities are suggested to further more extensive understanding. The information is not intended for use as a method of categorizing, nor as a way of putting people in boxes. The danger of any model is that the helper will use it too precisely, and so indulge in an unproductive travesty of true science: the game of labelling. Knowledge must not become a straitjacket.

There is an alternative to labelling which is found in the concept of 'naming', a concept used in Near- and Middle-Eastern cultures and with which we are familiar in the Judaeo-Christian tradition (Jacobs 1976).

Claire introduced the distinction between naming and labelling implicitly. She had been in counselling for several weeks when she opened one session by asking, 'What's wrong with me? Am I a manic-depressive? Am I neurotic? Do I have an anxiety-state?' The counsellor replied that he was not interested in attaching such labels to people. Claire very promptly and rather angrily came back at him, 'Well, if you do, I want a category all to myself.' She came from a very large family, in which she was the middle child. Time and again she had spoken of situations, past and present, where she felt she did not matter. She was left out of invitations to parties, people ignored her, her parents teased her when she showed early signs of intellectual promise and asked perceptive questions which the other children had not. She desperately wanted to be treated as an individual who mattered (yet also felt guilty when she was), and she was prepared to insist on that in any 'diagnosis'.

It is the uniqueness of the individual that is apparent in the ancient idea of naming. Even today in some places in the East it is felt that to give one's true name to another is to surrender power to them. Leslie Weatherhead recalls that Indians serving in British regiments used to keep their real name in a little cylinder around the neck, and would not give their true name to their officers, lest the officers acquired even more power over them (1963, p. 64). I recall a priest, who had been working in Syria more recently, confirming this example from experience of a village where all the men were introduced to him by the same name. He was not permitted to learn their individual names. Weatherhead reminds us that this same concept is present in the familiar New Testament story of the man possessed of devils, where healing depends upon Christ asking his name, which is Legion. It is also seen in the Old Testament myth of the angel who wrestles with Jacob. The angel asks Jacob his name, and he gives it. But Jacob is not permitted in return to learn the name of his adversary.

This ancient idea has been reworked by Ursula Le Guin (1971) in the novel *A Wizard of Earthsea*. In the world of Earthsea everything has a common name, used in everyday speech, but it also has a special secret name. Plants and animals have their secret names in an ancient language, passed down the ages. People on Earthsea are given their true name at a ceremony not unlike baptism, either in infancy or at puberty. Wise men, the magi, can only control people or the natural world when they are able to speak the true name. Therefore, as in Weatherhead's example, you only give your true name to those you trust.

In the novel, the hero Sparrowhawk conjures up a shadow from the dead which nearly destroys him. After he recovers the shadow pursues him. Sparrowhawk tries to flee from it, without success. An old wizard, who had given Sparrowhawk his true name, tells him to stop running, to turn and face the shadow, and to name it. Sparrowhawk protests, 'The evil thing, the shadow that haunts me, has no name.' 'All things have a name', he is told. So Sparrowhawk turns, becoming the pursuer of the shadow whose turn it is to flee, until at the ends of the earth Sparrowhawk names it.

The object of this digest, which does not reveal the twist in the tale, is to emphasize that it is the individual whom we have in mind in the following chapters, should features of normal and abnormal development which are common to many people appear to make everyone the same. The permutations are infinite. With each separate client we need awareness of what is special, perhaps even secret; and to add to our fore-knowledge the knowledge which comes from the client, to help them name what troubles them. 'Labelling' can so easily become the imposition of technical definitions. 'Naming' tries to help people find their own shadows and to name them — a process which the counsellor assists, but does not dictate. In counselling it is not usual to talk about psychodynamic theory, but only about what is close at hand. 'The wise man can only control what is near him, what he can name exactly and wholly' (Le Guin 1971, p. 60). The stories from clients, and the summaries which are included here, are used as illustrations and not as glib blueprints. The developmental model provides a way of finding clues to possibilities which ultimately only the client can confirm or deny.

Human development is not a science with which to blind others, nor can it be used to answer their questions for them. To dole out diagnoses, even if they are accurate, will only temporarily reassure. There will be some occasions when the counsellor can translate common experience into plain words, in order to help the client feel 'normal', but the counsellor is also looking for that which is unique to the experience of each individual; or what seems unique, because learning from one client may, at a later time, throw light upon the problems of another. Ursula Le Guin puts it well when the old wizard says to the young inexperienced and impatient Sparrowhawk:

> When you know the fourfoil in all its seasons, root and leaf and flower, by sight and scent and seed, then you may learn its true name, knowing its being: which is more than its use. What, after all, is the use of you? Or of myself? [. . .] He went on for a half-mile or so, and said at last, 'To hear one must be silent' (1971, p. 29).

If this summary of human development in all its seasons is to have any value, it will not be because of mind-knowledge alone, but because it is integrated with those inner senses of which counsellors are already aware from their initial training. Combining the knowledge of the theorist and the insight of the artist is a delicate skill.

References

Jacobs M. (1976) Naming and Labelling *Contact: Journal of Pastoral Studies,* 1976:3

Le Guin U. (1971) *A Wizard of Earthsea,* Puffin Books (Penguin), Harmondsworth.

Malan D. H. (1979) *Individual Psychotherapy and the Science of Psychodynamics,* Butterworth, London.

Rayner E. (1978) *Human Development* (2nd edn), George Allen and Unwin, London.

Storr A. (1979) *The Art of Psychotherapy,* Secker and Warburg, London.

Thomas D. M. (1981) *The White Hotel,* Penguin, Harmondsworth.

Weatherhead L. (1963) *Psychology, Religion and Healing* (2nd edn revised), Hodder and Stoughton, London.

THEMES...

· 3 ·

TRUST AND DEPENDENCY (OS)

Introduction

If we were to go purely by appearances, it should be relatively easy to describe early human development. When we look at new-born babies, we are tempted to imagine that life is straightforward for them, and that it only gets more complicated with age. Unfortunately for our purposes it is the other way round, although, to be sure, it is not normally until later in life that complications appear. It is a mistake to see babies simply as helpless creatures, unable to do anything for themselves except suckle and sleep. It is true that they appear passively to respond rather than actively to initiate, and that they are largely dependent upon others to feed them and make them comfortable. But parents know that this is not all their baby wants — nurturing includes holding, cuddling, and the primitive communication between parent and child we call 'baby-talk'.

Yet already this is too idealistic a picture. Babies are not always contented, as we see when they screw themselves up in pain and rage — hunger is painful when you have not learned to wait. Far from being passive they are able to express themselves with considerable force; not just when they are hungry, but equally forcefully when refusing attention. Again it is a mother who knows that in the first few months her baby allows her little independence. Our picture is becoming more balanced. Babies are more than sweet, contented little bundles. They are demanding, they do not hide their frustration and discontent, and they make themselves well and truly felt in their immediate environment. Not surprisingly, even if said tongue in cheek, they can be 'little monsters'.

Even then we are still only scratching the surface. The description above represents only a fraction of what is observable both by sensitive mothers and by perceptive child analysts and paediatricians. The information available to us about the earliest months of life has been extended by the close observation given particularly by the latter to babies and mothers; by inference from older children and adults whose phantasies provide clues to infancy; and by attempts to conceptualize the inner experience of the infant. Such information is relevant to counsellors, not only in helping to identify seriously disturbed adults (generally known as psychotic or borderline personalities), but also in providing better understanding of more 'normal' clients.

Personal boundaries

It is not easy for an adult to unlearn many years of experience and perspective. Very few people have memories of being a baby; even the leap of imagination fails us. Just as it is very difficult to imagine a state of being unborn, or of being dead, so it is hard to imagine the thoughts and feelings of a baby. As adults we can anticipate daytime when it is night, and we can visualize summer when it is winter. We are able to do this because we have memories with which to recall a former time which we have every reason to think will return. Imagination and phantasy are in such instances based upon reality. There are other times when we have not experienced 'reality' — visiting a new place, or a person we have never met but only spoken to on the telephone. We form an idea of what the place or person will be like, and are often surprised that the reality is scarcely like our imaginings. Even then we have sufficient knowledge to be right in some respects, and the experience of reality is usually not too disturbing.

Like our other senses, we take this ability to imagine for granted, and rely upon our having sufficient knowledge and experience for the phantasies not to be too wild. Most day-to-day experiences can be assimilated readily into some frame of reference. The new-born baby, however, has no frames of reference, and only slowly learns to set experiences in perspective. He learns that the pangs of hunger are relieved by sucking and swallowing something warm, sweet and wet, and that the discomfort of cold is assuaged by something warm and secure. Milk, blankets, the surface of the mother's skin — none of these have the objectivity and substance which even the older child recognizes. The external stimulus is only known through the internal response, just as when the sun is shining I only know it through the warmth on my face and its light in my eyes. I need experience and knowledge to be able to imagine that the sun is still shining when it is behind the clouds or behind the other side of the world. Experiment: put your thumb into your mouth — where is the focus of sensation? It is your *mouth* which experiences the thumb, and it is not until you gently bite your thumb that you become aware that it is actually part of your own body. Before biting it would not have mattered whether it belonged to you or to someone else.

Such crude analogies hopefully take us a little further in imagining early experiences, which in turn lead us to conceptualize some of the features of personal development at this age. The boundary between what is me and not me, between self and not-self, the space between the skin surface of the baby and the skin-surface of the mother — all are only gradually perceived. The needs of the baby — to be fed, to sleep, to feel secure — are met by objects not yet recognized as persons. Hence the use of the term 'part-objects' to describe those parts of the person which the baby experiences. The line between subject and object is as yet non-existent. The relationship between mother and baby is sometimes called 'symbiotic' — each dependent upon the other. Although the baby will not survive without mothering, it is true that a mother can survive without her baby. But the term is used to describe the psychological relationship, where the baby is unaware that mother is not part of self, and where the infant is for many mothers still intimately connected to her self-image.

To describe this as 'unity' would be deceptive. Perhaps we can coin a word and call it 'binity' — two in one and one in two. We catch glimpses of this state in adult life in those mysterious moments called 'oceanic feelings', where for a fraction of time, time itself seems suspended and we feel a sense of harmony which cannot adequately be conveyed in words — although music sometimes expresses it better. It is also seen in the confusion of space and time boundaries which can result from the use of hallucinogenic drugs, both in good and bad 'trips'. It is the bad experience which is more likely to bring people to the counsellor:

> Diana had been slipped LSD in a drink. She described the terror of time sliding backwards and forwards, together with frighteningly vivid confusion of herself with two people whose deaths she had witnessed years before. At one moment she felt she was them, at another that they were her, and she was convinced that she was going to die too. Fortunately this was an isolated incident, and after she had been able to describe the terror, she was able to go on to look at the significance her neurotic guilt played in her memories of these two deaths.

The confusion between self and another person is another example of confusion, as are confusions of time (as in the example) and of spatial boundaries. When a client refers to such a confusion, particularly to feeling apart from the world about him, or even from his own body, the counsellor needs to consider the possibility of a borderline personality, in whom any interpretative counselling might trigger off psychosis; or whether there is evidence of drug abuse, in which case again specialized help might be necessary.

The confusion of self and not-self is not confined to the seriously disturbed. It arises in most of us, including people who appear fairly stable. It will not always be troublesome, although can lead to strained relationships, when, for instance, we project a personally unacceptable part of ourselves on to another, or when we identify with negative aspects in another person. At such times personal boundaries become confused between one and the other. The counsellor can often help clients identify what it is in a relationship which belongs to them and what it is that belongs to the other. Those who project can be helped to own *their* feelings and responsibility, but also, those who swallow whole what others say negatively about them sometimes need help to see the contribution others have made to their difficulties; and, if not to disown, at least to temper their sense of over-responsibility for things that have gone wrong. Confusion of boundaries can also be seen, and is a common experience, when people fall in love. The language which lovers use expresses frequently the interpenetration of each by the other. If this phase of love is perpetuated, not permitting separateness to be re-established, a person may fear losing himself in the other:

> Edward became desperate when he realized how his love for Fleur made him so dependent upon her that she was able to play him along, always calling the tune. He needed Fleur so much that he was afraid to say anything which might destroy the relationship. At the same time he felt resentful at being treated like an object that could be picked up and dropped at her whim. Things got to such a pitch that he resolved to break off seeing her, and was able to do so. Immediately he felt so different that he told the counsellor, 'I have got my *self* back again'. He had feared being desolate and alone, but found himself able to relate to others much more easily. Edward was then, and only then, able to see parallels between the confusion of his self with Fleur's, and the relationship of his parents. He remembered a time when his father was cutting a piece of wood, but cut it to the wrong length. He had

immediately blamed Edward's mother, with the result that Edward was bewildered. He could not understand what his mother had done. His mother also confused him, because she would say, 'If you do this, or don't do that, you'll kill me.' He remembered feeling puzzled as a child about how such things could happen, and what it meant about the way people interacted. He had had to distance himself from his home before he felt he found any sense of identity; but had lost it again in his relationship with Fleur. One of the aims of counselling was to help Edward to establish the boundaries of his own identity. Only when he had done this would he be able to get close to another without fearing loss of self.

Basic trust and dependability

The boundaries which are familiar to the mature adult are not clear to babies. Their limited ability to experience only what is close to them means that their world is, in adult terms, very small, but it is for them the only world they know. It is therefore legitimate to call the symbiotic relationship of mother and baby 'the world', providing the first experience of a world which enlarges as the child grows. First impressions count for much, especially at such an impressionable stage. When the baby feels good, even though the source of that feeling is not yet clear, the world as a whole is good; when he feels bad, everything is bad. It is an all-or-nothing stage of existence. Of course there will often be times when all feels bad: no mother can be ever present, and even if she were there are some pains which she can do little to relieve. Nature must simply take its course. Moreover, too concerned a mother can give rise to later problems. It is not only the neglectful mother who sows seeds of doubt. What is important is that the mothering is reliable and dependable, so that where there is pain there can also be comfort, and so that if all is not well there can also be a feeling that it will become well. The good-enough mother (a phrase of Winnicott's) is able to *contain* the painful feelings in her baby. She will not blame herself. She knows when to fuss and when not to fuss, so providing the foundation for the emerging view of the world that in later life recognizes that not all is heavenly, but that on balance it is a good enough place to be. Such trust, built on a dependable mother-figure, lays the foundation for basic trust in the world, and, because the symbiotic relationship means that what belongs to her also belongs to me, a basic trust in myself.

There are clients who have serious problems about dependency, but such little trust that they withdraw from intimacy [p. 35], perhaps into phantasy [Phantasy and reality p.55]. But issues of trust and dependability are present to some extent in every client. The reliability of the counsellor is maintained by keeping to appointments, by being able to listen without fussing, and by being able to contain the 'bad' world into which a crisis temporarily throws a person. Thus the counsellor provides hope, without being glib and without promising more than can be achieved, so enabling, in Alice Miller's words, a

> freedom to experience feelings which are spontaneous. It is part of the kaleidoscope of life that these feelings are not only cheerful, beautiful and good, but that they can display the whole scale of human experience including envy, jealousy, rage, disgust, greed, despair and mourning (1979).

Perhaps the need for reliability goes without saying. Yet no counsellor can be so reliable as to be ever-present. Apart from illness and those occasional but unavoidable times when she cannot keep an appointment, the counsellor builds breaks into the meetings — holidays, and regulation of the frequency of appointments. She cannot avoid those lapses of concentration or failures to understand which make her appear, despite her generally careful attention, to be fallible. No counsellor can fulfil the need some clients have for a substitute mother. Where clients have experienced unreliability in their parenting, such moments of 'failure' provide occasions to take up the clients' feelings of disappointment, sometimes intense, their anger or their sense of loss in relation to the counsellor. If such feelings can be vented, they may be linked to past experience where it is known, or can even be the occasion for enquiring into past disappointments. With clients who are either clinging or distancing in their current relationships, the fear of being let down can be observed. The counsellor aims to be reliable enough (even if it is the nature of things that she cannot be perfectly dependable) to allow feelings of vulnerability to be voiced.

Basic trust leads to more refined forms of trust. Blind trust may be appropriate for babies, but not for toddlers [p. 7]. Although suspicion is not likely to win one many friends, awareness of others' difficulties and weaknesses is a necessary part of relationships:

> Gwen was distraught: she would never be able to trust a man again. Her husband had walked out on her suddenly, without her being aware that there was anything wrong in their relationship. It was clear that she had

idealized him, and had trusted him blindly. But she had gone through five years of marriage with her eyes closed. The counsellor used an analogy to describe trust in relationships: 'It's like crossing a wooden bridge every day on your way to work. You trust it is secure and that it won't let you down. But you don't cross it blindly. You have your eyes and ears open for any signs of weakness. Neither do you refuse to cross it until you have examined every plank in detail. But you need to be alive to signs of change.'

It is this type of trust which parents have to learn as their children grow, not just in the exploring stage (A.S.) but also in adolescence. It is not a nonchalance which appears uncaring, nor an idealization of their children which fails to recognize pitfalls. Neither is it an intrusive or restrictive fussiness which fails to let them experience the less pleasant effects of their actions. It is never easy to get the balance right. This type of trust also applies to the counsellor, who recognizes the freedom of the client to make mistakes, but who also attempts to foresee, through discussion and interpretation, the likely pitfalls in any contemplated action.

Dependency and withdrawal

In reaction or response to mothering which is either neglectful or over-indulgent, and by this we mean not feeding and physical comfort alone, an infant can adopt different defensive ways of coping. These are not necessarily linked specifically either to neglect or to indulgence but can apply equally to both. Such contradictory responses abound in human behaviour. A child may become clinging, or withdrawn. Both defences can be seen at work in those who cling to drugs, alcohol or food, or who live in a phantasy world, in extreme cases becoming psychotic, and who at the same time withdraw from intimate contact with people. In general, but especially where there is evidence of a disturbance to the continuity and effectiveness of early mothering, such people will require long-term counselling or psychotherapy, or other specialized help. Where change occurs, it will often be very slow. But our concern is also with those whose dependency or withdrawal is not so extreme as to overtax the skills of the ordinary counsellor.

As an example of dependency, and anxiety about dependency, take Hazel. She had fallen in love: everything was heavenly, her boyfriend was 'super', her work going 'very well'. Even her terminally ill father had begun to rally. But none of this eased her problem of over-eating. When she was on her own she ate and ate. She could not see anything to cause it, except to acknowledge that the only cloud on the horizon was her fear of being let down when she was so happy. A previous boyfriend had left her when she least expected it. Her counsellor wondered whether eating was a way of trying to store up happiness. He made several interpretations which had no effect on her voracious appetite, until one session he suggested that it was almost as if she were saying of her boyfriend and her father (both of whom she feared losing), 'I'll eat you up — I love you so much.' His remark appeared to have a dramatic effect; from that session on her eating became more normal, and she was able to move towards owning the discontent she felt at her present boyfriend's occasional lack of consideration for her.

Nothing was known of Hazel's early life. Counselling concentrated on the present situation, but used imagery which fitted the presenting problem. Relating her difficulties to a developmental stage seemed to be valuable.

Other people fear becoming dependent. In the following case, the family history had some relevance in what was also short-term work:

Ian had fallen in love. This had created some turmoil for him, because he was a 'fiercely independent' late adolescent, following his father who had laid great stress upon that quality. Ian's father was the child of a broken home, and had been shunted from one part of the wider family to another, and from one institution to another. Subsequently he had been successful in his career, and brought his sons up to think of career first, marriage a long way second. Ian had also been successful to date, ahead of his peers in achievements, and yet was afraid of being caught up in a close relationship. He was not only worried what his father would think; he was scared in case he ceased to love his girlfriend, or she stopped loving him. But she, Ian said, 'has got into the pool, whereas up to now I have only allowed my close friends to dip their feet in'. The way she had 'got inside him' was a disconcertingly new feeling, though fortunately it only temporarily threw him.

Some clients fear dependency on the counsellor or on counselling. This may be expressed openly in the first session, but may be expressed obliquely. 'I don't want to depend on Valium' is a reasonable statement for a person to make, but it can sometimes mask fear of becoming dependent upon anybody. Others provide clues in speaking of outside relationships:

Joan said in her first session that she tended to see people two or three times, and then break off relationships. The counsellor was thereby alerted to the possibility of this happening with him, and indeed after four meetings Joan aired the idea of stopping. The counsellor was able to point back to her own words, and suggest anxiety about closeness.

Joan illustrates the withdrawn person well, one who fears close relationships, but deep down longs for comfort. She came for counselling because she was so isolated, spending much of her time on her own, eating and sleeping. It soon emerged that her infancy had been traumatic. She had been born prematurely, her mother dying soon afterwards. Her first weeks of life were spent in an incubator, and it was several weeks after that before she left hospital. Father had been looking for somewhere to place her. She went into a foster home, where food or a dummy was used whenever one of the children was upset. When Joan's father married again, she rejected her step-mother, after she had been brought back to the new family. Joan also experienced later losses of other members of the family who became important to her. Little wonder that she could not allow herself to depend upon another person, for fear of losing them. She found herself hating people once she had got to know them a little, which was a way of forestalling any rejection they might make of her.

Joan is typical of that personality type known as 'schizoid', where emotional, and perhaps physical, distance has to be maintained at all costs. Counselling was limited by time in her case, and could not hope to shift the problem in any major way. The counsellor was content to work towards the building up of sufficient trust to make long-term therapy a possibility.

Clearly one of the difficulties in counselling a withdrawn person is creating a relationship in the first place. The opposite is true of the dependent person, who latches on to the relationship offered, and hungrily demands more and more time, help and attention. The counsellor can feel 'drained' (an oral image again), frustrated and angry, mirroring in herself the dependent client's own feelings of emptiness and anger which cannot be assuaged. The compulsion to make demands can make some dependent people feel guilty. They are afraid of their hunger for love in case it drives people away — which it often does. The counsellor, who is normally not trained sufficiently to handle a full regression, needs to be able to preserve her own and the client's boundaries, remaining steady but reliable over time limits and frequency of meetings. In all probability this will lead to quiet grumbling or open hostility in the client, but if this can be brought out into the open and accepted by the counsellor, without retaliation on her part, the client can often appreciate boundaries, recognize the separateness of the counsellor, and fear rejection less. Greed comes not just from hunger alone, but from fear that food is going to be taken away. We do not normally bolt food unless we fear it will be snatched from us.

It needs to be said, however, that it is easier to recommend a balance between limits and love than it is to effect it. It can be difficult to weather the storms which blow up, even if the client stays in counselling. Until a client feels secure in the relationship with the counsellor, and understands that the frustrations are not linked to feelings of being 'bad' or 'punished', it will be difficult to move from the counsellor to other relationships outside the session, and to wider areas of concern. The link between being 'bad' and being demanding is seen in the following case:

> As a child, Katherine clung to her mother for many years at those times when mother was home from the mental hospital. She was a frequent non-attender at school, until the age of ten, when she overheard her mother saying to a neighbour that her most recent spell in hospital was because she was worried about Katherine's clinging behaviour. Although it was initially mother's absences which had made Katherine so, the situation was now turned on its head, with her demands, so she believed, driving mother away. She also recalled an early occasion of mother's absence when an aunt with whom she was staying refused to let her see 'Watch with Mother' on the television, because she had not 'performed' on the potty after lunch. We might restate that situation as: 'If I cling on to what is in me, that prevents me seeing mother too.' After Katherine had heard mother speaking to the neighbour she determined to become self-reliant, and went to school without making any fuss. But the problem had been pushed underground, because in her first session with the counsellor she used the phrase 'You can't rely on anyone' several times. The counsellor observed that she was probably wondering if she could even rely upon her, but even this was not enough to help her come and talk again.

Consistency and dependability are important with all clients. With demanding clients it will help them to learn that however badly they think of themselves this does not alter the constancy of the counselling relationship. For some this will lead to greater trust in themselves and the counsellor, and perhaps to looking at appropriate and inappropriate demands from a different perspective.

Narcissism and self-respect

Demanding people often treat the counsellor as if he only belonged to them. This is an indication of narcissism, which is a natural and normal stage in early infancy, before the baby has learned to recognize limits and boundaries, and before he has learned to live with them. The narcissistic person can easily become at least a bore and at worst an object of hostility, but perhaps we can be more tolerant if we understand what lies beneath the preoccupation with self and the wish to have everything his own way. In the symbiotic phase of infancy the mother figure is inseparable from the baby. Therefore love for the mother, because she is not yet a separate and whole person, is also a form of self-love. It is appropriate that a baby should therefore be described as in love with self. The following words, which Winnicott wrote for new mothers, would be just as applicable to new babies, were they able to understand them.

> Enjoy yourself. Enjoy being thought important. Enjoy letting other people look after the world [. . .] Enjoy being turned in and almost in love with yourself [. . .] Enjoy having more right than you have ever had before or will have again? — author to do just what you feel is good (1964, p. 26).

A mother can enjoy herself and love herself, because as Winnicott says the baby is part of her. If therefore she enjoys and loves the baby, she helps the child to acquire a sufficient sense of self-love. It is from the security of being loved that we learn to love others. The narcissistic person in adult life, so often thought of as self-centred, has not in fact acquired sufficiently strong a sense of self-love to be able to express that love outwardly in concern for others and for their well-being. He therefore appears selfish, but has a weak sense of self. He seems self-opinionated, but has not actually reached the stage of being able to take his own worth for granted.

> Larry was described by a psychiatrist who had seen him as one of the most narcissistic people he had met. We might be tempted to think that it was being an only child which had 'spoiled' him, but in fact his mother had had little time for him, and sent him out of her room whenever he went to talk to her. He keenly felt the status of an outsider, which his nationality and religion reinforced. The issues which so often aroused

his anger were those where his 'private space' was threatened. When he lost his own office at work, and had to share; when the presence of his third wife in the living room, bedroom or kitchen interfered with his wish to watch television, sleep or cook a meal respectively; and when doctors refused to take his hypochondriacal symptoms as evidence of physical illness — Larry got wild. He saw himself looking after his wife in a generous and selfless way although it appeared that she represented a part of himself that wished to be looked after. In his phantasies he devised schemes for robbing banks of money, of which they had plenty and which therefore they would not miss. He was always looking for an ideal job with status, yet gave up opportunities where he could have done well after a short time when negative aspects of the job appeared.

Although he liked to think of himself as important, he was taken aback when the counsellor offered to see him for a year: he clearly felt he would never be offered so generous a time. It took a year before he was able to recognize how he had treated people, and in the penultimate session he acknowledged how he had made his three wives insecure. The counsellor felt obliged to point out that he too had been made to feel insecure, and that his behaviour sprang from his insecurity. It was important to support Larry's self-respect at those points when he was able to be honest with himself, since the inflated sense of self hid a fragile and frightened person.

The narcissistic person appears self-centred — Larry wanted the world to fall at his feet, and found frustration very difficult to tolerate — but in fact has a damaged self-image. Since narcissism entails clinging to self, there may be difficulties for the self-centred person in mid-life, when physical faculties begin to wane, illness becomes more common and the intimations of mortality more acute. The fragile sense of self beneath the grandiose self-image is threatened by the very dissolution of that self. Death, of course, is no respecter of persons, and cannot be controlled. It may be denied, but with increasing age even this defence becomes strained. Death and ageing are particularly feared by the narcissistic person [Ageing p. 186]. 'Death exposes the superficiality and triviality of many of the ambitions and aspirations on which men spend their energies' (Macquarrie 1966). Letting go is more gracefully accomplished when we feel secure enough in ourselves. Just as in intimacy, where the sense of self needs to be established before it can be partially merged with another's, so in death and loss and disappointment of all kinds, acceptance is possible when we have a strong enough sense of value to tolerate the wounding of narcissistic pride [see also: Pregnancy p. 166; Early adolescence and sexuality p. 137; The adolescent adult p. 148; The client's faith as an indication of maturity (narcissistic faith) p. 194].

Pride is a defence against feelings of worthlessness. So the narcissistic person may find it difficult to accept what the counsellor says, not simply because it appears critical, but because it strikes at the root of his being. The person who has a basic sense of self-worth will be less anxious about observations made upon various features in himself. We are here describing something different from shame or guilt. The person who shows O.S. difficulties will say, or feel, 'I do not like my *self*', whereas in shame or guilt (A.S. and G.S.) the expression is more likely to be, 'I do not like this aspect of myself'.

Some clients, far from seeking praise and attention, show a type of 'humility' which provides evidence of their defence against their narcissistic needs, and of their lack of self-worth. It is seen typically in the statement, 'You must have people who are much more in need of your time than me' — used partly as a defence against counselling, but also demonstrating inability to claim time and attention for themselves. They may be afraid of their wish for love and affection, in case it is never achieved; they therefore deny themselves to prevent intense feelings of later disappointment.

> Martin expressed doubts early in the first session about counselling being self-indulgent. He went on to talk at length of various family situations in which, as a child, he had to defend mother against father, sister against mother, and look after a sick brother. Such concerns meant that in late adolescence he had to abandon his own plans and wishes. He saw that he had had to assume an adult's responsibility for others which did not permit him to enjoy his own childhood. The counsellor related all this material to Martin's difficulty of having the counsellor for himself, because that seemed self-indulgent. 'You seem to be saying that no one cared for you, you had to care for them, and you aren't at all sure you can allow someone to show care for you.' Martin's eyes filled with tears, confirming the accuracy of the counsellor's intervention.

> A middle-aged woman introduced herself to the counsellor as 'second-hand Nancy'. In the session which followed there were many examples

of allowing others to be indulgent at her expense. When the counsellor had to alter the times of their meetings two sessions running, she acquiesced and denied any feeling of being put out. She was grateful that she was able to see her at all. 'You have to put yourself second here too, even though it would be natural to feel something, just as you put yourself second with others', the counsellor observed.

Nancy often said that she felt selfish about coming to counselling, although later she was able to accept that she could sometimes put herself first. She found it difficult to relate freely to others: she was continually concerned not to offend them, needing to make sure of their favour, but at the same time suffering because they (themselves more obviously narcissistic) took advantage of her.

The complaint that counselling is too self-centred and introverted is by no means rare. Yet it is through becoming aware of their own needs that, paradoxically, people are able to care better for others; treating them not as persons upon whom their own needs are projected, but as people in their own right.

Loneliness and being alone

In adult life there is a substantial difference between being 'lonely in a crowd' (a not uncommon description of people who are depressed), and the ability to be solitary and yet content. Early infancy throws light on such feelings. Self-respect and self-worth depend upon a person being able to say, 'I feel comfortable about and with myself.' We notice the two personal pronouns 'I' and 'myself', indicating thereby an internal relationship between two parts of the one person. The capacity to be alone without discomfort depends upon this internal relationship, which is not to be confused with either narcissism on the one hand (a desperate attempt to like oneself), or schizoid withdrawal upon the other (the need to be alone because relationships present too great a threat). Winnicott throws light on the capacity to be alone when he describes the need for a mother and her baby to be on their own, and yet in the same room, without the mother needing to fuss the baby, and without the baby needing mother's active attention (1965b). The narcissistic person shows such a lack of self-assurance that relaxation and contentment in solitude become difficult. Loneliness in a crowd describes the inward feeling of being at odds with oneself, no matter how much external affirmation is forthcoming from others. A person in such a state could be said to have become their own worst enemy. J.S. Dunne describes it well:

> What makes a man happy when he's alone and happy? What makes a child happy when he is playing alone? There may be a clue in the word 'alone'. The word is a combination of the two words 'all' and 'one' (1979, pp. 104–5).

He goes on to suggest that loneliness can never be cured by another person: 'We are alone, you and I, and we cannot make one another unalone' (1979, p. 106). The only real solution is to be 'all one' within.

The capacity to be alone therefore depends upon being content with oneself, yet not self-content, and upon loving oneself, yet not upon self-love. It is another of those delicate balances which we shall see at many points. It is of crucial importance not simply in the next stage, where children learn to play, frequently on their own before socialization begins, but also in adult life. Coming to terms with being single — between adolescence and marriage, or after a bereavement, or for some throughout life — clearly hinges upon the right degree of inward harmony [The single person p. 153; Bereavement p. 199].

Idealization and splitting

At this point we may summarize, to the effect that in the early stages of life, given good enough mothering, the baby acquires sufficient sense of well-being in the face of the natural vicissitudes of living, so as not to be afraid of his world. It is still a very small world, but it is his whole world. This experience also influences his basic sense of self, upon which much yet has to be built.

In the face of distress and vicissitude, especially where they are more than the innate disposition of the baby can tolerate (individual babies bear different degrees of stress), ways of trying to preserve a basic sense of worth are adopted. These are seen more clearly in adults than in infants. The dependent person continually needs to 'top up' an empty sense of value; the withdrawn person tries to keep well away from the risk of rejection and the wish to be dependent; the narcissistic person surrounds the undervalued self with self-praise and flattery; or even puts others first and meets his needs by meeting them in others. Parents sometimes do this with their children, not permitting them to develop a self of their own; while they appear to be encouraging the child's development, they may be doing this in order to feel better parents.

A major aspect in developing a more harmonious sense of self is learning to integrate good and bad experiences, so that the growing child can learn that while life is not wholly good, it is not all bad either, and that on balance the good outweighs the bad. This is essential if we are to make realistic assessments of the relative merits and faults of ourselves, of others and of situations in which we find ourselves. It is clearly a lifetime's task. Writing of her adolescence, in *Lark Rise to Candleford*, Flora Thompson records that 'older people saw things more in proportion, for they had lived long enough to learn that human nature is a curious mixture of good and evil — the good fortunately predominating' (1973, p. 479). It is not surprising therefore if this is difficult to learn in the early months of life. We commonly use the term 'ambivalence' to describe mixed feelings, although analysts use it to indicate more extreme swings of feeling, and the difficulty of holding together loving and hating emotions towards self and others. For some people, relationships are all or nothing, while many more find it difficult to reconcile contradictory reactions in the same situation. Flora Thompson continues that 'tart and tears should be separated by at least a decent interval' (1973, p. 479). If adolescents find mixed emotions difficult to bear, and they *par excellence* swing dramatically both in mood and in their views of others, how much more must children, and babies, find life's experiences confusing and puzzling.

We come back to the difficulty of imagining: what is it like to feel full, comfortable and good at one point, and hungry, cold, frightened and angry at another? It has been suggested by child analysts such as Melanie Klein (Segal 1973) and others, that a baby copes with this, as yet incomprehensible, phenomenon by splitting, and believing that good experiences come from a good mother, while bad experiences must come from a bad mother — so separating into compartments their own positive and negative feelings, where bad feelings cannot damage the good ones. Such thinking may be difficult for an intelligent adult to comprehend, but we need to remember that we are dealing with a primitive form of logic which somewhat like a computer's can only 'think' in compartments. An infant is as yet incapable of the lateral thinking more typical of mature intelligence.

In fact such 'primitive' thinking is also encountered in adults. In some religious belief systems the problem of God as the apparent cause of bad experience is 'resolved' by splitting so that a 'demi-god', the Devil, is given responsibility for all that is evil. Despite their claims to be monotheistic, some such religions encourage dualism: the belief in two gods, each with a different attitude to creation. Splitting is also seen in much political rhetoric, together with paranoid projection; an external enemy is lampooned as all bad, and threatening the all-good homeland; or one group promises to save society from the depredations of another group. Realistic assessment of people and the world is not as common as we would like to think, even amongst so-called educated men and women.

Splitting, at its most extreme, leads to idealization on the one hand, and denigration on the other. The counsellor too may be seen as an idealized person, while another, perhaps a person in the client's family, or a different helper, or even the client, is spoken of in the lowest terms imaginable. When faced with such idealization, the counsellor can adopt certain approaches; she may:

(1)   observe that she is being elevated into being a perfect person/object;
(2)   suggest that the client is making her out to be good but is denying his own value and strengths;
(3)   interpret the negative feelings voiced towards those outside the counselling relationship as belonging also within the relationship between them — the greater the idealization of the counsellor, the more rigorous the defence against discontent and anger with her;
(4)   draw out the positive features in those people whom the client runs down, so that the splitting is not so readily perpetuated in those relationships.

There may be occasions, albeit fairly rare in counsellor–client relationships, where this idealization of the counsellor is so extreme that she finds herself worshipped like a god, and the dependency upon her becomes almost impossible to cope with. This has been called the eroticized transference. Such situations are delicate, and require not only full understanding of the client's history but also of the course of counselling. It is impossible to give general advice on handling these matters. In such cases the counsellor will want frequent opportunities to discuss the client in detail with a skilled supervisor, preferably one who is experienced in more intensive psychotherapy.

Anger, paranoia and envy

The child — or the child in the adult — struggles to preserve the good
against the ravages of bad experiences. Idealization veers towards putting
all that is good on to another, such as the counsellor, leaving the client with
all that is depressing and bad. Anger may be turned upon self, or upon
someone other than the 'good' counsellor. The paranoid client also splits,
but projects all the bad feelings outwards, seeing either the world, or
people generally, as hostile and persecutory, attacking an innocent and
good self. Such a person is struggling to keep bad feelings at bay, by denial
and projective defences. In extreme cases such paranoia takes the form of
plots and devices, human or otherwise, which are so 'real' that the
counsellor recognizes the client's need for psychiatric help. The suspicion
of such a client often has the effect of making other people wary of him,
thereby compounding in reality his phantasies. Making a referral is difficult.
While the idealizing client sees referral as rejection, the truly paranoid
person may see it as confirmation of the plot against him, and as a way of
delivering him into the hands of the enemy. The skill of referral lies in first
becoming and then remaining a good enough person, working with every
hint of the central rational part in the client, so as to quell, at least partially,
the irrational fears. Very careful choice of words, a gentle manner, refusal
to show irritation or even panic oneself — all this is easier said than done,
because seriously disturbed people test our skills to their limits. Such,
however, are the aims of the referring person, who recognizes that he
plays a most significant role, even if it is a fairly brief one. If it is carried out
well, a referral provides an example of an alternative world-view, more
positive than the one which the client has come to fear. Badly done, it
simply confirms the negative world-view and makes the task of the next
helper even more onerous.

Paranoid tendencies are present in all of us, and are not the burden of
the seriously disturbed alone. When life takes a turn for the worse, it is not
unusual to project one's frustration and anger outwards, to wonder why
others, or indeed why life itself, should have it in for us. It is a common
way of dealing with negative feelings. The counsellor needs to discriminate
between justifiable feelings and more paranoid ones; and of course it is not
just in racism and sexism that we witness prejudice. At the same time, the
counsellor cannot rule out the possibility that some people invite or incite
hostile reaction, or interpret current situations adversely on the basis of
former experience. Such situations are often complicated by clients

selecting, as their persecutory figures, people who indeed demonstrate prejudice. The examples given therefore have some basis in reality, but frequently are selective. Caring people, or caring actions are either unrecognized, or dismissed as having some ulterior motive. The counsellor therefore tries to assist such clients to disentangle their own feelings of anger, and to own them, even when prejudice is real.

The nature of anger and aggression is still much debated, particularly how much it is innate, and how much it is a response to frustration or fear. Certainly it takes various forms at different stages of life. The anger typical of this stage (O.S.) is frightening to all except the psychopath (one who has no moral check on his behaviour), because of its potentiality for destructiveness. When a baby is frustrated, his whole body can become contorted with what an adult might call rage. If the force behind a baby's physical movements were translated into an adult's strength, the ensuing destruction could be immense. But it is not the physical expression which interests us so much as the phantasy, difficult for adults to picture, of having irreparably damaged the source of love and goodness.

Such a statement appears extreme, so let us try once more to pursue the limited logic in the 'mind' of a baby who struggles with the frustration of his demands for food and comfort. Feeling hungry or uncomfortable, the baby cries, but mother does not immediately respond. The frustration rises, and the cries become more angry and frightened. Still mother does not come. We catch glimpses of the type of construction a baby might put on this when, even as adults, we are kept waiting by someone who does not arrive. If that person is special to us, we begin to wonder if they are all right. Are they hurt? How dare they keep us in suspense? And, perhaps, did I say or do anything last time which has put them off?

The reader will be able to add other constructions and phantasies which, when that person arrives, are soon forgotten in the relief at seeing them again. It is not far-fetched therefore to wonder what constructions a baby puts upon mother's absence — without, of course, the hundred and one explanations which older people have to draw upon. Various possibilities occur: is it my need for her, my greed for her, my frustration with her, or my anger with her which has driven her away? Mother eventually returns (only minutes late in her eyes, but an eternity in his); and such phantasies are set at rest. The repetition of this experience enables most babies to learn that she comes, even if they have to wait, as surely as an adult knows the sun will rise each morning. Yet in babies where toleration of frustration is low, or the frustration continually goes beyond what they can take, a residue of fear is left that it is they themselves who have driven mother away.

Is this perhaps far-fetched? I suggest not, when we remember the myths in primitive societies which attempt to explain what has happened to the sun as it rises and falls in the heavens, or the fact that primitive people may hold themselves responsible for the sun's disappearance and reappearance in an eclipse. Neither is it far-fetched when we recognize that in bereavement the words 'if only I hadn't thought, said or done that', can be the precursor of thoughts that in some way the bereaved was responsible for the death. Nor, yet again, when we remember those occasions when we have become so angry that we have wished someone dead. Of course we did not mean it, but that is easier to recognize as long as the person survives and reconciliation enables the thought to be laid to rest. This does not prevent memories of such thoughts surfacing when a death occurs, and some adults *feel*, even if rationally they *know* otherwise, that their death wishes might have been responsible. It is not far-fetched to surmise that the irrational mind of the infant and child can make false assumptions, amongst which is the thought that it is 'my anger that has driven her away'. Analysts themselves differ in the relative weight they give to anger, greed, or even love, as the imagined cause of loss, but they all accept the power of the child's irrational phantasy.

Just as the degree of idealization is proportionate to the strength of rage, unconsciously felt but repressed, or split off on to another person (an equal but opposite force), so rage is proportionate to the degree of need and its consequent frustration:

Oliver collected clocks and watches — his room was full of them. But whenever he detected a blemish in one he had bought, or when one of his time-pieces went wrong, he got into a frenzied rage, in which he smashed the offending object to pieces. His early history threw light on his behaviour. His parents had divorced soon after he was born, and he was sent to live with a spinster aunt who spoiled him and, in his own words, 'let me get away with murder'. He was visited occasionally by his mother, and once by his father. It was his earliest memory that father had tried to comfort him when he was distraught by holding a watch to his ear — soothing him to sleep with its rhythmic ticking. From the age of three Oliver remembered wanting clocks and watches, and his mother would bring him old clocks, which no longer worked, when she visited him.

We have to guess that the old aunt, while giving him much, was unable to give him the body-contact and the nurturing which he needed. Being 'Victorian' in her own upbringing, she may even have been of the school that felt babies should not be given too much attention. Father's watch became a symbol of closeness, comfort and intimacy: what Winnicott calls a 'transitional object' — a representation, like a thumb or a teddy-bear, of mother and of mothering. The thumb is the best transitional object because it cannot be dropped from the cot, and is always to hand! But whereas most children grow away from their transitional object, Oliver was always looking for the perfect one. He could not get enough watches in his search, and when the objects he thought were perfect showed their obvious imperfections, they had to be destroyed. Oliver was not so disturbed as to think that the clocks and watches which were imperfect became persecutory objects (like the Duke in James Thurber's tale *The Thirteen Clocks* (1962), where time itself is the persecutor). But the borderline was slender. It was only Oliver's fear of his new father and his mother, when she remarried and he returned home, which prevented him from smashing them up when they frustrated his wishes. It was ominous that his old aunt had been the person he continued to attack physically right into adolescence. Becoming frightened of his aggression, he sought help.

The counsellor who works with a client who feels or fears this destructive anger can follow a number of lines simultaneously. She

(1)   helps the client to hold on to those aspects of self which are positive and good, especially when wishing to explore with the client those aspects which might otherwise overwhelm him with fear or guilt;

(2)   attempts to get the client to verbalize the anger in the session, rather than act it out in self-destructiveness or damage to objects or people outside;

(3)   demonstrates, through the relationship she has with the client, that expressing anger (especially towards the counsellor) in thought and word does not actually destroy either the counsellor or the relationship — the client can 'bite the hand that feeds', and knows that it will not be taken away;

(4)   makes connections between the past and the present which help to explain the intensity of the anger and the guilt accompanying it; at the same time the counsellor draws a distinction between what was an age-appropriate response in infancy or childhood and what is inappropriate now (in Oliver's case, the imperfect watch is not his mother);

(5) tries to help the client express appropriate anger about current situations. (Oliver was in counselling for some time before he was able to go back to the shop to complain about a clock which turned out to have a fault);

(6) helps the client distinguish between realistic guilt resulting from expression of anger which has hurt others (Oliver's aunt) and unrealistic guilt, where the damage is much more to the client's sense of well-being. Where there is realistic guilt, she encourages and supports the client's wish to make some direct or indirect reparation: being able to mend situations is a sign that destructiveness need not be final.

(7) Lastly, the counsellor does not forget that beneath the anger there may also be deep sadness, emptiness or a profound sense of helplessness and weakness, all of which are defended against by rage. The person who is wounded may prefer to respond angrily rather than show how hurt or weak they really are, but acknowledging their own pain may help them more.

Since those who act out their aggression are in the minority amongst clients, we must not neglect the subject of anger in those who form the majority — those who find it difficult to express their hostility openly because they fear that if they do so, it will be destructive. Their aggression is often turned instead upon themselves, in depression or in destroying opportunities for self-enhancement: breaking off relationships, for instance before they get angry with others.

> Pamela is more typical than Oliver. She had great difficulty acknowledging her own anger, more usually feeling that it was others who were angry with her. She was constantly trying to please others in order to stay in their good books. After a year's counselling she was able to acknowledge her destructive phantasies, and even said to the counsellor on one occasion: 'If you say that again, I'll go for your jugular.' Having come to terms with what she felt, she was able to say, 'It's been good to find the anger in me, and to begin showing it here without feeling so guilty.'

There is also an angry, sometimes destructive, component in envy, an emotion which is believed to be present in infancy. Envy is similar to, but not the same as jealousy. Jealousy normally involves three or more persons: for example, a husband is jealous of his wife's attention to their baby. Envy more usually describes a two-person situation, where one person envies and does not possess what another person has: a thing, or a quality. Melanie Klein uses envy in such a sense, of a baby's wish to possess all the good milk in the breast, while Freud uses it in a similar sense when he writes of penis-envy in women [Castration and penis envy p. 89]. Though not taking up these issues here, it is useful to notice that envy springs from a feeling of inferiority, and that it can lead to anger with the person who 'has it all', to fear that the person will turn upon the one who has little or nothing, and sometimes to wishes to destroy what the other has, on the principle, 'If I can't have it, then I'll make damned sure he doesn't have it either.'

> Queenie told the counsellor how angry she had been the previous week. She had returned from a break to find him suntanned and relaxed, not even listening to her, or so she felt. She envied him such a good life, when hers seemed to be full of disasters. She denied that she wanted him to suffer as she did, but the counsellor nevertheless took up her anger with him for being away and withholding his listening from her, and he linked her feelings about his inaccessibility while on holiday, with the anger she felt at her mother's withholding herself from Queenie when she was little and mother was so often ill.

The destructive component in envy (and jealousy, which also features in the following example is seen more obviously in the case of Robin. Whenever he got close to a woman, he found himself so possessive of her, and so jealous of other men that it always led to the break up of the relationship. One of his sessions deserves recounting in detail, since it illustrates the type of envy which Melanie Klein decribes (Segal, 1973):

> Robin was remembering incidents in early childhood. When he was five he was taken by some slightly older boys to a wood which was out of bounds. They were going to collect birds' eggs. The other boys said there were dinosaurs in the wood, and hid behind bushes making roaring noises. Robin became so frightened that he ran home, and arrived there crying. He could not tell his mother why he was upset because he should not have gone to the woods in the first place. In her frustration with him, she shook him to try and find out what had happened. He wanted comfort from her, but she only succeeded in making him more frightened.
>
> The counsellor said, 'Perhaps it also felt bad to have stolen birds' eggs.' Robin paused, agreed, and then went on: 'I've just remembered something else, but I'm too embarrassed to tell you.' The counsellor tried to take up the resistance, saying, 'Perhaps you are afraid I'll shake

you like your mother did.' This helped Robin speak of his second memory. When he was very young he was sent off to bed early, and lay in bed thinking that he wanted to cut off mother's nipples. He himself wondered whether what he felt then, and re-experienced now in his possessiveness of girlfriends and his jealousy of other men, was associated with the birth of his younger brother, who always (so Robin felt) received more understanding from mother than he felt he did. He also wondered whether brother's arrival had meant that he felt pushed away from his mother's breast. His insight certainly made sense.

A Kleinian, we can speculate, might have gone on to suggest that the stealing of birds' eggs was associated with guilt (the persecutory dinosaurs) about his wish to destroy in his envy the eggs in mother's body, and so prevent a rival appearing on the scene. It would of course be inappropriate to use such a theory with the client, but such associations might provide further links, if there were evidence from the client to make them plausible. It was Robin who made the links, and not the counsellor.

Another phase of early infancy, when cutting teeth makes feeding at the breast more painful for the mother and when in our culture weaning takes place, may prompt a link in a baby's mind between biting and the removal of the breast. If biting is associated with aggression, there is further reason for believing the phantasy that anger is destructive. Biting might be added to the repertoire of aggressive images linked with the O.S., together with greed, envy and destruction.

Children's stories, especially the traditional fairy tales (of the Brothers Grimm for instance) and their modern equivalents, often contain very powerful images which are associated with the developmental conflicts of the early years. Perhaps this is why such gruesome stories are so popular with children. One such modern example is *Where the Wild Things Are* by Maurice Sendak (1970), which is well worth looking at, for the illustrations as well as the highly significant text; and which evoked a minor storm of protest from some protective parents when it was first published, as being too frightening for their children.

In this story the young boy Max is a 'little monster' and his mother sends him to bed without any supper. In his room Max 'dreams' (we are not sure whether it is a dream or a waking phantasy) that he travels to the land of the Wild Things where he tames them, despite their terrifying attempts to frighten him. He then gets them to join in a wild rumpus which he calls to a halt by sending them off to bed (as he was himself) without their supper. But then he feels lonely, wanting to be where he is loved ('best of all' — the one and only of the O.S.). He leaves the land of the Wild Things, despite their protest that they will eat him up (words he used to his mother when she got angry with him); and he returns to his room where his hot supper is waiting for him.

Max's own wildness at home is thus re-lived and relieved in the dream, projected on to the terrifying Wild Things of his own imaginative world. Max tames his wildness, which has got him into trouble, by taming the Wild Things and controlling the start and finish of their rumpus. Having punished them (as he might have wished to punish his mother) he then feels unloved and empty, and needs to return to reality, where he finds that his supper is waiting for him after all. Thus the loving relationship with his previously angry mother is repaired and restored.

Such a story encapsulates some of the principles of counselling too, through which clients are helped to face both the strength and cause of their own feared or actual wildness, by looking it straight in the eyes, as Max himself does when he first encounters the Wild Things; then expressing it (as in the rumpus) and controlling their aggression, as he does when he commands the rumpus to stop. The constancy of the counsellor, who goes on attending to the client, even when the client has been angry with him, helps to demonstrate that relationships need not be broken irreparably if aggression is expressed, and that supplies of love, especially when they can be internalized, need never be permanently cut off.

Guilt, anxiety and concern

Although the term 'guilt' has been used above, it is not one which sits easily in this stage. Guilt describes the reaction of the older child or adult, although it may be linked to feelings which first appear in the O.S. A baby is more likely to feel anxious than guilty — *anxious* that rage has been destructive, for instance, rather than *guilty* that it has been so; and often the adult's neurotic guilt is a form of anxious concern for oneself, whereas real guilt, that is constructive guilt, includes concern for another or others.

Yet it is in this stage that the first stirring of guilt and concern is felt. Both depend upon the capacity to imagine what another person might be feeling as a result of one's actions. This capacity will be examined in the next section, where it is referred to as 'identification' or 'empathy'. Empathy is not possible until the separateness of the other has been recognized, since empathy requires us not to confuse our feelings with another person's situation. Concern for others and our effect on them, is a positive consequence of guilt. It is not altogether selfless, since we wish to repair broken or damaged relationships for our own well-being as much as for the other's. Pure altruism is a difficult concept: it may be seen in the readiness to suffer and die to save the life of a child, although children still represent the continuation of one's own life in them. Nevertheless it is the relatively selfless concern of the mother for the baby with which the infant identifies in his concern, first for the mother, and then for others. As the sense of self becomes more secure there is greater freedom to show concern for others, without projecting one's own unloved features on to them and loving oneself at one remove.

This is particularly relevant for counselling, because the counsellor who feels relatively secure and free from anxiety about himself, will be more attentive to the client. Times of personal stress and anxiety can play havoc with counselling, even though, once worked through, they provide experience from which to empathize. When a counsellor lacks an inward sense of security, it is much harder, for instance, to interpret and to permit the anger and frustration which the client feels about the shortcomings of the counsellor, because he is too concerned to maintain a good self-image with the client to be open to criticism or attack.

Phantasy and reality

Tales such as *Where the Wild Things Are*, fairy stories and science fiction, contain more true phantasy then other imaginative works of literature. Worlds are constructed which sometimes have little semblance to the reality of the world as we know it. These worlds provide settings for human situations which are indeed found in other literature, but with fantastic creatures sometimes symbolizing aspects of the 'inner world' — like the dinosaurs in Robin's memory [p. 51] and the wild things in Max's dream. Dreams, indeed, are phantasy *par excellence*, and serve the purpose of working over unfinished anxieties, most commonly from the previous day. Clients' dreams are not usually an easy medium to work with, yet clients who learn to associate freely to their own dream images are often able to find their own clues to a dream's possible meaning. The temptation with dreams is to try and understand them straight away: yet often it is later material in the session which throws light upon a dream image. Full dream work is normally too time-consuming for once-weekly sessions.

Phantasy can provide insights upon our internal world. Phantasy, in the form of day-dreaming, can also temporarily fill a gap: day-dreaming of a good meal enables a hungry person to defer eating much during the day so as to enjoy going out to dinner that evening. Day-dreaming of a loved person from whom one is temporarily separated usually makes the interval and absence tolerable. The ability to imagine situations which might take place can act as a useful way of 'rehearsing' one's words and actions, so as to be better prepared for them.

At other times phantasy is less helpful. The nightmare is the dream which has gone too far, when the phantasy becomes too much and uncontrollable, even in sleep. I have already cited examples of phantasy constructions upon experience which often lead to false conclusions, and may lead to perceptions of the world, and of people, as hostile or fearful, or both. Some phantasies provide security and satisfaction, but because they keep a person introverted and collude with anxieties about real relationships, they impoverish the opportunities for fuller and more mature relationships.

In either case the phantasies of the client provide rich material for counsellor and client to work upon, providing the counsellor can help the client to feel unashamed of recounting them. In sexual problems, for instance, masturbatory phantasies frequently provide clues to what it is in real relationships which the client wants or fears.

As far as the O.S. is concerned it is necessary to distinguish between phantasy which is recognized as such (and therefore provides the opportunity for greater insight), and phantasy that has become so real to the client that the world of make-believe and 'as if' has become confused with the real world. Making such distinctions is important for the counsellor, since there are some people in whom phantasy has become so close to being their reality that they are unlikely to benefit from the counsellor's skills.

The psychotic — paranoid or schizophrenic — person is one of those who might find such distinctions difficult. The old and somewhat 'black' joke runs: the neurotic builds castles in the air, the psychotic lives in them, while the psychiatrist collects the rent. Anyone who is so caught up in their own phantasy world that they cannot recognize 'reality' is unlikely to be suitable for counselling. Of course, like the baby's phantasy world, that of the adult psychotic also has its own logic, and protects him from the feared devastating effects of the real world. Trying to convince such a person that his thoughts are pure phantasy is unproductive, because such thoughts serve a purpose and cannot lightly be given up. Where the counsellor detects evidence of more mature and rational thought, as he might do, it is helpful to support those ideas, especially in guiding such a person to more specialized help:

Stephen had a problem with hand-washing — an obsessional symptom (A.S.) but in his case with psychotic features. He believed that when he was walking down the street he might tread on glass; so that when he came to take off his shoes, splinters of glass might get transferred to his hands; and that if he then rubbed his eyes, he might damage them. He asked whether this was a possibility. The counsellor said that it was a possibility and that it certainly made sense to wash at times, but that the chances of damage to his eyes were very slight indeed. The counsellor suggested there might be other worries, and that it would be wise for Stephen to see his G.P. That degree of support appeared to encourage Stephen to visit the doctor, who was able to prescribe a drug which calmed Stephen's obvious anxiety and 'erratic' thinking. (We notice that his thinking is not illogical, but too literal; and that words like 'might' and 'possibility' indicated less rigid a phantasy than words like 'does' and 'probability', which Stephen might have used if he were more disturbed by the thoughts).

A further example of the power of phantasy can be seen in Tim. He had met the girl of his dreams, but his difficulty — as the counsellor saw it — was that it was all a dream: a day dream, a phantasy. Tim believed that she would marry him, but she (who had also seen the counsellor because she was unable to handle Tim's attentions) was clearly angry at his pestering. She had tolerated his visits to her, but made it quite clear that she had someone else — which was true. She had said, 'Let's just be friends', even though she did not like Tim at all and only felt sorry for him. Such a straw was enough for Tim to cling to, and he redoubled his efforts. She moved away, refused to answer his telephone calls. He wrote, but she did not answer, until one day she grew tired of his persistence and replied, to tell him about her new job. Once more Tim grabbed the straw, and sent by return an erotic love-letter. Nothing could shake Tim's conviction that he was going to marry her. 'But he's not in love with me', she said despairingly, 'he's in love with himself.'

Tim was certainly in love, but in love with an illusion, a mirage, an object of wish-fulfilment, an idealization of the girl and of their relationship. When Tim himself saw a counsellor he provided an opening in what could so easily have been an intractable situation when he said, 'It's God's will that I marry her.' The counsellor replied. 'you seem to be very sure that you know God's will, but I wonder whether God's will can ever be known for the future — it is only afterwards that you can say such things. Perhaps you are trying to tell God what you want.' This oblique reference to Tim's wanting things to go his way, without pausing to think of the other, seemed to make some slight impact upon his thoughts about the girl. Tim replied at that point, 'Perhaps I should wait and see what happens between us, and try not to push it too much.' The counsellor was not confident that things were resolved, but it was a step in the right direction.

Phantasy and imagination have their limitations. What Tim was unable to imagine, as in the first few months the baby also finds it difficult to do, was what it might be like to be the other person. He could not put himself in the girl's position, and see the effect he was having upon her. Learning to recognize what others might feel, how they might react, and what their own needs are, is a life-long task, which begins in the growing separateness of mother and baby, and in the growing recognition that the other is a separate person. The early weeks are filled with experience of fusion (in adult life more appropriately called con-fusion). Love in older people involves, in Rayner's words 'being together but being separate' (1978, p. 34). In analytic terms, the infant moves from primary identification, where the distinction between 'me' and 'you' does not exist, to secondary identification, where separate identity leads to the ability to identify with the other.

With such complex concepts, it is scarcely surprising that there is some confusion in analytic writing between words such as identification, internalization, and introjection, reflecting the extreme difficulty we have in identifying and expressing what is special to us, and what belongs to another; whether we act from our own unique identity or influenced by another who has become so much part of us that the difference is undetectable; and whether in understanding others we are ever able to understand them as they are, unless in some respects we can identify their experience with part of ours. Perhaps these are philosophical distinctions which in the event need not interfere with the counsellor's practice. The confusion also reflects the difficulty of putting into words that intuitive capacity and emotional rapport which Winnicott calls 'primary maternal preoccupation': 'she knows what the baby could be feeling' (1965a,

p. 15). Whatever is written in these pages is no substitute for that intuitive way of knowing.

Yet the capacity to know what another might be feeling (the counsellor in the maternal role) also needs self-understanding, and a healthy questioning, doubting attitude to our own perceptions, if we are to avoid projecting on to another person parts of ourselves which bear little or no relation to what is being offered us by the client. The ability to imagine the client's situation, and to empathize, must be tempered by the reality of what the client says, just as phantasy needs to be tested against reality. There is always a danger, given the dependence of many clients upon the counsellor, and when some clients swallow whole what their counsellor says, that the counsellor, unknowingly, prevents them from developing their own identity.

Transition

The development of the baby in the first few months entails finding trust and faith in self, in the other (who represents the world), and in life itself as basically good. This is achieved, not by an infancy free from frustration, but by beginning to learn to integrate painful and difficult experiences which are not good in themselves, with satisfying and pleasurable ones. In later life such a foundation permits the development of a multi-faceted view of life and the world. The baby also begins to distinguish between self and the external world, to recognize the separateness of others, and to use phantasy constructively to tolerate frustration. At the same time, the baby should not be afraid to face new developmental tasks — phantasy should enhance, and not prevent personal growth. The infant of a few months is beginning to discover a sense of 'self' with which to enter the second stage, where learning to cope for himself and with himself becomes a major issue. Recognizing the separateness of others, relationships to them are tested in the second stage in matters of authority and control, and in the third in matters of sexuality and socialization.

It is tempting to idealize early infancy, but hopefully closer observation of babies, and of the 'baby' in the adult, corrects the imbalance of phantasies of bliss. It is tempting too to idealize motherhood — yet counsellors will no doubt work with mothers where idealization has turned in the event into deep depression when all the other facets of mothering become real. It also appears in some writers that there is a temptation to idealize the role of the counsellor as a maternal figure. Clients sometimes do this, but counsellors need to be wary of collusion. To describe the counsellor–client relationship in O.S. terms with any accuracy, we need to set alongside each other two contradictory statements of Winnicott's:

> It is the mother–infant couple that can teach us the basic principles on which we base our therapeutic work (quoted Guntrip 1968, p. 361);
> he can never make up to clients for what they have suffered in the past, but what he *can* do is to repeat the failure to love them enough . . . and then share with them and help them work through their feelings about his failure (quoted Malan 1979, p. 141).

References

Dunne J.S. (1979) *Time and Myth*, S.C.M. Press, London.

Guntrip H. (1968) *Schizoid Phenomena, Object Relations and the Self*, Hogarth Press, London.

Macquarrie J.(1966) *Principles of Christian Theology,* S.C.M. Press, London.

Malan D.H. (1979) *Individual Psychotherapy and the Science of Psychodynamics*, Butterworth, London.

Miller A. (1979) Depression and grandiosity as related forms of narcissistic disturbance, *International Review of Psychoanalysis,* 1979, 6:72.

Rayner E. (1978) *Human Development* (2nd edn), George Allen and Unwin, London.

Segal H. (1973) *Introduction to the Work of Melanie Klein* (enlarged edn), Hogarth Press, London.

Sendak M. (1970) *Where the Wild Things Are*, Puffin Books (Penguin), Harmondsworth.

Thompson F. (1973) *Lark Rise to Candleford*, Penguin, Harmondsworth.

Thurber J. (1962) *The Thirteen Clocks*, Puffin Books (Penguin), Harmondsworth.

Winnicott D. W. (1964) *The Child, the Family and the Outside World,*
Penguin, Harmondsworth.

Winnicott D. W. (1965a) *The Family and Individual Development,*
Tavistock Publications, London.

Winnicott D. W. (1965b) *The Maturational Processes and the Facilitating
Environment,* Hogarth Press, London.

· 4 ·

AUTHORITY AND CONTROL (A.S.)

Introduction

The physical development of the infant towards the end of the first year brings many new issues to the fore. With muscles becoming stronger and co-ordination better, the baby now sits up, shuffles along, crawls, stands and eventually walks; at the same time manual dexterity increases so that it is now possible to manipulate toys and other objects, to use a spoon to feed, etc. These significant achievements include muscular control of urination and defecation, an activity which is given singular importance by our own culture, and by many others, ancient and modern. All these new activities bring new ways of relating between parents and child, since the baby's achievements, or lack of them, will be significant not just to the child, but also to the parents. We may therefore see this stage, where children are learning to do things for themselves, as one of 'doing' more than 'being', and where they are valued as much for what they do (or do not do) as for who they are.

We move therefore from faith in self and the environment, to faith in our personal competence and ability. Properly negotiated, this stage lays the foundations of self-esteem and pride in achievement, together with the pleasure of self-expression. Negotiated less well, this stage sows the seeds of doubt, shame and inhibition. And whereas being able to depend was a key issue in the first stage, being able to be independent is at the heart of the second.

We have seen how easy it is to idealize early infancy as a blissful stage, without acknowledging the many other feelings present. Likewise it is tempting to see 'toddlers' one-sidedly. It is a period of rapid extension of physical abilities and of vocabulary, and the adult often praises the child as being 'a big boy (or girl) now' — not infrequently attributing to children more understanding than they actually have. Since verbal communication is now possible (particularly when speaking *to* children, even if the child's vocabulary is still limited), adults are tempted to think that everything they say makes sense. This is far from the case. If we take an example such as the child's difficulty with adult expressions, we notice that precisely the same skewed logic is used as we hypothesized in the first stage — the only difference is that now we have some evidence to support our argument. Even children who are much older can return from, let us say, Sunday School having learned the Lord's Prayer, thinking that 'thy kingdom come' is 'Vikings will come', or 'lead us not into temptation' is 'lead us not into Thames Station.' Finding it difficult to grasp words and concepts which are unfamiliar to them, they have to make some sense out of the confusion, and therefore 'hear' what they do understand, even if it makes as little sense to the adult, as the words used by the adult were to the child.

Such a trivial example helps to confirm the misunderstandings which can so easily arise over toilet-training. The child learns that it is good to perform, but then fails to understand, at least at first, why it is not good to perform in the wrong place. The 'pot' may be significant for the adult, whereas it is his faeces which are significant to the child. Having then discovered that the toilet itself is a 'sacred vessel' into which precious libations are poured, is it that strange that the child wonders why mother has got so cross when some other precious item has been placed therein? As adults we smile; as children we are bewildered, and perhaps even shamed by discovering that we are not as grown-up as we had been led to believe. The infant wishes to learn and copy the adult's rules, but as yet cannot comprehend the subtleties of the adult game. As Lowe says, he is sometimes 'damned if he does, damned if he doesn't' (1972, p. 49). It is a puzzling world to be living in. Just when they feel most pleased with themselves, their achievements are scolded. What was an achievement at one time, becomes a disaster at another. Energy abounds in short bursts and yet can be curbed as being too disruptive, while at other times the child wants to regress to being more babylike, and yet is forced to be active and conform.

In all this there is much more room for an active relationship with others, although often only with one person at a time. The growing use of physical energy and assertiveness, as well as the copying of parental behaviour, but then being told 'don't do as I do, do as I say', provides plenty of opportunity for battles of will, and frustrations of freedom, but of course there are opportunities also to please. All such factors make for the possibility of growing confidence and a degree of autonomy which lead naturally to the developmental tasks of the third stage (G.S.).

Controlling oneself

The emphasis upon toilet training at this stage obscures the ways in which other parts of the body also come under control and are co-ordinated, not only to survive (movement and feeding are essential for that), but also to learn elementary skills which will be employed later in life in making and using tools and materials, to make life more pleasant and efficient. With so much stress put upon toilet training — holding back and letting go at the right time and in the right place — characteristics develop which lead to different personality types. This emphasis on toilet training is not simply in analytic writing — it is only highlighted there because it plays such a significant role in parent–child relations. But parental attitudes about control are not confined to personal hygiene alone. A mother may go by the rule-book in providing feeds when the baby is young; a father may be disturbed by toys cluttering up the floor; parents can show anxiety about a child's performance at school which resembles the pressure to produce results as a toddler. In counselling, many of the pointers to the degree of control and to ways of exercising authority by parents are evident from later stages, and may provide hints about their possible attitudes in the A.S.

The counsellor will find clients falling into a number of 'types' which may well be related to the second stage handling of control and autonomy issues: there is the relaxed and confident person, who has negotiated the issues well; there is the rigid, uptight, controlled person, who is afraid of 'putting a foot wrong' or of 'making a mess of things'; there is the disorganized, 'let it all out', uncontrolled person, who may enjoy freedom, but at the same time wishes to get things together more; and the person who antagonizes authority figures, and appears to get pleasure from 'wilfulness' in situations where authority figures are not in fact oppressive.

Some clients remember, or have been told of their early days, and anal issues may be identified clearly from their accounts:

Ulric had great difficulty letting go of his feelings and emotions. He could only express himself in a distant intellectualized fashion. He discovered what his early weeks had been like when his sister had her first child. He had visited her at the same time as their mother, and heard mother telling his sister off for not putting the new-born baby on the pot straightaway. 'You and your brother were put on the pot from the first day out of hospital.' Ulric was amused, relieved (he realized it was not all his doing), and somewhat angry as he told this to the counsellor. It certainly helped him understand his problem of not being spontaneous, when his early life had been so ordered.

Victor had problems with premature ejaculation, and found it very difficult relaxing when making love. Although he 'let go' too soon, his tension contributed to his difficulty. He recalled an early memory of walking in the country with his parents, and bursting to pee. He asked if he could go behind a bush, but mother forbade it — he had to wait until he got home and do it in the right place. Not only did Victor find sex rather dirty, but he also recognized that whenever he was asked to produce results, from academic work to sexual performance, he worried inordinately in case he did not do things correctly.

We need not ourselves get too hung up on toilet functions, for, as already noted, other examples of parental attitudes also lead to rigid self-control:

Wendy was a quiet girl, who was very tense when trying to relate to others. She found it difficult to enjoy herself, and particularly feared losing control when with a man, in case the playful initial stages of the relationship got out of hand. She found it equally difficult to let go of her thoughts and feelings in counselling. The counsellor felt he was always having to draw her out, and that what she wanted above all from him was guidance. Wendy remembered a time in her early adolescence which typified the attitudes of her parents towards her, when she had some cousins to stay. They were all excited, and were bouncing up and down on the sofa, when her parents came in, and told Wendy off, but not her cousins. She felt very small and ashamed. This 'down' on getting too excited and letting off steam, which pervaded her home, influenced her even when she had left home behind her.

These three examples all show people who have inhibitions about being spontaneous; in two of these clients the spontaneity was missing from the sessions with the counsellor too. They feared feelings of shame, and feared what would come out if, as they saw it, they lost control. Such characteristics can also be seen in the person who is very precise and exact in the counselling session, planning out all that is to be said, perhaps afraid of letting something slip, or speaking in a measured way, detailing precise times and dates, as if each session is a minute-by-minute report to the counsellor. 'Getting it right' seems to dominate:

> Yvonne began to irritate the counsellor because she always introduced so many qualifications into a sentence that he almost forgot how the sentence had begun by the time she got to the end. For example: 'I was pleased to be able to go to London — well not exactly pleased, but to go to London — well not to go to London, but to get away from Birmingham — it wasn't like a few years ago when I went to London . . .' by which time the thread was lost. She seemed so afraid of making a mistake in her choice of words, that the counsellor eventually put this to her, linking it to her dread of the future, in which she felt things could only go wrong.

> Arthur began every session by alluding back to the last. 'I'm sorry I said . . . I didn't mean . . .', etc. The counsellor observed to him: 'You seem to leave here each time afraid that I have got you wrong.'

Rights and wrongs, 'oughts', 'musts' and 'shoulds', seem to feature highly in those who exercise rigid self-control. It is even a relief when such a person can actually come late to a session (when normally the counsellor would wonder why) without having to apologize:

> Brian was an over-ordered and precise person. It felt important to his progress that after a missed session he could come the next week, quite gleefully saying that he had hired a car for the day; and how much he had enjoyed sitting on a hill at the time of the session feeling that he could pay for the counsellor's time but did not have to attend. It was, of course, also an unconsciously aggressive act towards the counsellor; but in that context it felt like a bid to be independent, without feeling guilt, since he could at one and the same time meet his obligation (he would still pay), yet also assert his freedom of choice. The counsellor needed to be free enough too to detect the positive side of rebellious acting-out.

Conscience and internalized parents

It is valid to ask why many adults, who have left their parental home behind them, should still go on acting as if their parents were around; or indeed acting as if their parents were still the controlling figures they might have been in their childhood. We saw how in the O.S. the infant takes in (internalizes) an image of the mothering figure, which helps form a self-image, either a good or a bad one, or in all likelihood a 'mixed' one. Likewise the child's personality is augmented by taking in the type of authority figures whom the parents represent. This internalized figure may be exaggerated; we have already seen that a child does not perceive people or situations accurately as a mature adult does. He may therefore overestimate how 'bad' he has been especially if the parent's anger was sudden and forceful. While the parent's anger soon abates, it continues to echo in the child unless an obvious gesture of reconciliation is quickly made. The parent's anger may be felt more intensely when the child attaches to it his own anger projected outwards. Children cope with tellings-off in a variety of ways: they try to be better next time; they copy their parents in telling off their dolls, cuddly toys, or younger siblings; they get cross with phantasy companions, disowning their own responsibility. In these different responses we see both introjection of the critical person (they themselves become critical), and projection of their own naughtiness on to another. Such introjection takes up a permanent position within the child's mind, forming the basis for the conscience or super-ego, learning what is right and wrong in the family and in the culture or sub-culture. In fact, while popularly these two terms may be used interchangeably by those who know something of Freudian thinking, conscience is more aptly used of a rational, conscious, self-observing and self-controlling function in the personality, based upon considered judgement (the ego as a discriminating observer); whereas the term 'super-ego' more aptly describes part of the personality that becomes unreasonably hostile, often unconsciously as much as consciously. Other terms used to describe this latter function are 'the internal saboteur' and 'anti-libidinal ego' (both from Fairbairn 1952), libido here referring to love felt in relationship to others) or 'the persecutory object' — this last term aptly describing a super-ego which is endowed with self-destructive aggression, and which tortures the central ego.

> Colin had been terrified for some days that he was gay. He had recently challenged his father with all that he had been doing to his mother over many years, and was fearing father's retaliation. He knew rationally that he was not gay, and was never aroused by thinking about men sexually — women had always been the focus of his sexual phantasies. But he could not get rid of this anxiety. When the counsellor said to Colin, 'It's almost as if one side of you is persecuting the other', he

seized on the phrase: 'That's just it — that's how it feels.' The use of even such a technical term brought some relief to him, helping him to feel that he was understood, and moving him further towards exploring the issues which had been raised.

Clarification of these different functions of the personality, in terms with which a client can identify, can strengthen the central ego. Sometimes the terms used in Transactional Analysis (Berne 1968) fit well: 'There's a critical parent inside you getting at your child'; or 'it feels as if you are at war with yourself' — 'you' and 'yourself' describe two different parts or functions of the one person. In Doris's case the imagery came from her own words:

> Doris was saying how restricted she felt in her digs. She could not play music late at night, because it disturbed people; but others also disturbed her, the walls were so thin. Doris was one of those who find it difficult to enjoy themselves. She always felt she ought to be working. Her parents were still protective of her, never allowing her proper freedom, in case she got hurt. What they said when she was with them continued to exert a strong influence upon her when she was on her own. 'Working' was the only safe activity. The counsellor used her words about her digs to suggest that there were thin walls within herself too, and that when she tried to enjoy herself she heard her parents saying 'Do be careful', 'you should be working', etc.

A strong super-ego is not the only critical, warning or punishing voice that such a person as Doris hears. Authority figures in particular, and others in general, in current situations, will be heard as critical and punitive even when they are not, and even when the person has done nothing to warrant such a feeling. (Many people feel fleetingly guilty when they see a policeman, even when they have not broken the law.) The counsellor needs to listen for indications of the way he himself is perceived by the client, who may project his super-ego on to the counsellor. What are intended as helpful observations can be heard as judgements. Counsellors need to phrase their observations and remarks especially carefully with those who are prone to self-criticism. Confrontation, which must always be used sensitively, is doubly difficult to get right with the client who sees his counsellor as a critical parent-figure.

Yet no counsellor can go on 'wearing kid-gloves', not daring to comment. It is by trying to lessen the severity of the client's own self-criticism, that the way may be opened for the client to accept the observations that the counsellor can usefully make. If the client appears to have to defend himself, following the counsellor's interventions, the counsellor might observe, in this or similar ways: 'You appear to think I'm being critical of you — I think you are very critical of yourself.'

Shame and guilt

It sometimes seems that the terms 'shame' and 'guilt' are interchangeable, like 'envy' and 'jealousy'. Yet there are differences which may be usefully defined as long as we do not press too hard for clear-cut distinctions. Shame describes the inability to do things, feelings of incompetence, a self-image of being immature, a failure to reach the aspirations set either by oneself or by others. Such a definition makes sense of Erikson's scheme (1965), where shame is one of the signs of failure to negotiate the tasks involved in the muscular-anal stage. Erikson places guilt in the third stage, where it is a response more to what a person has done, than to what he has been unable to do. Such clear placing of each term in different stages is nevertheless misleading, since guilt is also experienced at this stage, particularly in relation to anal-aggressive behaviour. Although we replaced the word 'guilt' with 'anxiety' and 'concern' in the O.S., followers of Melanie Klein also detect its presence there.

Shame, however, comes from feelings of failure to achieve control, for instance, and from a sense of letting oneself down, or of letting others down. It is a kind of disappointment, sometimes intense, rather than anger with oneself. Sometimes shame is expressed in obvious anal language: 'I fouled it up . . . I made a mess of it . . .' although such language can also be used of more aggressive feelings such as the wish to spoil or soil as a token of defiance. Probably the tone of voice used is a clearer indication of the different feelings. Using control of toilet functions as an example, we might say that the child who inadvertently messes elsewhere than on the toilet feels shame — the opposite of the confidence felt when he achieves his 'aim'. If the child deliberately messes elsewhere as an angry protest, he is more likely to feel guilty. Eric gave an interesting example of the difference in another setting:

> He had returned with a chum to a former school one holiday to see their old classroom. They both climbed over the fence, and were wandering around the outside of the building when the caretaker caught them. Eric felt very guilty at having been caught trespassing, but his friend simply

unconditionally. It is probably of little permanent value for a counsellor to demonstrate unconditional acceptance, one of the marks of good counselling, unless it is coupled with enabling a person like Gillian to accept herself, without laying down conditions, and without having to conform blindly to accepted or self-imposed expectations.

Obsessional rituals and perfectionism

One form in which such 'conditions' are seen, and which have to be met before a person feels secure, are obsessional rituals. Certain actions have to be performed, either in the correct order, or so many times, before a person feels relatively calm and at peace with his conscience/superego. Obsessional tidiness, checking, hand-washing, repetition of actions: all serve the same purpose of warding off a threat. Sometimes this is the threat of attack, sometimes of danger, sometimes of guilt. What is kept at bay is both the expression of strong desires, sexual or aggressive, and also the punishment for having such feelings at all. In general it is difficult to shift such behaviour through counselling, unless the client is prepared to branch out from preoccupation with the rituals, to explore wider experiences and thoughts. Since 'bad' feelings are defended against in the first place, this wider exploration will be fruitless unless shame or guilt can be alleviated to some extent. What tends to happen is that the client's attention is constantly turned upon the ritual itself. Even though it may cause him considerable inconvenience and worry, he finds it impossible to give it up, for fear of what will happen if he does. But the situation is complicated because the ritual itself sometimes expresses the very desire which is repressed:

> Harry had to wash his genitals so thoroughly after masturbating that he worried lest the soreness he then experienced meant he had damaged himself. Further masturbation was necessary to see if this was so, which meant more washing — and so on: a dreadful vicious circle, which dominated Harry's thoughts. Although he denied feeling guilty about masturbating, the reader will see the parallel between masturbation and washing his genitals — both of which meant pleasure, as well as fear and guilt in his handling of himself.

Since rituals are themselves a disguised form of acting out repressed wishes they can become so functional that they are not easily relinquished.

As with phobias, a behavioural approach to modify the actions might be used alongside the attempt to uncover unconscious wishes and the guilt and shame attached to them. In cases of monosymptomatic presentations (as perceived by the client for whom nothing else seems wrong) behaviour modification may be the only treatment suitable, with the aim of achieving change, if not deeper insight as well:

> Ivan worried about every choice he had to make, in case he got it wrong. It was not easy to shift this obsessional pattern, although the counsellor achieved some success with Ivan's need to check all the calculations involved in his work at least five times. He got Ivan first to check only four times, then three, and finally to do the calculation just twice, a reasonable check, and to leave it there if the results were consistent. Although it may have been coincidental, it did appear to influence other areas of life. Having achieved this small change, Ivan became less apprehensive over other decisions, although still appeared back in the counsellor's office whenever there were particularly crucial choices to be made.

> Karen's ritual checking of all the doors and drawers in her room when she was on her own at bedtime, lest there was a man in her room also seemed intractable. She had been able to tell the counsellor of an incestuous suggestion made by her father when her mother was away, but this made no difference. The counsellor felt that such an event went a long way towards explaining the checking. However, it was not until she was able to break her relationship with a boyfriend who slept around with other women that the checking ceased. The counsellor was far from sure that it would not return (since counselling ceased about that time) if Karen were to form another relationship which had similar oedipal complications [The eternal triangle p. 96; the seducing parent p. 100]. In Karen's counselling the focus was on the difficulty she experienced giving up a man whom she shared with other women, linked to the parental situation, and not on the rituals themselves.

Although constant checking may be involved in perfectionism, it is the obsessional element which is far stronger, even if not often expressed in ritualistic terms. The perfectionist too has to feel blameless, and although often fearing external judgement, he is normally his own most severe critic. The following example demonstrates perfectionism in a work setting, taking us into the next section, and also providing ample evidence of characteristics associated with the A.S.:

Lionel was a young doctor who had failed a professional membership examination because the recent separation from his wife had interfered with his studies. It soon emerged that one of the reasons she had left was because he constantly complained about her untidiness about the home.

Many other features came out. He had himself become quite 'lazy' (as he put it) in his work. He had lost the capacity for hard slog which had seen him through his training, and he felt guilty about that. He found himself irritated by one of his partners whom he described as a perfectionist. We notice how he condemned perfectionism, but also the lack of it, in significant people around him — his work partner and his marital partner. His parents had both felt failures compared to their own siblings, and had put all their aspirations to brilliance into their son. His father was continuously afraid of 'doom striking' — lest he fall ill and could not keep the family. This must have communicated itself to Lionel. His father went to the toilet at least five times a day to empty his bowels. At the age of eleven Lionel was admitted to hospital with severe constipation, and still felt very angry at the humiliation of enemas and other treatment: he thought he should have seen a child psychotherapist, and not a physician. So in some ways he hated the medical profession, but had identified with his aggressors and had become a doctor. If you can't beat them, join them. In his training he realized how much he feared illness in himself, as his father did, and how depressed he became when the patients did not respond to treatment. His father, incidentally, worked in quality-control and hated his job, but he was doing a job which perhaps expressed some of his own desires for perfection. Lionel felt that the life of a physician was 'purgatory' and himself recognized how close this term was to his being 'purged' when in hospital as a child. He was constantly struggling with a lifetime's identification with 'perfection' against anxiety, and had lately reacted against this.

All work and no play

Work can easily become an obsession for the A.S. personality, as if life only consists of the need to produce results. Play, or hobbies, where permitted, take on the character of hard work. Yet play is a vital part of the development of the child of this stage. Toys cease to be transitional objects [p. 49] when they provide substitutes for mother, and are reserved for bedtime. Cuddly toys are replaced by play things which provide opportunities for building, opening, filling in, tearing apart, knocking down, and moving about, as the child also becomes more mobile. Later, in the third stage, they often represent masculine and feminine characteristics, nursing dolls, fighting soldiers, etc. Play is therefore a way of expressing internal development, but at the same time provides opportunities for building up manual skills, problem-solving skills, and pleasure in the completion of tasks (Anna Freud 1973, pp. 72–3). When people are rigid and unable to let go, pleasure in play, or indeed the self-expression involved in any artistic venture, becomes very difficult.

Matthew initially came for counselling because of difficulties breaking away from home, but he clearly had problems too in his work. He was so particular that he was always behind schedule, felt weary, and wanted to give up his job and return home. His parents had protected him against making mistakes: he had been discouraged from going out to play with other boys, from climbing trees, and from doing anything which could lead to him getting hurt, or getting his clothes muddy or torn.

Over the weeks of counselling Matthew was less obsessional in his work. He was able to take short-cuts, he brought his schedules up to date, and surprised himself with his accuracy which was as great as in his long-winded methods. He was pleased for a short time, and felt much better. But now he had time on his hands, and felt depressed and listless when not working. He felt guilty that he was not taking work back to his digs for the evening and at weekends. The counsellor began to explore what it was that made it difficult to take up other interests, to meet other people, etc., in his spare time. It seemed that again he feared making mistakes, appearing foolish, getting hurt. Play and other relaxing activities also demanded high standards. Other people who played sports (Matthew quite liked tennis) demanded only the best. It took a long time before he was prepared to risk looking foolish, and before he found real pleasure in 'play'. Yet when he discovered some excitement in that area of life, it also helped him appreciate aspects of his work as being more interesting.

Counselling is, of course, a serious activity, and requires work from both the client and the counsellor. However, the counsellor also needs to relax within the counselling setting, and she may even help the client to enjoy aspects of counselling. The use of humour can often lighten the heavy seriousness of a client, particularly when the relationship between counsellor and client is well established. There are some people who make such heavy weather of their problems that they cannot 'play' with their own associations and thoughts. Likewise, the counsellor who is too concerned about getting everything right is less able to allow free play to his own imagination and ideas. Playing with words, images and ideas, and the judicious use of hunches and shots in the dark is as important a component of good counselling as the already stressed need to look for evidence upon which to base interventions. It is surprising how often the off-the-cuff remark is the one which the client later says was significant, and not the well-thought-out interpretation!

Passivity

Play in the A.S. is a way of learning autonomy and control. We often find attitudes to controlling or being controlled becoming a battleground of the parent–child relationship in the A.S. One attitude is seen in the passive, and perhaps in some ways masochistic person. In such a client we find life lived at others' commands; pleasing others is high on the agenda; and seeking advice and approval is a constant factor. There are some clients who simply want the counsellor to tell them what to do, to answer questions for them, and to provide approval and advice. The counsellor who enjoys being looked up to may easily collude. Such clients are afraid to trust their own judgements. Living with uncertainty and at ordinary levels of risk is too dangerous.

> Nigel visited the family planning clinic and asked the doctor a series of questions about the effectiveness of the contraceptive pill. He had chosen a subject upon which an almost 100 per cent guarantee could be given as long as the pill was taken as prescribed. This led to another series of questions about abortion. The doctor at first answered the questions, but then changed tack and asked Nigel if these issues were important because of a new sexual relationship. He confirmed this, and went on to describe two areas of life where he felt uncertain: firstly he was unsure whether he and his girlfriend were right for each other; and secondly he did not know whether he was making the right choice over a change of job. The doctor observed that Nigel wanted 100 per cent certainties. He agreed: 'But life's not like that, is it?' This led on to other

worries, including guilt about engaging in a sexual relationship, and feelings of failure to meet the high expectations he felt his father had for him.

The counsellor who colludes with passivity, and cannot allow the client to learn, sometimes even through making mistakes, is like the parent who cannot trust the child with the new-found mobility of this stage. Children of this age like to walk away from the parent figure, then run back for safety, gradually pushing out the radius of detachment further and further. The counsellor likewise needs to encourage and permit the passive client to go off between sessions and cope on his own, even if the next session represents a running back to check that all is well.

> Odette was a student whose parents gave her everything that she wanted. She felt nonetheless a lack of trust on their part. Instead of allowing her to have her own money and to budget for herself, they had told her to ask whenever she needed more. She felt much more independent when she was able to negotiate with them to be paid a lump sum at the beginning of term, no greater than fellow-students, and when she determined to try to live within that, not asking for any more. She felt her parents were too possessive, and used the phrase 'tied to their apron strings'. Likewise in her counselling she eventually asked for appointments once a fortnight, and then once a month. This seemed a reasonable request, since she wanted to test out her independence there too, but only gradually. With some clients, and with adolescents in particular, the counsellor recognizes their need to be independent, and weighs this against any advantages there may be in encouraging them to stay in counselling.

When a client is distressed it is sometimes useful to give some reassurance. But the counsellor needs to weigh up whether in doing so he is acting as a nurturing figure (O.S.) or as an authority figure (A.S.), and whether to speak authoritatively might lead to more problems in the long run. The counsellor in the next example was acutely aware of the dilemma:

> Colin [see also p. 66] wanted the counsellor to tell him that he was not gay. He was in a real panic over his fears, which had come upon him suddenly, and never troubled him before. The previous weekend he had had a stand-up row with his father over the way father had treated his mother. Grievances nursed over the years were unleashed, and

father was taken aback. This challenge to the authority figure (although there were also clearly oedipal aspects — see chapter 5) had brought on, so the counsellor thought, anxieties about retaliation from father, and having to become submissive to a male. They also touched on feelings of neglect that Colin himself had experienced from father's distant manner.

The counsellor could fairly easily have given straightforward reassurance to Colin, especially since Colin had made his hetero-sexual preference clear. But he felt that if he were to do so he would be putting himself in an authoritarian and superior position, and that Colin might later feel equal anxiety that he had needed a man to tell him what he could find out for himself, and that he needed a man to 'comfort' him. In fact the counsellor used his dilemma by expressing it openly to Colin: 'I could tell you that you are not gay, and that might reassure you, but I think you would then feel anxious about me becoming the man you want to comfort you; you say you keep wanting men to comfort you, but then that in turn makes you afraid that you must be gay.'

Explosive anger

The above example shows how anger was held back for many years, and then released in such strength that retaliation was feared. There may also be explosive anger at being controlled by parents, seen typically in the angry young man or woman [chapter 7], but perhaps seen with equal force in the earliest words many children learn: 'No' and 'Mine'. This natural assertiveness is necessary in order to make claims on their own behalf, to stick to their aspirations, and to be able to become independent. The young child wishes to be like 'grown-ups', and is normally praised for his growing will-power.

Assertiveness can spill over into cruelty or destructiveness without the child realizing that this is wrong. It is the loving tie to the parents that enables a child to accept their restraints upon his aggressiveness. But when that love is missing, or is tenuous, the assertiveness can lead to destructive, quarrelsome and ruthless behaviour. It is concern for others, already nascent in the O.S., that must continue to develop in order to temper any natural expression of anger aroused in response to frustration of the child's will.

Typical of the expression of anger connected with the A.S. is a type of explosiveness not unlike a volcano blowing its top. It is often held back, like faeces have to be held back, bursting forth when endurance has reached its limit. People who fear their anger tend to bottle it up, but have to let it go every now and again. Controlling anger by suppressing it seldom works for long. It is hardly surprising that such held-back anger, let out suddenly, involves real risk of hurting someone more than a person intends, so confirming fear of expressing any anger at all.

Depression, sometimes caused by anger turned back on oneself, or irritability, or both, frequently indicate such held-back anger. Stories of having let it go explosively and disastrously provide sufficient reason for understanding a person's fear of expressing such strong feelings. If the client can explode at the counsellor and realize that it does not spoil the relationship, it helps; but that type of explosiveness is scarcely desirable in any other setting. The counsellor will want to understand the client's frustrations, and may usefully rehearse with such clients ways of expressing their frustration, which include their concern and respect for the other, yet which still convey their own point of view.

The passive-aggressive personality

The overt rebel, the type of person who seems to prefer hostile relationships to friendly ones, is not typical of the average counsellor's caseload, unless referred instead of or as part of a disciplinary process. Counselling may then be felt as a means of social control by the client (or indeed by others). Tempting though it may be to indulge in argument with the hostile client, win or lose the client will continue to see attack as the best means of defence against criticism. (We refer here to the A.S.: some hostility may, of course, be a defence against weakness and dependency needs.) Observation of the client's fear of being criticized is preferable to trying to convince the client by arguing the point.

More common in counselling is the passive-aggressive person — a term which does not mean swinging between passivity and aggression. It describes one who expresses aggression passively: the person who is apparently submissive yet provokes anger, and then has a disarming way of appearing quite 'innocent'.

> Peter was sent to the student counsellor because he was not handing in work as requested. His tutor described him as pleasant enough, but told the counsellor that he could never get anything out of him either by way

of work or of explanation; he added that Peter insisted upon standing up all the way through any interview, making the tutor feel that Peter was a submissive character. When the counsellor met him, Peter had no hesitation about sitting down. He formed a different impression of a confident young man, who took perverse pride in boasting how little work he did, and who obviously led an active life in college. As the session went on the counsellor suggested that Peter was actually quite angry with the tutor for expecting him to work, and that he enjoyed standing up, watching the tutor squirm in his chair. He seemed to want to impress people by turning on its head the idea that you earn praise for working hard. He got praise from his friends for getting away with it. Peter felt the counsellor had hit the nail on the head, and opened up considerably about his parents' aspirations for him, but his feeling that he would never be as well respected as his father was in his career. He agreed to meet again, and within a few weeks was working so hard that the tutor jokingly said to the counsellor, 'What did you say to him that I didn't?'

In fact there may have been some splitting here, which could have led to the tutor feeling bad at having failed where the counsellor had succeeded. Passive-aggressive clients may split authority figures, turning one against the other, getting them to do their dirty work for them, while they stand on the touchline and watch them fight. In just the same way a child soon learns how to run to one parent with a complaint about the other. Handled well the 'good' parent is able to provide some comfort, but is not drawn into an alliance against the other. Helpers and authority figures also need to watch for similar mechanisms at work. Such splitting differs from more primitive splitting [p. 43] in that the client uses one person to get at another with whom he feels angry.

Another expression of passive-aggressiveness is 'withholding', not through shame or fear of criticism, but to convey discontent. The client who misses a session, comes late, or having arrived has nothing to say, *might* be holding back angry feelings towards the counsellor for something which occurred in a previous session.

Ruth came very late two sessions running. On the first occasion she told of an incident when a man exposed himself to her. In telling the story she got very upset, so the counsellor, having time, let the session go on for longer, hoping that by helping her express her feelings it would make the incident less worrying for her. But when she came late the next week, she was reluctant to say anything. The counsellor suggested to her that she might not want to talk about the things which were so upsetting last week. His remark had some truth, but was too late. Ruth eventually said that she was very angry at being given more time the previous week, because it was *then* she hadn't wanted to say any more about the incident. It appeared that she came late the first week because she felt ashamed, and wanted to flee as soon as she had mentioned the incident; but the second week she had come late because of her anger.

Controlling others

When people reach adulthood, they have opportunities to exercise authority over others. The way authority has been experienced by them will influence their own management of adults and children. Some become very controlling and authoritarian, stern, rigid people who cannot allow their hold over others to be relaxed. Others have difficulty in exercising their legitimate authority:

> A student teacher found it impossible to control his classes, so much so that near-riots were taking place. As Simon told this to the counsellor he was laughing. Certainly he was covering up his own anxiety about the situation, but it also felt as if he was getting some pleasure from seeing the children do what he would never himself have dared do with his teachers or with his parents. Simon had decided that teaching wasn't for him, although his father had felt it a good and safe job, and he did not wish to let his father down. But, since Simon was a Christian, he had prayed about it all to God, and God had said, 'Go ahead, do a different job.' In fact this seemed a sensible decision, but Simon needed to refer to God's authority to carry it out, since God was more powerful than his parents! When the counsellor observed the different ways in which authority problems were causing difficulty, Simon asked the counsellor to repeat what he had said, so that he could write it down. He wanted to put the counsellor's authority on record, rather than make of it, if appropriate, something for himself.

In this example, Simon's control of others was made difficult because he identified with the children's reaction to control, and wished to express, in them, his own high spirits. Others find it difficult to exercise authority for fear of hurting others:

Trevor was the manager of a large office, and had achieved his position through efficiency and his ability to charm those who worked for him, by his gentle nature and example. But he had problems with the occasional employee who took advantage of his manner. In those cases Trevor could not bring himself to administer rebukes or warnings. He told the counsellor that he was afraid of hurting people. The anxiety he felt at having to play 'the heavy father' was similar to a time of his life when he had felt extremely worried. His best friend had died as a result of a heart attack when they were playing a rough adolescent game of football. This shock also corresponded with his own father's ill health after a series of heart attacks. Here there were issues connected with rivalry [Jealousy and competition p. 112], which threw light upon problems of authority and control.

Sadism and masochism

An extreme demonstration of problems of controlling others is seen in sadistic behaviour. This is a complex area, where, as Rycroft (1972) says, it is not clear whether the pleasure obtained by the sadistic person is due to the enjoyment of the suffering of others, or to the sense of power and control over others. Sadism can feature in each of the three early stages, being oral, anal or sexual in its expression. Masochism seems linked more closely to the anal character. Sadism differs from more ordinary forms of aggression in the pleasure which accompanies its expression.

Counsellors will rarely see clients who are blatantly sadistic, since the excitement is stronger than any concern about their behaviour, so they do not seek help so easily. Indeed, where there are indications of the acting out of sadistic phantasies, the counsellor would be wise to consult a forensic psychiatrist or psychologist, senior probation officer, or someone more experienced in working with offenders. Evidence of cruelty to animals (as a child or as an adult), pleasure from the idea of acting out sadistic phantasies, and more obvious signs of such actions indicate that the client is at risk, and should be taken seriously. The counsellor should not avoid closer questioning of such phantasies and of instances of their expression (Prins 1975; 1980). It is preferable to expose these issues with a client, and seek advice on whether referral is advisable, than to shy away from the subject for fear of encouraging a client. Most counsellors already know this is also the case with suicidal threats or anxieties, part of the masochistic end of this polarity.

If such instances will be rare, there will be more clients who have sadistic phantasies, which they have never acted upon, but which cause them tremendous guilt or shame. Here the counsellor can assist the client by uncovering his wish to get back at someone who has made him suffer: one component of sadism is the wish to turn the tables and compensate for intense feelings of inferiority, or the pain of being severely hurt and punished. The wish to attack women, for instance through indecent exposure, denigration, rape, etc, probably indicates direct fear of women, or an indirect fear of men, both threaten to rob the person of his masculinity. Women who have been subjected to this type of attack may similarly hide their own feelings of sadistic revenge. The object of the sadistic phantasy is often someone who is seen as physically weaker, and therefore easier to control. With sexual sadism in particular we are obviously seeing some overlap between two stages of the developmental plan. Unresolved issues from the anal-aggressive stage are carried over into the next stage, when coming to terms with sexuality (genitality and gender) is a further issue, and compounds the problem.

Masochism in the form of self-criticism and self-denigration has already been mentioned in this chapter. Where masochism is linked with sexual pleasure, we can again understand it better by reference to the child's struggle to make sense of experience — in this case of painful experience. If parents have been sadistic towards a child, showing more physical or verbal abuse than affection, the child may come to understand 'love' in such perverted terms. Being punished may even be the only way of being noticed, and of gaining a dubious form of recognition. It is not an ideal relationship, but it is a relationship. That may seem strange, but I recall hearing an anthropologist speak of her experiences researching Buddhism in a Japanese monastery. During meditation she found herself subjected to heavy slaps across her back. At first she thought she was being punished for doing it wrong, but she discovered that the 'beating' was a sign of encouragement and affirmation. She had to explain to the masters that as a Westerner it had the opposite effect on her, and fortunately they passed her over for the rest of her stay. If, in that culture, beating was a sign of the master's pleasure, it is not difficult to imagine a child (who in the early years knows no other culture) attempting to incorporate negative experiences into a more positive framework. Furthermore, the child's own anger, unexpressed because retaliation by the adults is so feared, is turned back upon the self, willingly accepting another's anger.

Masochistic tendencies may therefore be the result of learning about relationships 'through the looking glass': the child has got it all back to front. (Bearing in mind the Duchess's baby, perhaps *Alice in Wonderland* would be a better analogy.) Attacks upon the self are at least better than no relationship at all. There are, of course, other components: masochism can also be anger turned back on the self rather than expressed outwardly, because of guilt about sadistic feelings; and sexual pleasure linked to masochism may indicate guilt about sexuality, which has to be punished while it is also being enjoyed.

Transition

Before moving naturally into the next stage (since sexuality has already made its presence felt), I summarize the development which has so far taken place in the 'normal' child. The muscular-anal stage has its own transitional quality. At the beginning the infant was discovering independence. During this stage he has moved outward from the essential central self to explore the powers and pleasures of the body's movements, internal and external, learning to control and co-ordinate his muscles and limbs. He has learned to be more independent, taking control, testing out autonomy, challenging the authority and control of the parents. Mother and father have become separate persons, each with their own identity and each with their own physical characteristics. The child has learned the value of verbal communication, but has already discovered that life seems hedged round by all manner of rules. He has begun to ask questions, and enjoys learning: 'Tell me this . . . why that?' The external world has become larger, although it is only ready to be explored as long as one parent is within reach or sight. If in the first stage the foundation of basic goodness of self, of others and of the world was the major lesson, in the second it is that the world and others are basically fair and just.

So the child is ready to move into the third stage. Having for so long been the passive recipient of nurture and guidance from the parents, he now wishes to take his place alongside them, to give love as well as to receive it. Having begun to come to terms with his body, he is now ready to take a further step in identity. Having achieved a type of independence from other people, he now begins to evaluate relationships to others, and to recognize that in the case of half those around (those of the same sex) there are familiar similarities, and that in the case of the other half (those of the opposite sex) there are some interesting differences. In the next stage, running parallel with issues of autonomy and authority, which are still around, new issues stemming from sexual awareness and the wish to give love come to the fore.

References

Berne E. (1968) *Games People Play,* Penguin, Harmondsworth.
Bettelheim B. (1983) *Freud and Man's Soul,* Chatto and Windus/Hogarth Press, London.
Erikson E. (1965) *Childhood and Society,* Penguin, Harmondsworth.
Fairbairn W.R.D. (1952) *Psychoanalytic Studies of the Personality,* Tavistock, London.
Freud A. (1973) *Normality and Pathology in Childhood,* Penguin, Harmondsworth.
Lowe G. (1972) *The Growth of Personality,* Penguin, Harmondsworth.
Prins H. A. (1975) A danger to themselves and others (social workers and potentially dangerous clients), *British Journal of Social Work,* 5, pp. 297–309.
Prins H. A. (1980) *Offenders, Deviants or Patients,* Tavistock Publications, London.
Rycroft C. (1972) *A Critical Dictionary of Psychoanalysis,* Penguin, Harmondsworth.

· 5 ·

SEXUALITY AND RIVALRY (G.S.)

Introduction

Movement brings new perspectives. Just as adults see things from new angles by moving around them, or, by distancing themselves from large buildings and landscapes see them more in context and less distorted by perspective, so the child not only physically moves, but also psychologically moves, further away from the parents and sees them in new ways. They are seen more as whole persons, and they are perceived more obviously as in relationship to each other, as well as to the ever larger world the growing child is discovering. Through the A.S. in particular, he has gradually acquired such new perspectives: parents are no longer simply care-takers, the fulfillers of needs, protectors, boundary-setters, guides and teachers (i.e. doing things for the child): they are becoming whole persons with whom and for whom the child wishes to do things. Having been at the receiving end for so long, and yet having begun to achieve the first measure of independence, the child wishes to give; he has already learned the pleasure to be gained from giving, in his progress towards bodily control and achievement. In play also children of this third stage are beginning to relate more fully to other children, showing more concern for them than in A.S. play, where they are individuals playing in close proximity, but rarely *together*.

At the same time as this is happening, the focus of interest in the child's body gradually shifts, taking on a new centre of attention in addition to the pleasure to be gained from food (oral) and from retention and evacuation (anal). The genitals are the source both of curiosity (games of mummies and daddies, doctors and nurses) or even more straightforward exploration of each other's genitals, and of pleasure (what is misleadingly called masturbation, but much less self-conscious and deliberate than after puberty). If we put these two developments together (wanting to give love to the parents, and the first signs of interest in sexuality) we can begin to understand the tasks to which the child of this age is introduced, and upon which are built the foundations for the fuller expression of sexuality in adolescence and beyond.

Male and female

If we are asked to describe another person, the first and most usual distinction we make (except perhaps where the person is of another colour) is between male and female: 'an old man . . . a smart woman . . . a rough boy . . . a tall girl'. Gender is an obvious division to make: we immediately narrow down our description to one half of the population. Yet it is also one of the most natural to make, since male and female are also sexual descriptions, and sexuality is as basic for the survival of our species as food is for our individual survival. However sophisticated we like to think humanity is, able to rise above sexuality and able to divorce sexuality from reproduction, this fundamental part of our nature cannot be denied. It reminds us, as does our need to survive by eating, and by fight or by flight, that human beings are still animals. Of course, as mature adults the fact that another person is male or female need only be a rapid perception before passing on to relate to the other as a *person*, but even mature adults have their gaze caught by obvious sexual signals in another, and some people dress and act in order to accentuate their sexuality. It is not difficult to identify the gender of another adult: there are many physical signs, even when dress and hair length is 'unisex'. The shape of the body itself, mannerisms and pitch of the voice are generally sufficient for the quickly made discernment that we are talking either to a man or to a woman, and to some extent to use that perception in any interaction.

Such external signs are not so obvious when we look at children, or when children meet each other. There may, of course, be indications in ways of dress or by length of hair (although even in fairly recent times little boys were dressed like girls and had long hair, just as today girls are likely to look like boys). There is only one sure way of distinguishing gender, and that is by looking at the genitals. When a baby is born, and the parents ask whether it is a boy or a girl, the doctors do not need to take a chromosome count: they simply look to see whether there is a penis or not, and are more than 99 per cent sure they can trust their judgement.

I labour the point, but of necessity because it is less than fashionable to dwell on sexual differences in a society which, at least in some quarters, risks blurring the differences in what is an otherwise proper concern for equality. For children, particularly of this age, and later in adolescence, gender is important: and remains so for many adults.

The physical differences between men and women, mother and father, brother and sister are significant to the young child, since they are part of the wish to understand anything that is new and puzzling. We shall look at this attempt to understand in the next section. At this point we need to make a necessary distinction between the terms male and female, which describe given factors and are rarely changed, and the associated, yet different, terms masculine and feminine. Psychological characteristics and gender roles have been tagged on to the physical signs of gender in every society, although not in the uniform way that early analysts-cum-armchair-anthropologists believed. Such psychological characteristics are not 'given' or innate factors, but acquired in the course of socialization, within the family, at school and in society at large. Since counsellors have themselves experienced that process and are working with some clients whose attitudes are sexist, we cannot pass over these distinctions as if they did not exist. In an ideal society perhaps they might not, but the culture in which we have all grown up does not change simply by surface changes. Acts of parliament against sexual discrimination, changes of words in advertisements, or the banishing of sexist language help to change male/female stereotyping and discrimination, yet they cannot undo (at least in one generation) the inbuilt stereotypes which men and women, conservative or radical, chauvinist or feminist, have of each other and of sub-groups within their own sex.

A writer who is also a male cannot, however, be blind to the possibility of unconscious or implicit stereotyping when dealing with this subject. He hesitates, for instance, about using distinguishing phrases that appear in the literature, such as boys being intrusive and girls inclusive (Lowe 1972, p. 92). There is however some confirmation in such matters from those working in the feminist therapy movement, where there are some writers who believe that there are significant differences not just in society's views of men and women, but also in the different treatment many mothers give to sons and daughters. They also suggest that there may be something distinctive about the female psyche: for example, 'the basic feminine sense of self is connected to the world, the basic masculine self is separate' (Chodorow 1978, p. 162). Such feminist writers who are involved in therapy press the case for enabling women to develop the capacity for separateness which men have, and observe that men are by and large afraid of relatedness.

It may yet be that with advances in understanding of these matters we will be able to identify psychological differences between men and women which are linked in some way to sexual differences, and not simply to roles in the family or in society. At the same time, the counsellor needs to take notice of the false dichotomy between masculine and feminine which is prevalent in society — and indeed in many clients — and which feminists rightly challenge. What is fascinating is to see a partial return to Freudian thinking (at first rejected as completely chauvinist) by some of the writers on female psychology in the feminist movement. In fact Freud himself challenged the use of the terms masculine and feminine to describe anything other than anatomical differences. Although he was as puzzled about the 'riddle of the nature of femininity' (Freud 1964, p. 113), he writes that these terms terms add nothing to our knowledge. Masculinity and femininity have come to describe qualities such as active, aggressive. independent (all seen as masculine), or passive, intuitive and sensitive (feminine). Freud's belief in a bisexual component in physical development (at least up to the genital stage) underlines the importance of the counsellor assisting clients to accept what we might call the bisexuality of personal qualities: that is, men *and* women have the capacity to be both active and passive, scientific and poetic, assertive and sensitive. Jung (1953) expresses similar ideas, although he uses different terms. Each man needs to acknowledge and find greater expression for the 'anima' (female principle) within himself, and each woman for the animus (male principle).

Examples abound in counselling practice of clients who fear that they are homosexual because, for instance, they appreciate or write poetry, or who fear they are 'butch' because of their aggressive feelings. There is no need to expand such examples here. What is important is not only to help such clients recognize that their fears are often based upon stereotypes and derogatory remarks made to them by peers or parents in current or past situations (because these critics find such qualities threatening), but also to work towards helping such clients express their genitality sufficiently confidently, so that other personal qualities are unassailed by fears of being less than masculine or less than feminine. The case of Vernon illustrates the point:

> Vernon's concern that he might gay was based upon his love of music and literature, which some of his male sporty friends felt was 'queer'; but also upon a sexual difficulty — secondary impotence (i.e. he was only impotent in certain situations). Vernon tried for a time to

emulate his male friends by joining the football club, and going for long training sessions with them. It was not until the problems in intercourse were resolved (related to various factors which are introduced in this chapter), that he felt able to give up his attempts to be a 'macho' sportsman as not being his scene at all. His maleness was then firmly based upon sexual confidence, and so his masculinity was not threatened by others' remarks about his interest in the arts.

This chapter is much more concerned with male and female identity in sexual relationships than it is with masculinity and femininity in the sense mistakenly used by our culture. I believe that when issues about sexual identity can be resolved, sexism itself will assume less significance. For the first time in this account of development, the psychological paths of boy and girl diverge to some extent; this is, of course, a description of what is believed to take place, and is in no sense a value judgement about the relative worth of men and women.

Relationship problems in adult clients related to this stage are the most common ones presented in counselling, with authority problems running second, often as an integral part of the 'oedipal' difficulties. Modern psychoanalytic writing has tended to concentrate on the first year of life and problems related to it, but it was with this third stage that Freud's initial investigations began. It is still the starting place for many adult relationship problems. Even those who write extensively about the earliest period of life acknowledge that oedipal problems cannot be by-passed, even when deeper disturbances are clearly present. When Guntrip writes that 'the first few years of analysis' will be concerned with this oedipal period, it is clear that it is also going to be the one which predominates in the much shorter times involved in counselling (Guntrip 1968, pp. 278–9).

Castration and penis envy

One of the difficulties of using psychodynamic theory is that its terms are sometimes used literally, sometimes symbolically, and sometimes as a mixture of both. Thus when Freud writes about the fear of castration in the male (or little boy) or penis envy in the woman (or little girl), he bases his arguments on the symbols he finds in his patients, translating them into what may appear to be very narrow concepts, unless we in turn use those terms symbolically. We have to remember that we are dealing with phantasies, and that phantasies have subjective validity to the person experiencing them, even if they are distortions of more objective truth.

We have recalled already that children of this age ask many questions. Sometimes they provide themselves with the most delightful answers, which can bring a smile to the adult, but are taken seriously by the child. We often do the same with Freudian imagery: we smile, without always pausing to think that the child in the Freudian patient takes the phantasy seriously. Remember that the young child is interested in and puzzled by sexual differences, and it is not difficult to imagine how a boy (without adult knowledge) *might* react to discovering that mother, sister or a play friend does not have a penis; or how a girl reacts to seeing a penis on father's, brother's, or another boy's body. One possible explanation (for the girl) is that hers has been removed; and one possible phantasy (for the boy) is that his might likewise be. That does not mean that every child imagines that. Equally bizarre explanations may be a substitute for the truth.

Alternatively, such phantasies may arise not so much from the child, as from the threats used by parents: we may wonder what effect was caused by the words used by a mother when she noticed her young son handling his penis: 'Do that again and I'll call the doctor to cut it off.' That may seem an isolated case, but a group of young mothers said, when they were discussing such ideas in a W.E.A. class, that they recognized a parallel in an expression several of them used with their own children (sons and daughters): 'If you're naughty I'll cut your tail off.' It was an expression that had been used by their mothers to them, and which unthinkingly they used with their children. We have to ask how some children *might* interpret such words, when the only 'tail' they can see is the penis. The literal statement about castration and the metaphor can easily become confused. Similarly there are examples of literal penis envy in women, although there are many more obvious examples of such envy in men of the size of another man's penis; while Karen Horney observes that some boys wish to have breasts or children (Rubins 1978, p. 149). Thus, before throwing out Freudian ideas because they seem too narrow, we need to consider whether Freud's ideas in fact could be extended, in the way in which Karen Horney does, making fear and envy of the genitals of the opposite and the same sex a much more common occurrence. There is also evidence in more recent theory (e.g. the French analyst Lacan) that each gender wishes to rediscover early feelings of completeness and unity, and that this is represented by the desire to possess the opposite sex, of which the breast or the penis is a part-object symbolization.

The following examples suggest some evidence for, firstly literal penis envy in a woman, symbolizing wider envy of men; and secondly symbolic envy of a man by a man, which has links with more literal penis envy:

Win had come for counselling because she was unable to enjoy sexual intercourse with her husband. Much that she said pointed to her wish to be a man, although she did not use so open an expression. She liked 'to wear the trousers', and did not permit her husband to take the initiative in sex. She was very excited by pin-ups of women, and could only allow penetration if she was on top of her husband. She preferred watching him masturbate, or bringing herself to a climax with a vibrator (her own penis). She was turned on by reading letters in male magazines about men's erections. In addition to all this she enjoyed rifle-shooting, and had once cornered an instructor and told him what a 'lovely cock' he had, although she would not permit him to have intercourse with her. Although Win never acknowledged that she envied the penis, she often expressed envy of her brother, who was very successful in his career, and whom she felt was her parents' favourite. She also envied men all the privileges they had, but was as opposed to the feminist movement as if she had been the most chauvinist type of male.

Alec had great admiration for his father, who was a 'big man' in his business, admired by everyone, but who in fact was frequently denigrated by Alec's mother as not being assertive enough of his own rights. Alec wanted to be like his father and rise to the top of the same profession, but he could never follow through the opportunities which might have led to this. The only time he had ever criticized father was when he had given him a wallet, because it was a plastic one, and not like the large leather one his father had. Alec threw it through a closed window in his temper. It seemed to symbolize his feeling of inferiority.

Alec treated his wife as the 'inferior' one in the partnership, as if she embodied the inferior side of himself. He constantly drew attention to her mistakes, denigrating her (as mother had done father). He was deferential to his male counsellor, although he spoke of relations to other authority figures as fraught: he was often angry at their power over him. He usually made such situations worse by lashing out at them in a manner which reminded the counsellor of the way a child can hit out at an adult — ferociously but ineffectively.

In his dreams Alec would sometimes see himself as a woman, with other men whom he would identify as homosexuals he had met. The counsellor used such imagery to illustrate how Alec felt inferior (like a woman in society), and that he felt weak and powerless in his transactions with other men. In his dreams he 'castrated' himself, and submitted to men. Alec was thrilled one day when he was able to stand up to the driver of a huge lorry who had forced him off his pedal bike, even though within he felt like running away. The imagery used throughout (lorry/bike, man/woman, leather/plastic wallet) appeared to link in with the symbolic terms penis envy, or penis inferiority. This was confirmed when the counsellor drew Alec's attention to his envy of his father's wallet. Alec responded (without any prompting by the counsellor) that he remembered once seeing his father's penis, and thinking how big it was compared to his.

We do, of course, live in a culture which has absorbed much Freudian imagery, and we must always allow for some clients using such images in order to please the counsellor. But as long as we translate the symbolism into the wider context of human relationships it is often effective; and on occasions can even be taken rather more literally in its own right.

Oedipus — myth and symbol

In the first two stages of life the relationship between the child and the parents is mainly between two persons alone. In the O.S. it is mother who is the more important of the two parents, even when father takes a more active role in sharing the nurturing. In the A.S., although fathers are traditionally seen as authoritarian figures, it is still often mothers who carry the bulk of the responsibility. So while in both stages the child also relates to the father, father is sometimes a substitute for mother, not yet a person in his own right. This is not to denigrate his role, which is vital in supporting and sharing decisions and worries, but mothers do in practice normally provide more continuous care of the child.

By the time we reach the third age, one-to-one and one-by-one, relationships broaden out, siblings are related to more fully [Jealousy and competition p. 112], and there is a recognition that the parents have their own relationship. This relationship may be seen as a co-operative and relatively harmonious one; it may be full of arguments; it may be an unequal one with either partner dominant over the other. In sections that follow, we shall see how the tensions which exist in the relationships between the parents, or between parent and child, affect the child's attempts to make intimate relationships later in adult life. But here we also consider the likely course of events when the parents relate reasonably well to each other and to the child, since it is this that forms the basis for successful negotiation of what is called the 'oedipal stage'.

If we are to understand this central feature of Freud's early work (also known as the Oedipus complex), it is essential that we distinguish the term 'oedipal stage' from the Oedipus myth. The story of Oedipus concerns what can go wrong in family relationships. The oedipal stage covers all normal development as well, and culminates in a satisfactory resolution when adults can relate to a sexual partner of their own as man/woman to woman/man, without the child/parent relationship distorting their partnership. The oedipal stage will always contain some elements that are symbolized in the Oedipus myth, but in healthy development the extremes of that story do not occur. We think we know the Oedipus story well — the young man who kills his father and marries his mother and who then blinds himself when he discovers what he has done. In fact, as Bettelheim (1983) points out, the myth which Freud knew so well contains far more than that: Oedipus is abandoned by his real parents because they want to *avoid* the incest and patricide that is foretold of their son, but instead of dying he is adopted by the king and queen of Corinth, and he grows up believing them to be his real parents. When the oracle informs Oedipus too that he is to kill his father and marry his mother he leaves Corinth, again because he wishes to *avoid* such heinous crimes, unaware that he is in fact safer where he is. So he kills his father and weds the widow not knowing that he has fulfilled his fate. Bettelheim observes that when he blinds himself it is as much for failing in knowledge (not seeing) as for the crimes themselves.

Fuller acquaintance with the myth shows that what is at issue is a natural wish to *avoid* incest and patricide, which is only thwarted when 'fate' intervenes. In a child's development there is a wish for closeness and intimacy with the first love object, but also the natural wish to avoid incest, so that Oedipus' fate is only repeated either when parents reject too strongly the child's love and sexuality, or when either over-stimulates the child. In successful resolution of this stage children learn that their love and their nascent sexuality are accepted, and through a positive relationship to both parents learn to identify with one (of the same sex) and form a good enough but not over-close relationship with the other (of the opposite sex), thus providing a basis for their choice of a sexual partner in adult life. But from this point also they learn that their wish for intimacy has limits set on it by both parents; they recognize their parents' own intimacy, and so begin to leave mother and father behind them. To repeat, it is when there is either rejection of the child's love and sexuality in a harsh way, or rejection of one parent by the other and thus over-stimulation of the child's wish for closeness (usually with the parent of the opposite sex), that oedipal problems arise.

So in healthy development the child does not constantly wish to marry mother or father and kill the other. To be sure there are times when such thoughts occur, as when a six-year-old boy said 'If anything happens to daddy I'll marry you mummy', or when a slightly older girl said to her mother 'I'll never find anyone as good as daddy to marry.' There will be times of rage when a child will wish one of the parents dead — we all have such thoughts when tempers are boiling. There will be times when a child feels jealous of the parents' relationship, wanting to come into their bed either to share their closeness or to separate them so that he or she can have one or both to himself or herself. A child is not normally conscious of the wish for sex with a parent (although it can appear in dreams), but a child does have to struggle with sexuality when one of the parents appears to require a physical intimacy which oversteps the natural limits. This is particularly noticeable in adolescence when sons and daughters, and parents too, do not quite know how to manage intimate feelings which previously came naturally — such as a hug, or a kiss on the cheek, since they are conscious of the sexuality of the other. Trouble arises when the natural adjustment to sexuality and its limits are made more conscious through parents or children allowing them to be acted out: as we shall see in following sections, when a child or young person feels that one parent's attention to himself takes precedence over feelings for the other parent, or when death or separation takes one parent away, or a child feels his own love and sexual identity rejected, then the Oedipus myth is repeated. Where the approaches of a parent are directly or indirectly sexual, as we shall see in examples in the following sections, the problems are even greater. The need to leave mother and father and form sexual and intimate relationships of one's own, however, is a common task for all, and the Oedipus story, in differing degrees of intensity, will find echoes in normal as well as abnormal development.

There is one more aspect of normal development which merits attention before we look at the problem areas. Boys and girls have followed a common path of psychological development up to this stage of life, but the oedipal stage introduces a further step for girls. Both sexes started life attached to mother, so that the most obvious person to whom they relate in the early years, and with whom they wish to share their love, is her. Boys have to make the transition from directing their love towards mother to intimacy with other women in adolescence, normally making one close partnership in early adulthood. This woman will often have some psychological resemblance to his mother. The path is not quite so smooth for girls, since their first love object, being mother, is a homosexual attachment, and they need to move from this to heterosexual love. Father is therefore, even in development that goes fairly smoothly, the second love object, and they have to make yet another shift away from father towards other men. A double shift carries with it more risk of problems than a single shift of object. Furthermore some feminist therapists (e.g. E. Belotti, 1975) have suggested (as Freud himself said) that mothers tend to give less nurture to their daughters than to their sons — we see here oedipal feelings in the parent; indeed a mother is often more jealous of her son's wife than a father is of his daughter's husband. If there is truth in these arguments, it may also be less easy for a girl to detach herself from mother from whom she still wants more love. Certainly men often fail to recognize that women want mothering as much as men do; in some partnerships there are problems because the man takes the woman's wish for comfort as a sexual sign, and not as an expression of her wish for him to be maternal. This is seen in the following example, where the young woman was still attached to a mother-substitute, and in this case not even ready to integrate the sexual:

> Bridget did not know how to cope with her fiancé's wish for sex. As long as he was caring, did things for her, bought her presents, and was kindly towards her, the relationship went well. But when he wanted to sleep with her, not only did she feel anxious and refuse him, but she turned to her close girl friend for sex. As long as her fiancé was maternal Bridget appeared to be happy; as soon as he wanted to be 'male', she was driven back to a homosexual love-object, and to her need for a mother-figure alone.

It is perhaps the greater difficulty of detachment from mother that helps us to understand the greater tempestuosity in the teenage years in the mother–daughter relationship. Since the girl has to make such a major change, from female love-object to male love-object, not just a change of person in her object choice, she needs more assertion if her wish for detachment is to overcome her wish to remain attached. Just as a rocket leaving the gravitational pull of the earth needs greater energy than one which is leaving the moon, so the fire in the daughter helps her to push away from her mother.

The eternal triangle

Novels, films and plays so often have plots based upon triangular situations that we can be sure that three-person relationships — two women and one man, two men and one woman — present us with unresolved issues that we like to see played out before us. Indeed we might be so bold as to say that there can be very few marriages where there has not been, at some time, at the least a hint of a triangular situation, sometimes within the parent–parent–child relationship, and sometimes in the phantasy or fact in one or both partners of an extra-marital affair. Whether or not such phantasies are acted out, the counsellor will often find evidence of unresolved oedipal problems.

The triangular situation is not always outside the family. If children have their wishes to have mother or father for themselves, so too can parents easily bring such phantasies to life in the way they use their children as allies against each other. The child becomes the confidant (sometimes from an early age), the person with whom complaints about the partner are shared. The child can even be told the intimacies of the parents' sexual life, and feel both excited and yet guilty (or even disgusted) by what they hear. Children are not necessarily slow to exploit the differences between the parents: not, as in the A.S., playing off one authority figure against the other, but trying to achieve closeness with one to the exclusion of the other. Should the parents separate, or the hated/feared parent die, then guilt in the child at having brought this about is quite possible. John Le Carré writes of what a child can feel in *Tinker, Tailor, Soldier, Spy* (1974), and in a television profile since has identified his own experience with the young boy in the novel:

> Most of all he blamed himself for the break-up of his parents' marriage, which he should have seen coming and taken steps to prevent. He even wondered whether he was more directly responsible, whether for instance he was abnormally wicked or divisive or slothful and that his bad character had wrought the rift (p. 15.).

Triangular relationships seldom consist of one triangle alone — each apex can be the apex of yet another triangle. The case of Charles illustrates this well:

Charles was a mild person, married to a woman who was something of a tyrant. He was pushed around by her, always feeling unable to make his own decisions. The relationship survived for some years, with Charles willing to take this role. Then his mother died. (The death of a parent sometimes leads to a shift in the balance of the 'child's' marriage.) His mother had been a fairly timid and distant person. Charles, meanwhile, found himself involved with a woman who was engulfed by her husband, and her situation aroused anger in him towards her husband. He identified how she felt with his own relationship. They started an affair, which after a few months was discovered by her husband, who forbade her to see Charles. This she refused to do, trying to seduce Charles away from his wife, yet at the same time taking fright whenever he seemed prepared to do it. At such times she distanced herself from Charles.

Charles began to feel guilty, but also very angry with this woman, and he described in counselling how he felt just as he did when a child, with mother being distant, and father making life hell for him. His father would express violent jealousy of mother's affection for Charles, although Charles himself never felt that mother dared to express what she felt for him. He was therefore angry with the woman's husband for being like his father; and with her for never being brave enough to follow her feelings through. He also felt angry with his wife for being so tyrannical. We see in his marriage an inverted oedipal resolution where Charles has identified with his mother, and married someone like his father. In his extra-marital relationship he was attempting to set that situation right by choosing a woman more like his mother. But, as so often happens, it was a false solution, with the new woman reinforcing the negative side of mother, and compounding the problem for Charles. In despair he left them both, and chose a third woman who was divorced, only to discover after a few months that she was periodically going back to her former husband.

The rejecting parent

The last example shows the importance of allowing expression of affection between mother and son, father and daughter, without it becoming too intense, as well as the expression of the love between the parents which helps the child to move away from them. A child wishes to reach out, and to say, as it were, 'Let me give you, let me love you, let me touch you', with the emphasis here upon 'you', as distinct from the emphasis upon 'me' which has been present in the first two stages. Rejection of what the child offers takes place not only through open hostility, but also through passive distancing; and such a rejecting parent so easily becomes translated into the rejecting lover in adult life, or fosters in the child fear of rejection in adult relationships, and difficulty in becoming a person who dares to express love. The child's love and sexuality need to be affirmed as being good, and yet deflected so that they can later be given to and accepted by another when the child becomes an adult. Yet in many triangular situations there is eventually as much frustration as there was in the original parent/child relationship. Some men and women always seem to be in search of the unobtainable.

Debbie's father was often abroad on construction work during her childhood and adolescence. Not unlike other teenagers, she developed a crush on one of her male teachers at school, and worked especially hard for him. She remembered being very disappointed when he did not remark on her special efforts to please him. We might expect this in youngsters. However, Debbie went on to university, slightly later than usual, and again idolized one of her male tutors. She pursued him via her work, and felt sure that he also loved her. When, however, the tutor appeared to respond to her (although it seemed from her account only a friendly gesture, not a sexual one) Debbie became angry with him for wanting to seduce her, and she left university at the end of her first year. She then got a job in an office, where a manager of a different department would come in and flirt with the typists. At first she thought he was 'dishy', but then began to feel he had his eyes on her. She engineered a meeting with him, and confronted him, asking him what his intentions were. Taken aback, the man was angry and unfortunately told her she had a screw loose. So Debbie left that job. When she came to the counsellor she was experiencing these feelings all over again in a second job, although by now she had recognized that she was projecting her wishes for a sexual relationship on to an unattainable father figure, and that she needed to look at the reasons for her turning down the genuine advances by men of her own age.

The counsellor is another of the unobtainable figures whom such a client encounters. The oedipal situation is therefore also implicit in counselling, especially where the counsellor and the client are of the opposite sex. There is a fine line to be drawn by the counsellor (as there is for the parent) between accepting and affirming the client's sexuality and attractiveness, and being seen as seductive and encouraging sexual feelings. The counsellor cannot be the client's lover, anymore than a parent can be; so the disappointment, anger or feelings of inadequacy or unattractiveness in the client at the counsellor's 'distance' will be understood better when related to the frustration of sexual and loving feelings towards a parent. Such a link is more constructive than any explanation along the lines of: 'You realize that as a counsellor I can't get involved with you.' Just as the counsellor working with very dependent people has to draw out their feelings of her failure to be the ever-present source of care, or with submissive people their feelings of her failure to tell them what to do, so the counsellor works with a client's feelings at her failure to become a sexual partner or lover; while at the same time delicately affirming the client's worth [p. 59].

Exhibitionism

The wish for affirmation and admiration of his sexuality is one of the explanations of the insecure man who exposes himself to women, although we shall see later that there is also a hostile component. Exhibitionism is not confined to flashers, or indeed to strippers. It is seen in the enjoyment of being admired, although often at a safe distance. It has some connections therefore with narcissism [p. 39–42]. The stage is one place where such needs can be expressed, and where alternative roles can be taken on temporarily and acted out, without having to own that the role is also oneself. There is also the element of admiration and affirmation from the audience, safely seated beyond the footlights. Although the following example includes the theatre, there are other metaphorical stages where people take on roles, and hide behind masks:

> Elaine had never felt affirmed as a young woman by her father, who spent his spare time fishing, away from home. She was unable to allow herself any sexual relationship, and was even afraid of being touched. Yet as an amateur actress she not only received some sense of value from the audience's applause, but was also able to play the sexual

woman on stage. But if one of the cast asked her out, she always refused, even steering clear of post-production parties. There is more to Elaine's story than this, and we shall add other experiences in the next section [p. 101].

The seducing parent

One of the earliest errors Freud made was to take literally what his patients told him about being seduced as children by an adult. Later, although not before the damage had been done to his reputation, he revised his theory, and said that such stories were in fact *phantasies* of being seduced. The taboo on incest (and its breaking in the Oedipus myth) remained central for him. We have noted how prevalent the theme of triangular situations is in literature. The same can be said for the incest theme, whether in those picaresque tales where lovers turn out to be siblings, or in the modern examples of television drama in which incest is a pivotal theme: 'I, Claudius'; 'The Borgias'; 'Cleopatra'; and 'Bouquet of Barbed Wire', to name some in recent years. That incest should be a taboo makes sense when looked at genetically. Evolution is served better by the mixing of genes, so leading to variety within the species, better able to adapt to the changing environment. Most species breed out because the choice of mate is wide, and inbreeding need not occur. The inhibition on inbreeding is instinctive in some species, but the taboo is culturally acquired and almost universal in some form or other in most human societies. But whatever the explanation of the inhibition, the acting out of incest in the phantasy world of literature and film seems to hold a fascination, as long as it is safely confined to the imagination.

The inhibitions upon, and conversely the interest in, incest appear to work as long as relationships do not actually become incestuous, or symbolically so. Where they do, there can be serious effects. What is strange is that Freud's original 'error' may not have been that far from the truth at least in early adolescence. Social workers and counsellors can cite many examples (which do not have the ring of phantasy about them) of sexual relations between members of the same nuclear family. The counsellor learns not to be surprised when a presenting situation, with incestuous imagery implicit in it, turns out to have some substance in the past. (J. Masson (1984) has made the same point, though appears to underestimate the significance of phantasy in his wish to restore actual incest to its original Freudian significance.) The case of Freda is an example.

Freda visited her doctor when she became very upset after an interview for a job. The interviewer had asked her for a date, and she had refused him. He, in turn, declined to give her the job. This, of course, would be upsetting for anyone; and allowing her to express her feelings helped calm her down. The doctor invited Freda to return for a longer session the next week. She already felt better and she took the opportunity to talk about her relationships with men. She had noticed how often men tried to pick her up — in the pub and elsewhere. She felt she must be giving off some signs to them, and since she was sitting in the chair in a short skirt with her legs wide open the doctor thought there might be something in this! Freda went on to talk about her father's sexual advances when she was in her teens, stroking her breasts while sitting next to her. She managed to control the situation by sitting in another part of the room and resisting his invitations to sit with him. But, at the same time, she regretted that she had to lose out on the closeness which, in her pre-pubertal years, she had always enjoyed with her father. The doctor pointed out how she may indeed have felt she seduced the interviewer to some extent, but was very upset when he had inappropriately asked her out, and she had lost the job she wanted; just as father's approaches were inappropriate to their relationship, and yet turning him down meant that she lost out there too.

The dilemma of wishing to have a close relationship, and yet at the same time wanting to stay clear of sexual complications, appears time and again, with resulting damage to other relationships:

Grace could not allow herself to get too close to men: she preferred a series of casual sexual relationships. She was told by her stepfather, when she resisted his wish to come into her bed when her mother was away, 'But you're not my real daughter.' This added a deep wound to the sexual threat, and she tended to get caught in relationships where she was 'the second woman'. Other examples could be given (though less frequently seen in counselling) of men who have been seduced by a close female relation, in whom there appear similar difficulties.

Let us return to Elaine [p. 99]. Her father had remarried when she was still small and she acquired a new 'mother' and a step-brother ten years her senior. She idolized the brother (perhaps as a substitute for distant

father), content just to sit at his feet and enjoy being in his presence.
When she was twelve he suddenly left home to join the army, and she
was heart-broken. Two years later she received a further blow when he
married. He and his wife came to stay, and when everyone was out
except herself and her brother, she cuddled up to him for comfort, but
the closeness led to intercourse. Elaine felt so guilty afterwards that she
could not speak to him, and had not done so since. She was unable to
let men near her (except on the stage) and could only be friends with
'older married men on a sisterly basis'. Although she thus described
men with whom she felt safe, she did not recognize that they
represented the one man with whom a sisterly relationship had gone
wrong.

The counsellor working with Elaine tried to remain sensitive to her
wish to end her isolation from men, but also to her fear of a man getting
too close. As a man himself he tried to demonstrate to her that he could
be trusted, so that she could learn to trust in turn her sexual feelings for
men. She tended to see men as the ones with designs on her, rather
than acknowledge her own desires. The anger with the step-brother
gave way to feelings of the love she still had for him. So, although the
counselling had to finish before the issues could be resolved, the
counsellor felt that Elaine made some progress towards talking about
intimacy, and towards the expression of love (including affection for the
counsellor) without fear that it would turn sexually against her.

The critical parent

Although the critical parent may appear to belong to the A.S., criticism
also influences sexual development, and the child's ability to feel close to
each parent, either as an adult to love, or as one with whom to identify.
The parent who cannot permit a child to share his wish for closeness
through criticism of his wish to give, or the parent who frightens the child
from feeling affection for the other partner are two examples of the critical
parent, as is the one who comes down hard against sexual play and
exploration. Sex, in the last instance, may be seen as dirty, and become
linked to the A.S., so that in adolescence, for example, menstruation or
wet-dreams become associated with shame, yet another product of the
body which is felt to be 'disgusting'. But there may also be evidence of
parental criticism of sexual exploration in childhood:

Hugh was terrified (by the phantasy, not reality) that he would want to touch a child sexually if ever he got close to one, and that he would then be imprisoned. He told an illuminating story of his mother's reaction on discovering that a boy two years older than Hugh and himself had 'compared' penises in the woodshed. Although Hugh was only five at the time, he remembered his mother threatening to call the police, and himself hiding under the table in fear. Mother may have been concerned, of course, and perhaps wanted to punish the older boy, but Hugh felt that he himself had committed the crime. She did not realize that homosexual activity at this age (and even later) is the normal precursor of heterosexual development, and not indicative of perversion or corruption (see Anna Freud 1973, p. 159).

We should also note the scorn of some parents at behaviour in their children which seems disconsonant with 'being a boy' or 'being a girl', and that this can lead to unnecessary anxieties such as those outlined earlier [Male and female, p. 86–89]. Boys (and men) do cry, and girls do like to get muddy, climb trees, etc. Criticism, particularly by the parent of the same sex, may lead in fact to doubts about being able to identify with him or her, even pushing the child towards further identification with the opposite sex.

The opposite sex as a threat

Where, for any of the reasons above, the growing sexual identity of the child is threatened (by rejection, hostility, criticism or seduction) there will often be difficulties in relating fully to the opposite sex. One way in which difficulty is manifested is in splitting relationships and the different aspects of love: some clients can only relate to one person as a mother/father figure, to another as a sexual object, and to a third as a friend and companion. The integration of all these aspects into one intimate relationship proves impossible. Others can only relate to the opposite sex as long as there is no obvious sexual attraction; presented with a sexually exciting person they clam up and do not know how to conduct a conversation. Some people (less likely to become clients unless they begin to feel the shallowness of their relationships) do not seem to be able to talk to a member of the opposite sex without actually or in phantasy taking them to bed. The ability to inhibit sexual feelings towards the majority of people we encounter is as important a sign of maturity as the ability to relate fully to one person.

There are however more sinister ways in which the threat presented by the opposite sex is dealt with. Sexual perversions — exhibitionism, voyeurism, and sadistic sexual attacks upon women — naturally arouse our anger, although as counsellors we also need to pause to consider what sort of man perpetrates them. Beneath the bravado is a frightened man, whose masculinity is theatened by men or women, or by both: women because they represent genitally the damaged man he feels himself to be, or because they represent the woman he feels has damaged him or will emasculate him. (Note the symbolism which is used here, which needs to be taken much more widely than just the genital.) Hugh [p. 103] associated one of his dreams of a shark with the vaginal 'jaws' which he feared. By interpreting such imagery symbolically we can relate it to the fear of being swallowed up by a woman, not just genitally, but existentially. According to one feminist writer it is because the hand that rocks the cradle is female that men

> fear the will of women and the helplessness of infancy, and employ such strategies to avoid facing their fears as the segregation of men and women at work, in religious activities, in legal and social restrictions on women's rights, and the separation of physical and emotional love to avoid the 'melting' experience of intense intimacy (Dinnerstein 1978, p. 236).

We need to add to this list sexual attacks on women. Although our horror at such attacks rouses our antagonism to these men, working with sexual offenders requires understanding of the very primitive fears which they have.

Not surprisingly, given the enormity of some offences and the publicity afforded them (some of which, surely, actually feeds on the sadistic or masochistic tendencies of the more normal person?), women can feel men generally to be a threat. No counsellor can overlook the reality of their fears. At the same time, especially when these fears are paralyzing the woman's freedom to make relationships, the counsellor might need to look for evidence of past experience which needs working through, so that men in general do not become stereotyped. Most men are not sexual assailants. It is proper caution not to trust a stranger, but some extreme feminists deny that it is possible to trust men at all. In this respect — the fear of the opposite sex — chauvinism and a type of extreme feminism have something in common.

Imogen's feminism, which was based on a serious and convincing analysis of sexual politics, nevertheless contained a hostility to men which led to a wish to humiliate them intellectually and socially. It was not her political analysis, but rather the extreme terror on being raped when she was eighteen that had led to this position. Such an event cannot but have made an indelible impression upon her. She imagined, as she walked along the street, that every man she passed had a gun in his pocket. The symbolism was obviously a reference to her horrifying experience. The male counsellor tried to help her to talk about that time, which up to then she had shared with no-one not even her women friends, and helped her to understand her wish to exact revenge. What was interesting was that Imogen not only began to enjoy the company of men (although remained cautious about getting too intimate) but that she also began to develop a critique of the sexism present in some of her feminist friends, which she felt was as damaging to good relationships as the sexism present more generally in society.

Hysteric or histrionic?

There is one type of client whom helpers are taught to fear: taught not formally, but by innuendo and implication. This is typically the woman who seduces men and the male helper to the point of arousing their interest; then she 'cuts and runs'. Such a woman is called 'the hysteric'. To be sure there is sometimes a nod in the direction of men, with the description of the Don Juan character. In the helping mythology he is the one who seduces women and leaves them, although in this case intercourse is assumed to take place.

Yet if we look in the classical psychoanalytical literature we are hard pressed to find this type of man or woman being called 'the hysteric'. In Fenichel's encyclopaedic work *The Psychoanalytic Theory of Neurosis* (1946), the term does not appear in the comprehensive index. Hysteria refers there either to phobias (anxiety-hysteria) or to the loss of function of part of the body from psychological rather than physiological cause (conversion-hysteria). There is a link to the term 'hysteric' since such symptoms are seen as attempts to cope with sexual excitement, but there is no description of the man or woman described in the paragraph above. The closest we get to it is in Fenichel's section on character disorders. When he describes the histrionic person and the schizoid character we find some parallels to the 'hysteric', and in a digression in the chapter on organ neuroses he outlines the hypersexual person (referring to the Don Juan type and to nymphomania).

In both these last sections Fenichel suggests that there are pre-oedipal factors. What men and women of this type experience is an intense hunger for love, and for incorporation with mother. 'Schizoid' is a term we have already used in the O.S., thereby indicating the level of disturbance [p. 37]; and 'narcissism' is similarly referred to there [p. 39]. Fenichel has no doubts about the narcissistic needs of this type of person. Sexuality is used as a substitute for a more primitive need, the wish to be reunited with mother; and the sexual greed which is often apparent is a substitute for infantile needs of love. Alternatively the 'flight' of such people indicates their ambivalence about closeness.

This digression is important because there is a tendency to classify the hysteric as the castrating woman who is out to wreak vengeance on as many men as possible, and as a woman who makes male helpers very angry and frustrated. I have no wish to deny the existence of such women (as long as we acknowledge that there are men like that too, even if counsellors see fewer of them because they see fewer men in general). But to see them simply as castrating and as playing with sexuality is to miss out on the fear that they have that their needs for love will never be met. As a result they often have to flee before they themselves experience rejection.

> Jenny was very honest, and indeed perceptive, about her feelings whenever she seduced a man, and dropped him the next day. There were three clear gains for her at the time, although she felt regret afterwards. First, she wanted to give a man such a good time that he was left with a picture of her as someone really special, whom he would always remember. Second, she chose men who thought themselves macho and proceeded to so dominate them in sex that they felt weak and inferior. She compounded this by never speaking to them again, just nodding at them if she ever met them, in a condescending way. She admitted she got great pleasure from seeing such 'fine' examples of men become submissive. Third, Jenny enjoyed other girls admiring the bravado with which she picked up her men and spoke of them so disparagingly afterwards. They would ask her, 'What was he like?', and envy the domination she had gained.
>
> Jenny's insight was so clear that it was possible to make a direct link between this behaviour and her childhood, when she was for years the special favourite of her father, but was suddenly pushed from favour

when he remarried and pushed her out of his attentions, his new wife coming between them. She hated her father for this. At the same time, while much of this material was obviously linked to oedipal problems, Jenny described the need to treat men in this way as 'like a drug' — indicating a deeper hunger which has associations with the O.S.

Keith spoke for many sessions of his relationships with women and his phantasies about them, in ways which indicated that he saw women only as sexual objects. When the counsellor chanced a remark about all the sexual talk being something of a red herring, Keith broke down and cried, and talked of feeling unloved and unwanted and useless, particularly in relation to his mother, and for the first time the counsellor felt they had reached a much more genuine feeling than all the previous bravado.

While there are histrionic people who flaunt their sexuality, or who use hypersexuality as a way of expressing their anger with the opposite sex, the counsellor who encounters the 'hysteric' will also need to look for problems which run deeper than sexuality; considering the possibility that such a person is desperately unhappy, hungry for love, and yet terrified of rejection. The counsellor will then not be seduced by the excitement of the sexual presentation or repelled by her distaste of it. She will look for opportunities to interpret deeper levels than the sexual. Where she recognizes the presence of oral complications she may even see her task as one of steering such clients towards longer-term counselling or therapy, if she is inexperienced in handling this type of problem.

Homosexuality

If counselling is first and foremost about listening, then counsellors need to listen to homosexual pressure groups, not only to understand the ways in which homosexuals come up against irrational prejudice, but also to consider their arguments that their homosexual orientation has no simple explanation. It is easy for 'psychological' to be used as a pejorative term: homosexuals rightly remind us that 'it's only psychological' is a glib way of labelling them, just as the equation of homosexuality with some mental illness is hurtful. The pressure groups have surely been right to reject the type of classification of their difficulties which makes them into social outcasts: whether they are right to claim that their sexual orientation is 'normal' is not so clear. However, these theoretical matters cannot be compressed into one paragraph, and our concern is with counselling the homosexual in practice. Just as in all counselling, what makes the greatest difference is whether the client wants to change, or wishes to stay as he (or she) is. If an authoritarian person comes for help, but does not wish to change his authoritarian attitude, the counsellor will find it hard to be effective. Likewise if a homosexual comes for counselling, and is quite sure that he wishes to be a homosexual, the counsellor can only work on those areas that make the client feel unhappy. In the course of counselling the counsellor may wish to allude to the authoritarian attitude of the one client, or the homosexuality of the other, and this may indeed throw light on the difficulty in such a way as to help broaden the dimensions of thinking — even if a person feels he cannot change. But in all counselling, the counsellor can only take his cue from the client.

In this section our concern is more with the man or woman who fears that he or she is homosexual, and who wishes to be heterosexual. This is in no way to deny that some clients are homosexuals and wish to remain so, but have other difficulties — a punitive super-ego, a tendency to get into masochistic situations, etc. Such difficulties are looked at in other sections of this book. Neither is it implied that heterosexuals do not have problems, nor that indeed hypersexuality may sometimes be a 'cover' for homosexual anxieties. Homosexual feelings are probably present in everyone, and the ability to accept such feelings is as important for the wholeness of the heterosexual, as is the acceptance of repressed heterosexual feelings in the homosexual. The suspicion and vilification of homosexuals is often the result of projection of personal fear and shame.

The age and sexual experience of the client who comes for counselling will influence the counsellor's approach. Sexual identity is still plastic into the early twenties, especially when there has been little or no sexual experience. Young people can easily convince themselves that they are homosexual when the evidence they produce is slight. The fact that as teenagers they have had crushes on members of their own sex, or have engaged in mutual masturbation, does not of itself indicate that they are homosexual — such experiences fall well within the range of normal adolescent development. Asking about their masturbatory phantasies, the counsellor sometimes finds that they are of sexual relations with the opposite sex, often with the 'partner' taking the initiative. Attraction to members of their own sex sometimes takes the form of admiration of one who represents the man, or the woman, whom they would wish to be, with physical or personal characteristics which they would like to have. Reassurance that none of these features are in themselves indications of permanent homosexual orientation, together with some supportive explanation about the normality of such feelings, particularly in adolescence, can be valuable in itself, easing the anxiety sufficiently to think about the problems encountered in translating heterosexual phantasies into real relationships.

> Lewis found himself looking at other men who were well-built, good-looking, and 'masculine' in their relationships with others; because he looked at them, he feared that he was a homosexual, even though the thought of sex with a man turned him right off. The counselling revealed that he swung between thinking himself 'top dog' (as he had been at home and at school) and a 'right little shit' (which he had sometimes felt at home, but more often felt now). In comparing himself with the men he looked at, he felt the 'bottom dog', a passive, and even in some ways an anal image; certainly in the canine world a feminine one. In his wish to be like these other men, there was a sense in which he wished he was inside them, or they inside him — which of course is close to a sexual (and homosexual) image; but Lewis was taking the symbolism literally. He also wished to be hugged by these men, which seemed to be a way of soaking up some of their strength — as the child who feels weak is strengthened by the hug of an adult. Hugging is of course more threatening to those from an Anglo-Saxon culture than it is for those from latin cultures.

Some clients, as has already been stated in previous sections, can mistake their awareness of 'masculine' and 'feminine' qualities within themselves (such as assertiveness or sensitivity) for signs of homosexual orientation. The counsellor cannot afford to overlook anxieties of a more obviously sexual kind, but often she will want in such instances to reassure such clients by affirming that such personal qualities are asexual, while looking to see whether it is they themselves, or their parents, peers and society in general that makes them feel otherwise.

> Mark was twenty and had over the last year visited gay clubs in search of a permanent relationship. When he came to the counsellor he was very depressed and disillusioned, since that year had consisted of one date after another, in which he had been picked up for a night, and then dropped. At first he had been disgusted by the sexual side, but had

persisted because he hoped to find someone who would be faithful to him. The latest rejection had made him think again. In counselling he saw for himself how submissive he was in the relationships, but said that this submissiveness (and its opposite, the difficulty of taking initiative) applied just as much to heterosexual relationships, which he had avoided for that very reason. Since he was a student, and did not wish to fail his degree because of his depression, he decided to keep clear of attempts to make sexual relationships with either sex, and to think again later about the personal difficulties which might be influencing his sexual orientation.

There are other factors which the counsellor may look for in the presentation of homosexual anxiety. Sometimes there is fear of the opposite sex, of damaging or being damaged by sex. The relationship with parents will be as significant, as it is in all the other 'problems' presented in these chapters; and examples may be apparent of over-closeness, or the opportunity for over-closeness with the parent of the opposite sex, sometimes through the distance, absence, or fear of the temper of the parent of the same sex. Identification with the parent of the same sex is therefore difficult, and identification with the parent of the opposite sex takes precedence. While it would need testing out more thoroughly by looking at the patterns of parental relationship in heterosexual clients, my own impression is that in a good many homosexual clients the parental relationships are heavily imbalanced — with perhaps a mother who is dominant and a father who is seen as weak, or a mother who is passive and frightened of a punitive and aggressive husband. Whatever the validity of such a general observation, the relationship to both parents obviously needs to be related specifically to the client's feelings towards men and women in the current situation.

Although some guidelines may be helpful to the counsellor working with clients who have not acted upon their homosexual feelings, or with younger clients whose orientation has not become fixed, work with older people who have a history of homosexual relationships, yet who wish to change, presents much greater difficulty. This is true of other chronic (i.e. long-term) conditions as well, which nearly always need long-term help. Whether the counsellor is able to offer this by virtue of experience and availability depends also as in other difficulties on the degree of motivation and commitment in the client. However, it needs to be said that in the selection of patients for brief focal psychotherapy at the Tavistock Clinic, Malan has indicated that patent homosexual problems are included in the list of those who are normally not accepted (Malan 1976). Long-term psychotherapy is the treatment of choice.

The gender of the counsellor

In problems related to the first two stages the gender of the counsellor is by and large immaterial. Whether male or female, the counsellor will detect a tendency in O.S. clients to treat himself or herself as a 'maternal' figure, and as an authority figure (stereotyped as paternal) when problems relate to the A.S. With problems associated with the G.S., and in particular when the problem is to do with sexual relationships, the gender of the counsellor may be more significant. The man who fears women, or the woman who fears men, may therefore find it difficult to feel relaxed talking to a counsellor of the opposite sex — although in the long run it may be beneficial for them to do so. The counsellor can provide a model of the feared opposite sex which in itself permits the testing of assumptions. He or she may also provide a 'screen' upon whom transference distortions are projected and are seen more clearly. Clients who specifically ask to see a man or a woman are saying something important about themselves which it is useful to explore, even where a counsellor accedes (if it is possible) to such a request and refers such clients on. In the relationship between counsellor and client there will be patterns of response (active and passive) which provide glimpses or even more obvious indications of that person's ways of relating to men and women outside the counselling room.

When the counselling relationship is felt to work, the client may deny its relevance for other relationships by saying, 'But you're different, because you are a professional . . . .' This is partially true, and it is in itself no guarantee that other men or women will be as positive for the client who fears them; but a good counselling relationship can indicate that not all men or women have to be seen as threatening, critical, etc. While there may be some areas in which it is more difficult for a male counsellor to empathize with a female client (and vice versa) this is compensated for by what may be a new experience of having such a man or a woman acknowledge the client's needs and value. It is interesting that some feminist therapists have challenged their more critical sisters' assumptions that only women can help women. The reverse situation is seen in the following example:

A woman hospital chaplain was visiting a very weakened man in intensive care. He (Mario) had collapsed after a violent argument with his wife, who had become an ardent member of the feminist movement. On one of the chaplain's visits, Mario had unleashed a flood of anger and resentment, pouring out his feelings about his wife. 'He was one of the angriest and most violent personalities I have ever encountered', writes the chaplain, 'We were two enemies with reason to be suspicious and hostile toward one another. I am a liberated woman; Mario is a machismo man. And still we met on common ground. Each of us represented, to the other, someone who had done something unspeakable to us' (Haines 1978).

When clients have homosexual anxieties [see section above] the gender may again be significant, bearing in mind the intimacy of the counselling situation. Those who are afraid of their homosexuality will tend to avoid a counsellor of the same sex, or may feel awkward with them. Where choice of counsellors is possible, such anxiety is well respected:

> Norma initially saw a female counsellor, who intuitively picked up some anxiety in her, and so referred her to a male counsellor. Her intuition was confirmed in the first session he had with Norma, who said that there were things she had been unable to tell the woman she had first seen. She never went to women doctors. She had once had a lesbian relationship which continued to upset her, and she obviously feared the re-emergence of such feelings if she saw a woman doctor or counsellor.

Jealousy and competition

We have already alluded to the observation that the child of this stage begins to learn how to share the parents with each other, the parents with siblings (even though brothers and sisters may have been around since the child's birth) and to share in co-operative play with other children. Difficulties involving such situations include jealousy and over-competitiveness, or sometimes the opposite, lack of necessary drive and competitiveness. The following example illustrates intense jealousy, seen in oedipal terms:

> Olivia's mother had died when she was twelve, and her father had married again a year later. Olivia was very angry, both for her mother's

memory, but also it seemed for herself, being pushed out of her special position with her father. As soon as she was old enough she left home to live with a man 'old enough to be her father'. But she continued to be 'insanely jealous' of other women, and would not permit him to go out for a drink with his friends, even throwing a tantrum many mornings when he was leaving for work. To compound the picture, this man's mother was also very jealous of Olivia, and had felt the same of previous girlfriends whom her son had known. Olivia's greatest fear was that her man would look at other women and lose interest in her. Her male companion, talking to the counsellor, did not realize the full significance of what he was saying when he described her relationship to him as 'almost incestuous'.

Learning to share parents with other siblings can be equally difficult, especially when a brother or sister is born before the older child has become relatively independent of mother [see also 'Robin', p. 51]:

Penny was apparently devoted to her younger sister, born when Penny was eighteen months old. Yet there were signs that beneath the devotion there was much jealousy. In her dreams Penny would sometimes scratch her sister (even doing this once when sleep-walking). She was fanatically anti-abortion, and as a teenager she had sorely tested a close friendship when she told her pregnant girlfriend that she was a whore. Penny had been told by her mother that she used to hug her little sister so tightly as a baby that mother thought she was going to strangle her — although Penny thought it was because she loved her so much. Penny was also over-competitive in nearly everything she did, jealous (but also very guilty about her jealousy) at anyone else doing well, even though another person's success did not prevent her doing equally well. Over a long period of counselling she was able to acknowledge that she could have felt pushed out by the arrival of her younger sister, and that this helped to explain the fury she felt, but also regretted, in some of the situations described above. What was interesting (because it was in an area never directly mentioned by the counsellor) was that she also dropped her campaigning against abortion, and became much more understanding of the moral dilemma facing women. It may have been that her fanaticism was a reaction formation against her own wish to kill her young rival while still in the womb.

The inability to be competitive, sometimes manifested as depressed feelings of being unable to succeed and not being good enough, can cause problems in a society in which a certain amount of competition is inevitable — however regrettable that it should be so. Competitiveness can be channelled into sport, but even then it can be overdone, spoiling the game both for those who are successful and for those who are not so talented. Interviews for jobs, the 'winning' of a partner against the opposition of other likely candidates, and even some leisure pursuits, mean that the person who is anxious in the face of competition starts with an inbuilt disadvantage. The problem frequently lies not in any lack of ability (or personality in the case of relationships) but in the guilt which would be experienced were a person to be successful, in having 'defeated' others. Beneath the apparent unwillingness of some people to enter quasi-competitive situations, even those where it really does not matter who wins or who does not win, we find not only people who have experienced some shame in the past at lack of success (a lack of confidence which is more indicative of A.S. problems), but also those in the G.S. who react against their wish to triumph over another.

There can be signs of rivalry present in clients towards other people whom the counsellor sees or knows. 'You must see a lot of other people' may be more than a pleasantry, or a need for reassurance that they are not the only ones. It may also be a way of asking 'How important am I to you compared to the others?' The client who introduces other clients to the counsellor, while flattering her by spreading her reputation, may also be hinting that he himself feels unable to come for counselling without feeling that others must share her too. The counsellor's outside relationships may also be the subject of enquiry, or occasions of jealousy:

> Quentin had always felt inferior to his brother. Quentin's wife, before he had met her, had been his brother's girlfriend. One night Quentin dreamed of anger and jealousy towards a dark-haired man. When he 'free associated' to this dream, he realized that it had occurred the night after seeing his counsellor at a concert with her dark-haired husband.

The third stage of development is also one which, in our culture, sees the start of school and mixing with many more children. Going to school provides a setting in which co-operativeness can be learned, together with the ability to compete without malice towards rivals. 'Mutual play is the keystone of social development', writes Rayner (1978, p. 83). Mutual play, of course, gives rise to more than co-operation: in play children make and break alliances, forge and forget friendships, often in a very short space of time. Erikson calls this period 'the infantile politics of nursery school, street corner and barnyard' (Lowe 1972, p. 91). Children's games and make-believe give them opportunities to fight and make it up, to share power and leadership, to relate to other boys and girls, as part of the preparation for living as adults in a wider society, with all its problems national and international. What is perhaps frightening (as Erikson suggests in *Toys and Reasons*, 1978) is not that children should play such games, but that adults (particularly some politicians and their hangers-on) do not appear to have grown beyond them.

Transition

It is important to remind ourselves that these three initial stages have introduced themes and developmental tasks to the young child, but that they are not resolved simply, and certainly not within that age span alone. Sufficient resolution is necessary in order to be able to move through the early stages, but succeeding stages provide many opportunities for further resolution, as well as further difficulties which can lead to setbacks. As this age is left behind, sexuality is still only at an infantile stage. In normal development there should be some indication that the child has been able to give love, and yet also to some extent begin giving up love of the parents, with a basic sense of being able to share them with each other and with other members of the family. There should be sufficient feeling for the child of his sexuality being accepted, and his love valued, together with an awareness that sexuality can be inhibited in its expression towards the parent of the opposite sex. In time, during adolescence, those feelings will then normally be directed outwards from the family into loving relationships with others. When that time comes, loving will be expressed in a variety of ways — in sexual relationships, in companionship and friendships, in care about and for others: sexuality and 'aim-inhibited love' will be able to be distinguished, so that others can be loved as whole persons, and not as sexual objects. Where such development does not take place, the young person enters adolescence at a disadvantage, and sexuality then may either be inhibited, or become too dominant so that all relationships are sexualized; or result in part-object sexuality, such as in fetishism.

In satisfactory development the child will have begun making a good enough relationship with the parent of the same sex, so that in their inner world there begins to be built up an ego-ideal, based upon identification with the positive features of that parent — as distinct from the super-ego which is largely based upon negative features. In both processes internalization is taking place; so that with both parents now becoming part of the inner world of the child in their different ways, the child is ready to move even further away from them — firstly through going to school and into the latency period — in preparation for the break at adolescence which enables the young person to make real the child's games of 'mother and father'.

Not surprisingly, when their child first goes to school, parents often feel proud of their son or daughter looking so grown up, and at the same time feel sad at the more obvious signs of losing them. There is of course a long way to go before the little person becomes a mature adult, with much learning of many kinds still to take place, but everything which will go to make up that adult is already present in embryonic form, waiting to be developed in the succeeding stages of life.

References

Belotti E. (1975) *Little Girls,* Writers and Readers Publishing Co-operative, London.

Bettelheim B. (1983) *Freud and Man's Soul*, Chatto and Windus/Hogarth Press, London.

Chodorow N. (1978) *The Reproduction of Mothering*, University of California.

Dinnerstein D. (1978) *The Rocking of the Cradle and the Ruling of the World*, Souvenir Press, London.

Erikson E. (1978) *Toys and Reasons*, Marion Boyars, London.

Fenichel O. (1946) *The Psychoanalytical Theory of Neurosis*, Routledge & Kegan Paul, London.

Freud A. (1973) *Normality and Pathology in Childhood*, Penguin, Harmondsworth.

Freud S. (1964) *New Introductory Lectures on Psychoanalysis*, Hogarth Press, London.

Guntrip H. (1968) *Schizoid Phenomena, Object Relations and the Self*, Hogarth Press, London.

Haines D.G. (1978) Paths and Companions *Journal of Pastoral Care* (USA), Vol. XXXII, 1.

Jung C.G. (1953) *Two Essays on Analytical Psychology*, Routledge & Kegan Paul, London.

Le Carré J. (1974) *Tinker, Tailor, Soldier, Spy*, Hodder and Stoughton, London.

Lowe G. (1972) *The Growth of Personality*, Penguin, Harmondsworth.

Malan D.H. (1976) *Toward the Validation of Dynamic Psychotherapy*, Plenum Medical Book Co., New York.

Masson J.M. (1984) *The Assault on Truth: Freud's Suppression of the Seduction Theory*, Faber & Faber, London.

Rayner E. (1978) *Human Development* (2nd ed), George Allen and Unwin, London.

Rubins J.L. (1978) *Karen Horney*, Weidenfeld and Nicolson, London.

. . . AND VARIATIONS

The major part of our concern has so far been the first four to six years of the development cycle. It may seem strange that what remains is proportionately less full, since there does remain the major part of life in numbers of years. In fact the three sets of themes in the preceding section have not been confined to early childhood. They have been linked, as is proper to the psychodynamic view, to present situations and to present work with adults as well, mainly through the examples given. Each age which follows early childhood gives rise to occasions of reworking some or all of the basic themes — with the possible exception of latency, where those themes by very definition need to be relatively latent for true learning.

The following chapters therefore draw out the three themes at work in the growing child, the adolescent and the adult stages of life; constantly reflecting back and yet at the same time looking forward towards the final stage of ego integrity. The quality of the reflection upon life which then finally takes place is a measure of how well the basic themes have been renegotiated as they are met throughout life; and how far phantasies and aspirations have become rooted in reality.

· 6 ·

LEARNING TO LEARN

Introduction

The term used to describe the fourth stage of development is a curious one. It may appear that 'latency' means that the developmental tasks (particularly the last one concerning sexuality) go underground for a few years, to re-emerge forcefully at puberty. Yet it is clear that children do not stop being interested in sex; the use of genital and anal imagery in the smutty jokes they tell each other indicates that influences from the G.S. and A.S. are equally in evidence. Nor do they cease being interested in the opposite sex, with many a child having a 'girlfriend' or 'boyfriend' at school, even if the relationship is often a distant one, more of admiration than anything else. Nor do they cease to engage in authority struggles at home or at school, nor cease having crushes on their teachers. While the intensity of all such feelings is obviously less strong than during adolescence, it is difficult to see their development as any other than a continuation of the previous stages.

Yet there are obviously new tasks as well, and latency refers to a stage of development where these tasks — of learning basic intellectual, manual and physical skills — are realized without undue interference from the concerns raised in the previous stages. To take a parallel example: the child who is able to control bowels and bladder is freed to engage in a whole range of activities, whereas the child who is still soiling himself is likely to be so concerned with problems of staying clean and dry, that little time will be left at school for concentration upon all the learning activities. Most children (unless disturbed by some family or classroom crisis) are able to be free of these physical anxieties. But other children may have concerns which are less physical, and more to do with attitudes or worries, which can be detrimental to their learning. If there is continued stimulation of issues from previous stages, attitudes to learning, as well as learning itself may be influenced detrimentally. Although some children use their school work (as adults sometimes later use their work) to defend against worries, others will find it hard to concentrate when there are more pressing issues — again this is something which adults know from their own experience.

There are no major physical changes until puberty. The child who can leave infancy behind is therefore more free to concentrate on the pleasures that come from work and play — sometimes inseparable in modern education — on their growing appetite for understanding and information, on the fulfilment achieved in the satisfactory completion of tasks, and on being able to make and do things well. Children learn to experiment (with objects as well as with friendships and social groupings), to tolerate the frustration of results taking time; they will ask questions, and look for proof (of a rudimentary nature) of observations and explanations. They learn to alternate between passively receiving instruction, and actively investigating. Learning presents opportunities to relate to and identify with other adults than those in the family, and with many more children than even the largest family can provide — especially other children of their own age, as well as those older and younger. It is a period of immense learning. The work of psychologists such as Piaget (1950) throws much light on the cognitive development of the child, and may be useful when looking at some learning difficulties. Here, however, we concentrate more upon the emotional difficulties which may impede the rapid progress made during these years.

Our concern is not only with the school age, because in all learning situations in later life (training, adult education, even aspects of counselling and supervision) the adult needs to be able to enter a 'latency mode' in order to maximize the opportunities presented. The difficulties outlined which interfere with the latency mode therefore apply to children and adults alike.

Morag Hunter (of the University of Leicester, in a private communication) has related all the Erikson stages to study and learning in what she describes as a 'mini-cycle of development' within the latency stage: the teacher needs to build up in a child a sense of *hope* that learning can take place, and the *willpower* to see the task through, especially in the early stages when the task seems too difficult. She needs to point towards a direction for learning that indicates its *purpose*, and to build on an appropriate method so that the child gains *competence*. This will lead to *independence* in learning, and a stage of ego integrity that generates reliability (*fidelity*), and *love* of learning and its potential for life, a *caring* attitude, and *wisdom*.

Such are the aims of the teacher, and of learning. What might go wrong?

Problems related to trust and dependency

While separation anxiety from mother and the home is one of the reasons for school phobia, there are other features of the first stage which may interfere with learning. The person who cannot tolerate waiting and frustration will find it difficult to tolerate the lack of special attention from the teacher, or even the frustrations involved in study itself. Problems with trust at home can lead to lack of trust in the teacher as well, or alternatively to wholesale acceptance of what a teacher says, without personally digesting or questioning it. The person who lives in phantasy, preferring the safer world of day-dreaming, retreats from social interaction, and may find it difficult to use constructively those periods of working on their own upon which most education depends. The person who finds the distinction between self and not-self a difficult one will be in a much weaker position to discriminate between subjective and objective thinking.

However, there are others for whom education provides opportunities of living in 'a world of their own'; it is not unusual to find that some of those whose minds are top-class also find difficulty in relating closely to others — their books, their research, their laboratories exercise a greater pull on them than their family at home. Sometimes there appears to be a revolt against academe, although this does not necessarily take them back to the relationships on which they have missed out:

> Rosie had been pushed back to school at the age of nine after a serious road accident which had disfigured her. After the accident and a spell in hospital where she was seriously ill her wish to stay at home close to her mother was very understandable. Yet her mother (as she later told Rosie) felt a dilemma: she wanted to comfort her daughter, and at the same time felt she should respect the child psychiatrist's advice that Rosie should go back to school as soon as possible. It felt hard within her to have to push Rosie out. But Rosie did not know that at the time, and having to go to school, she reacted by immersing herself in her books, and staying on the edge of the groupings of her school friends.
>
> In her books she found consolation. Her reading meant that her schoolwork progressed well, and eventually she went to university. Perhaps it was going away from home that triggered off the separation anxiety, or perhaps the defence had worn thin; but at university she stopped going out, stayed in her room, even in her bed, and read novels. When she first saw the counsellor she jokingly asked for 'magic pills' to make her less depressed. Like her mother before her she

wanted to 'go out' because that was the healthy thing to do; but she also wanted to stay away from people.

Later she told the counsellor that when she first went to see him she was concerned about him as a professional who might meddle with her mind. The child psychiatrist she had seen before had prescribed 'magic pills' to tranquillize her, after he had misunderstood her childlike way of expressing her school refusal ('It's like a voice telling me not to go') for incipient psychosis. So the counsellor, who at first had thought in terms of encouraging Rosie to go out and begin to mix with people, realized that there was a sense in which she needed to be able to retreat and find some safety, and to come out in her own good time, not under pressure. He was therefore content to link the dilemma to 'stay in' or 'go out' which she felt with her mother's dilemma, and indeed his own.

Counselling also involves a type of 'teaching', particularly when a counsellor makes such links. So the dependent, submissive client, on the one hand, or the mistrusting, distancing client, on the other, are not necessarily in a good position to make full use of the counsellor, whose interpretations are by and large aimed at the adult in the 'latency mode'. Where it is the music of his voice or his very presence which soothes or alarms, the transference relationship so interferes with the capacity to learn, that the client remains a clinging or distant child, and the adult in the client is unable to learn from the adult in the counsellor.

Alternatively, the person who uses an intellectual defence in order to avoid closeness may prove difficult for the counsellor, since the 'feeling mode' is kept at a safe distance. This is illustrated in the case of Stewart.

Stewart, like Rosie, had found solace in his books, and passed his exams at school well ahead of his own age group. He had been brought up in a home where there was not simply material poverty, but also extreme poverty in the quality of relationships. His parents' constant rows drove him to his room and to study. At school he made friends, but never close friends. It was not until his mother died that the dearth of love hit him, although his presenting problem was complete inability to progress with his doctoral thesis. He tended to talk intellectually in his counselling sessions, looking all the time for explanation — and always in a most affable way — but unable to get near to any feelings of sadness or of closeness. The most obvious feeling he experienced was anxiety about closeness, but he avoided that by keeping people at a social and comfortable distance. It took many months before he could begin to show any glimmer of sadness; the counsellor did not push for feelings to emerge, but rather used the 'intellectual' style of the sessions to point out constantly the fears which Stewart might have. Helping those who have deeper levels of pain can take a very long time, and requires respect for the defences that protect them.

Problems related to authority and control

The second stage of development has much in common with the latency period, since learning to do things, being able to achieve results, and accepting mistakes without fear of punishment all bear upon later learning. The ability to play is translated into playing with ideas, and into being able to give free rein to thought and imagination. The learner can take pride in his work and achievement, but is also open to learning from mistakes both in himself and in his teachers.

Where there are problems from the second stage, work can be feared as liable to show up one's mistakes, and this may lead to the work itself never being started. If work gets under way, there can be over-detailed preparation, with the need to get every fact and word correct. This type of perfectionism which tries to obviate all criticism from teachers, can easily become a burden. Some students even fear to ask their tutors for guidance with work they do not understand, thinking they will incur displeasure.

Thelma came to the counsellor as a desperate last measure since she was about to fail her exams. She had not worked for almost a year. Although initially there had been some adolescent acting-out of rebellion against her strict home and school which had led to non-attendance at lectures, the situation had got out of hand because she was afraid to approach her tutors to ask for help in catching up. She feared that they would tell her she was lazy, just like her father in the past. The counsellor pointed out that if she wanted to repeat the year, she would have to see her tutor — was it still fear of her tutor's criticism that prevented her from asking? Had she felt afraid of coming to see him too in case he told her she was just being lazy? Thelma decided she had to see her tutor, and returned the following week to say that in fact her tutor had been most understanding! But now she had to tell her parents. The counsellor wondered whether she really carried an outdated view of her father's criticism within her, and whether even he would be as severe as she imagined. Perhaps she even fostered his criticism by presenting herself as a naughty child expecting punishment, and not as an adult who had a mind of her own?

Problem-solving which is tackled with rigid perfectionism, and sometimes with strict categorization, may suffice at the simpler stages of learning, but sooner or later (particularly in higher education) such self-imposed demands become impossible to meet. The person who sees everything in black and white terms, or who has to be certain before passing an opinion, often fails to see other dimensions, or is afraid to express any opinion at all. Caution likewise prevents the imaginative leap which often lies at the heart of intellectual and even scientific discoveries. The wood cannot be seen for the trees. At later stages of learning it is necessary to learn to tolerate confusion, particularly about the interpretation of facts. The wish for certainty can sometimes foreclose the search for more information which will ultimately bring about a more comprehensive solution.

School phobia may also be the result of such fears: the child who is afraid of a weak performance, or that the teacher will shame him by criticism or punishment, or who feels that he is not as good as his peers, may try to opt out of the situation. Students like Thelma can feel this concern, even when later teachers have always shown themselves to be tolerant of mistakes and understanding of failure. Others wish to please teacher, and parents too, so that working hard becomes an end in itself, and not a means to an end. Typical of such is the workaholic, the person who can never relax, like Sir Jasper in Wycherley's *Country Wife*, who says to his wife that he must 'go to my pleasure, which is business, while you go to your business, which is pleasure'. While there are some who learn in order to appease authority figures, there are others who reject learning, as a way of expressing their reaction against the authority of the teacher or of the institution. This may be a rebellion against parents who have sent them to school when they did not wish to leave home, or against parents who were felt to be pressurizing them to go into further education when there was some wish to leave school and become more independent. Others will use authority issues as a way of testing out boundaries in the institution, which they have been unable to test out at home.

Ursula had got behind with her work, and saw her college counsellor when she realized that she was going to fail her dissertation. It soon became clear that Ursula was somewhat afraid of her father, and that she had elected to do her particular course because he wished it, and she felt obliged to respect him. Her elder brother had been a rebel and a source of worry to her parents. But she could not bring herself to ask her tutors for help with her dissertation — she wanted to do it all for herself. The counsellor was not sure at first whether this was a sure recipe for failing, whether Ursula was in fact trying to sabotage her chances and rebel against her father in a passive way. It was also possible that it was a way of trying to achieve some measure of independence, although it was a somewhat inappropriate issue and time to choose to demonstrate this. The counsellor felt confirmed in this latter interpretation when Ursula, who initially had kept asking him to provide the answer, to ring her father, etc., after a few sessions seemed in a hurry to get away early perhaps again out of need to feel independent of an older person who even if helpful was nonetheless still an authority figure.

Teachers need to have mastered their own authority problems in order to be both firm and yet flexible to boundary setting [Controlling others p. 80]. But we must not overlook the fact that there are some teachers, and some institutions, whose authority is reinforced by harshness and punishment, rather than by persuasion and encouragement. Even if the home has provided a good enough environment for the child, the sadistic or over-critical teacher, being a parent-substitute, can equally plant a strong negativism in the child, and reinforce the super-ego, often prejudicing a child's view of any activity which is called 'education'. This may well put them off further learning in adult life. Where both parents and teachers are cold or critical, the task of achieving confidence and self-esteem becomes doubly difficult; although there are of course teachers who can provide a different model, that of the accepting and caring parent-figure, and who can modify the harshness of the child's experience.

In counselling too the client can be afraid that the counsellor will be harshly critical, and will not therefore mention those things which arouse feelings of shame or guilt; the client may even fear to suggest ideas or take initiative [Passivity p. 75]. The counsellor too, if he is the type who always wants to be certain that he has got everything 'taped', might be tempted to categorize and fit the client into an apparently black-and-white scheme of things [pp. 23–4]. Yet the counsellor, like the good teacher or parent can provide a model which helps change a client's reactive patterns:

Vincent panicked whenever faced with a learning task if he was unable to get straight on with it. When he really needed time to think, he could not relax; so that unless he was getting something down on paper, he felt anxious, and began to fear that he would not complete his task on time. The counsellor was aware of this pressure too, because Vincent was clearly hinting that he wondered when the counsellor was going to make some constructive suggestion. The counsellor shared this sense of urgency with him, but in a calm and unhurried voice trying to indicate through her manner that she and he needed time to 'produce results'.

Problems related to sexuality and rivalry

With the move into the school environment, the child inevitably transfers some of the feelings toward parents to the teachers — the wish to please, to give, to copy — and many of such feelings encourage the process of learning. Anna Freud suggests that latency relationships will include love, admiration, dislike and rejection of teachers 'not because they are men or women but because they are either helpful, appreciative, inspiring or harsh, intolerant, anxiety-arousing figures' (1974, p. 159). So the sexual element need not be intrusive. Difficulties arise where the relationship is more than a positive working alliance: admiration and love become highly charged, and acceptance or rejection of the child's love inseparable from acceptance or criticism of the child's work ['Debbie' p. 98]. Problems can also arise where teachers (as can happen with those who teach older adolescents and adults in particular) take advantage of their 'parental' role to seduce their students. The damage to some of these students can be as severe as the damage from seduction by actual parents [The seducing parent p.100]. Teachers have to master their own sexuality and oedipal wishes in order to work with children, and especially with adolescents. But unresolved oedipal problems in the child's home can also make school attendance difficult, particularly where the state of the parental relationship causes anxiety about losing mother or father while away from home.

Obviously current problems have a major impact upon a child's ability to concentrate upon learning — that speaks for itself. The fights and threats at home, the trauma of a separation or death will almost inevitably prevent a child, or an older person, from giving his mind to activities at school, college or work. However, what I refer to here is the aftermath of such events, which may be long after they have happened, yet is still painfully influenced by them.

Wallace had lost his father three years before he had any difficulties which necessitated him coming to his university counsellor. He had initially deferred his place at university for a year in order to help his mother to cope and adjust. University had at first been an easy enough place for him, and also a relief from the sadness at home. But in his third year he openly admitted that some of his difficulty in working was because his mother had put so much hope into his success. This made him feel that any success was to be equated not with working hard because of her pressure on him (of an A.S. type), but rather with giving her the sort of pleasure she had formerly gained in her husband's success and popularity. He felt he had slipped too far into his father's shoes, and not working was one way of trying to get out of the predicament.

Rivalry with others in learning situations can become so intense that healthy competition (the wish to achieve what others achieve) disappears, and aggressive competition takes its place. Alternatively, inhibition of the ability to work may follow fear of failure by comparison with others. Co-operative work, in pairs and groups, and modelled perhaps in team-teaching by staff, is preferable to the subordination of learning to competitive tests and examinations. But, at the same time, the child benefits from learning that he and his peers have differing abilities in distinct areas, and that they have different interests; hopefully he is enabled to find personal success in one particular area of interest and ability. The pressure from some parents for academic success for their child (as if the child is as much a status symbol as the car, the house and the latest domestic appliance) may serve a child well in the examination system, but sometimes causes great difficulties when the young person leaves home [Jealousy and competition p. 112].

Success at school depends to some extent on the child's capacity to 'show-off'. In a home where this has been frowned upon, a child may be reluctant to stand out from the class. Certain subjects, such as creative writing, require not only imagination, but a certain amount of exhibition-ism in order to reveal oneself.

Yvette arrived for counselling with a beautiful smile and a striking red beret — these were the first impressions the counsellor had of her. She had recently started at college as a mature student, and could not go into lectures, because she felt faint in the crowded room. She was able to identify the first occasion she had felt this to the third week of term in one particular lecture.

During the session she told how she had once wanted to go to college to do drama, but had had to go out to work. She had been able to enjoy her interest in drama through amateur societies. She was fine, even now, in crowded rooms like parties, when she felt she was 'the life and soul'. She could not understand what had made her feel so bad in the lecture room. She did not want to faint and make an exhibition of herself.

The counsellor had by this time put a number of these phrases together in his mind, and tested out an interpretation; that though she did not want to make an exhibition of herself, she might also feel frustrated at having to sit still and listen when she liked to be up front entertaining. Her eyes lit up, and she capped his explanation with a forceful condemnation of the lecturer who was teaching when she first felt faint. He was dreadfully boring, he did not allow anyone else the chance to speak and ask questions or make a contribution themselves. It was as if she needed to 'protest' in some way (by fainting or walking out because she felt she might faint) both at the boredom of the lecture, and also her inability to 'show off' herself.

Other subjects (biology is a good example, since it is where sex and reproduction are introduced) may present emotional difficulties, since they touch upon important psychological as well as physical areas of development. Physical education also involves the body, and where there is shame about the body or co-ordination, such feelings can easily be reinforced through the hesitancy to become involved. Dance and drama may suffer likewise, as they did for the student whose obsessional need to get everything planned ahead meant that she was 'afraid to put a foot wrong' — scarcely the right frame of mind to express herself in dance. In order to be able to take full advantage of rather less sex-role-stereotyped education on offer in schools, boys and girls need to accept some subjects are not 'cissyish' or 'only for tomboys'. So it can be seen again how there is greater freedom and opportunity to learn when sexuality and sexual identity are not urgent issues but have become relatively latent, having been sufficiently resolved in early childhood not to intrude until they naturally come to the fore again in adolescence. One of the major problems for learning in adolescence is that of holding on to the latency mode, while at the same time engaging in learning tasks which give expression to the re-emergence of the old themes [chapter 7]. Some young people find the pressures too great, and either cast aside the learning, or so perpetuate the latency mode that they repress dealing with the dominant issues of their age. In early adolescence too, when sexuality forces its way to the surface again, some children (especially early or late developers) can be cruelly teased by their peers. Even where their home is a secure environment, school becomes hell. The effect of their body-image (so important for the young man or woman) may be crippling, seriously inhibiting the confidence of the growing person.

Again, much of this also applies to the working relationship between counsellor and client. The client needs to be able to step back from the highly charged emotions which are permitted to surface in counselling, so as to be able to reflect upon the experience and to learn from it. The counsellor who is embarrassed by charged emotions like sexuality will be less able to take up such material, while the counsellor who is over-excited by them will find it less easy to set them aside, or to set them in context. The counsellor also needs to rise above issues of rivalry with the client. Just as 'teaching is done in order that students finally surpass the teacher' (Hartung 1979), so the counsellor is not only prepared to be proved wrong (and so should not cling to his status as an authority figure), but also is prepared for the client to become an equal, or better than him, at the business of interpreting and understanding [The generativity stage in the counsellor p. 184].

The latency aspect of counselling

There is an important distinction to be made between two aspects of the counsellor–client relationship, known as 'the working alliance' and 'the transference relationship'. The working alliance is the latency part of counselling, where the turbulence and strength of emotions, feelings and phantasies can be temporarily set aside, and a 'cool' look taken at what has been said, and what has been experienced, including tentative explanations which are put forward for testing. In the latency mode counsellor and client are more obviously equal than they are at those times when the client reveals the more vulnerable 'child' aspects of the self, while the counsellor remains a quiet, watchful, caring parent-figure. Where the transference becomes too intense, and remains so, it is much more difficult for the counsellor to be heard in a rational way. The most useful counselling consists of a backward and forward movement between the catharsis of feeling and phantasy, and the working alliance, where both partners unpack the material, and try together to understand its significance.

Since learning is much more difficult when a person is in a highly emotional state, there are occasions when the counsellor has to permit the emotions to be discharged before she is able to say anything which might make some impact upon the client. It is rarely any use making a studied interpretation when a client is distraught or furious. Clients sometimes wish they could have seen their counsellor at the time of great distress, and feel frustrated by having to wait for the session time to come round: 'You would understand much more if you could have seen how I was then.' While this is the disadvantage of the fixed appointment, set against it is the advantage of being able to think more clearly about the stressful occasion when its turbulence has subsided. The counsellor's interventions would have been of a different nature had she been present during the stress. Counsellors therefore need to remember that their own contribution often differs according to the degree of emotional stress which the client is experiencing. Empathy, warmth, acceptance, accurate reflection and sometimes even gentle advice will be more appropriate when the client is in full flood; at quieter times the reflective interpretation comes into its own:

> There are some occasions where emotional factors are so strong that it appears to be impossible for a client to make use of the counselling at all. Zoe very much wanted help, and wished to unburden herself of a number of things that were troubling her about her behaviour, but found great difficulty in telling the counsellor about them. Fortunately she was able to tell the counsellor that she felt very nervous before coming, that she could not sleep the night before, and that she had been physically sick on leaving some sessions. Gentle empathic calmness and acceptance on the counsellor's part did not help her to feel at ease; but neither did interpretation of her feelings of guilt and shame and her possible fear of the counsellor's reaction should she voice her concerns. In the end, at least with Zoe, it was the silence of the counsellor — unhurried and unruffled — which appeared to help her to break through her reticence.

Just as the transference feelings towards the counsellor need, in some measure, to be put to one side when joint exploration and elucidation of the material takes place, so the counsellor himself, in order to function objectively, has to set aside his own counter-transference feelings, particularly those which tempt him to be the dominant, all-important, authoritarian, critical or seductive parent. This is easier said than done, since the most damaging counter-transference feelings are always those which are not obvious to the counsellor; but he too needs to have worked through the early developmental issues sufficiently to enter the latency mode or, as Hartung (1979) suggests, the generative mode of middle adulthood [p. 184].

Transition

I have treated the school years in somewhat peremptory fashion compared with the attention given to the pre-school age. This is not to deny that the school experience is a very formative one, equipping some young people (where education works) for work and life in society. The amount of basic learning to be acquired is immense — verbal, literary, numeracy skills, technical, manual and physical skills, as well as information about society and the wider world. For some children, success in learning can separate them more than usual from their family or their culture — especially when 'successful' children come from families of poor educational background, or from closed religious or racial backgrounds. We need also to distinguish between the low esteem present in many adults re-entering learning as a result of their failure to succeed at school, and the more basic low esteem which is more typical of the A.S. In addition, the basic themes outlined in chapters 3–5 provide useful guidelines with which to understand some of the difficulties which adult clients have had in their learning in the past, and which may continue to influence their learning in the present — problems of trust, of authority and control, of production of work, of over-intense relationships (positive and negative) with parent-substitutes, and problems of competition (or its inhibition) with peers. In healthy development this age of childhood is a relatively quiescent period free from such emotional issues, releasing the child's energies for the novelties of learning. But when earlier conflicts are carried forward into latency; or when they are experienced more intensely than before in relation to new adult parent-figures or peers; or when the onset of puberty resurrects such conflicts: then they will interfere with the potentialities for the enlargement of social and educational horizons which learning otherwise can promote.

References

Freud A. (1973) *Normality and Pathology in Childhood*, Penguin, Harmondsworth.

Hartung B. (1979) The capacity to enter latency in learning pastoral psychotherapy, *Journal of Supervision and Training in Ministry*, Vol. 2, (Chicago, Illinois).

Piaget J. (1950) *The Psychology of Intelligence*, Routledge & Kegan Paul, London.

· 7 ·

THE WATERSHED OF ADOLESCENCE

Introduction

We scarcely need the researches of psychologists to remind us that adolescence is a crucial time for both physical and personal development, and that the rapidity of change brings with it turbulent emotions. Each generation likes to think that its adolescents are 'a problem', although there is much evidence that adolescence is little different now from what it has been for many decades. G. Stanley Hall described American youth in 1916 with words which are just as apt today:

Energy, exaltation and supernatural activity are followd by indifference, lethargy and loathing. Exuberant gaiety, laughter and euphoria make place for dysphoria, depressive gloom and melancholy. Egoism, vanity and conceit are just as characteristics of this period of life as are abasement, humiliation and bashfulness. One can observe both the remnants of an uninhibited childish selfishness and an increasing idealistic altruism. Goodness and virtue are never so pure, but never again does temptation so forcefully preoccupy thought. The adolescent wants solitude and seclusion, while he finds himself entangled in crushes and friendships. Never again does the peer group have such a strong influence over him. At one time he may exhibit exquisite sensitivity and tenderness; at another time callousness and cruelty. Apathy and inertia vacillate with an enthusiastic curiosity, an urge to discover and explore. There is a yearning for idols and authority that does not exclude a revolutionary racicalism directed against any kind of authority (quoted R. Muuss 1968).

Adolescence is clearly a transitional time, between childhood and adulthood, although to call it such is to risk overlooking the number of issues that become more real than ever before. All the themes of early childhood are taken up and reworked, this time with greater opportunity of fully realizing them. But in addition the adolescent is still in education until at least the age of sixteen, so that the latency requirements struggle to stay active when strong emotions all too often threaten to interfere with educational tasks. In a small percentage of privileged adolescents, education may continue until early adulthood, and some young people can only succeed in their learning at the expense of emotional development. Intellectually mature adults are not necessarily emotionally mature — but then neither is there any compelling reason to think that those who leave school at the earliest opportunity are any more emotionally mature, despite their earlier introduction to the 'ways of the world'.

There is a danger in being too precise when mapping out development, especially of a time of life when moods and aspirations rapidly change; nevertheless, adolescence can be seen as a watershed in the Erikson model [p. xiii], especially if we follow the division of adolescence into three obvious periods — early, middle and late — as suggested by Laufer (1974) and others. Each of these periods takes up in turn one of the stages of infancy, but in reverse order, working back to the first stage. Thus early adolescence, with sexual development thrust into consciousness by physical changes, picks up the themes of the third stage of sexuality and rivalry, preparing the sexual identity of the young person for the sixth stage of intimacy. Each period looks back and also looks forwards. Middle adolescence is particularly concerned with issues of independence and autonomy, from parental morality in favour of self-direction, in terms of economic independence (at present not as straightforward as it has been in more prosperous times), and even sometimes setting up on one's own in early marriage, going away from home for work, or to college. In this period, therefore, issues of the second stage are picked up with considerable force, and the foundation is laid for middle adulthood (Erikson's seventh stage) where generativity is the major task, both as a parent and worker. The late period of adolescence, where there are often concerns about society and the world, includes experimenting to find a sense of purpose and 'faith' (including faith in one's own identity) and has obvious links with the first stage of trust and the emergence of the rudimentary 'self'; it also prefigures the final stage of the Eight Ages, that of ego integrity, where confidence in one's overall handling of life is a necessary step towards the acceptance of death.

I shall look at these periods in more detail, bearing in mind that any divisions are to some extent artificial. Although the issues which are most pertinent to each period often surface at that time, they are not resolved by the time the next period starts. Sexuality continues to be a major theme into middle adolescence and well beyond; authority issues continue well into adult life (it is probably not until most people are about thirty that they cease to be so concerned about what their parents think of them), while the issues around faith, hope and integrity remain a source of concern throughout life.

Early adolescence and sexuality

It is the physical change which starts at puberty that provides the first stimulus to the period of life which we call adolescence. The sexual characteristics of a boy or girl become more physically obvious, and re-initiate issues of sexual identity and attitudes, part of the overall quest for personal identity, leading eventually in adulthood to a more permanent heterosexual partnership for the majority of people. The issues which were examined in chapter 5 are therefore of major importance, although other features of the first two stages are also recapitulated within this early period of adolescence.

Thus, a young person at puberty often becomes very *self*-conscious. There is a natural return to the first stage of narcissism [Narcissism and self-respect, p. 39]. It is seen in the time spent in looking in mirrors, in great concern about appearance (even when their dress is not what adults would think smart), and with some young people in the writing of diaries. Masturbation brings more obvious orgasmic relief than it did in childhood, and is primarily a narcissistic activity — experimenting with sex, of course, but often with phantasies that initially emphasize part-objects (p. 31). Young people fasten at first upon isolated physical features in the same or the opposite sex — hair, breasts, ankles, eyes, etc. (Not that this is unknown in adults too! [Part-objects: pp. 31, 115]) Masturbation is also a source of comfort, and a way of relieving tension, even aggressive tension. Other people, first of the same sex and secondly of the opposite sex, are often idealized (pop stars, sportsmen and women, teachers, older adolescents) in a way which is reminiscent of the idealization of early infancy [Idealization and splitting p. 43]. All these aspects remind us of first-stage issues.

There are also second-stage aspects, particularly those concerning shame, pride and control. Masturbation is an activity which can be controlled, although sexual excitement itself cannot be, and the body often seems to have a will of its own: erections, nocturnal emissions, vaginal moistening are often spontaneous, and like blushing, sometimes difficult to control by will-power. Menstruation too cannot be controlled consciously, except by drastic measures like starvation and lowering body-weight. Rayner (1978, p. 91) suggests that menstruation gives rise to more seriousness in young girls since they cannot 'play' with that particular aspect of their sexuality in the way boys can, with their much more common playing through masturbation. Such issues of control might be linked to feelings about the control of bowels and bladder in the anal stage; the wish to suppress sexual feelings can lead to over-control and unnatural abstinence from masturbation in boys, or to abstinence from food in anorexia in girls, both sexes trying to put the lid on their sexual impulses which are felt to be wrong or shameful. (Girls also abstain from masturbation, and boys from eating, but in most young people with such difficulties the predominant 'abstinence' takes the above form.) Physical appearance matters not just to those who develop later than their peers, but also to those who develop earlier — feelings of strangeness and shame replace feelings of pleasure at the first signs of adulthood. If toilet functions in the anal stage have been associated with dirtiness and disgust, a girl's menstrual flow, or a boy's wet-dream can also have such associations [p. 68]. In middle and late adolescence A.S. concern about competence may also be apparent, making the idea of sexual exploration, sexual 'play' and intercourse anxiety-provoking. This may be because the young person is afraid of showing he does not know the 'how' of sex (there always has to be a first time); or it may be rooted in fears of being unable to perform sexually well enough to satisfy his partner [A.S. difficulties of intimacy p. 158].

> Adam had been asked out by a girl. He was delighted because it made him feel 'I'm not such a bad looker after all' — but he was also nervous because she had already had one boyfriend, and he himself had no previous experience. He looked radiant after their first date when he told the counsellor that he had discovered she was two weeks younger than him. Irrational though it was, feeling that bit older gave him a feeling of experience which no doubt compensated for other feelings of inferiority.

Just as a child moves from concern with the self to the wish to give to others, so a young person's sexual feelings move from self-consciousness to the development of an external aim or object for sexual expression. Often the feelings are directed initially to peers of the same sex, and are sometimes acted out in early adolescence. Such a homosexual phase in both boys and girls is common and natural, even if not always acted upon, and it is often helpful to reassure the anxious teenager on this point [Homosexuality p. 107].

> Barry (now a young man) recalled that at his single-sex school he and other boys in their early teens had played phantasy games of who was going to marry whom amongst the other boys. Like other boys of that age, they would also compare size of penis and growth of pubic hair. None of this felt to be homosexual at the time, nor did it worry Barry now, despite more recent anxieties about being homosexual. He spoke of that time as being completely normal.

The same sex acts as a mirror to the young person, and represents a rather better known, and therefore safer, genitality than as yet the opposite sex does. Then the relationships become less intensely identified with one person as the young person moves more into a grouping of his or her own sex, followed by mixed groups where there is still the safety of being with one's own sex, but some safety in numbers in being with the opposite sex. From such groupings often come the first dates, couple relationships, and, often after several brief partnerships, a more permanent, 'steady' relationship. The move from phantasizing about relationships to making them real is, of course, a risky one:

> Clive had admired a particular girl from afar, and eventually plucked up courage to ask her out. His inexperience at times made the counsellor feel she wanted to say 'Just get on with it', but she resisted the temptation to push him. Instead she took up the fear that the girl might reject Clive if he was too pushy himself, and suggested that in some ways he might prefer to hang on to the phantasy of going out with her because it was safer than 'risking the push' — using such an ambiguous phrase helped to condense two anxieties, one about pushing too hard, another about being pushed away.

Rivalry and competitiveness are also major concerns for some young people, especially since their peer group provides not only companionship and safety, but occasion for jealousy of and comparison with others [Jealousy and competition p. 112]. A young person can feel lack of confidence and self-esteem at not being as apparently sexually active as others claim they are, or as our sexually-anxious culture makes out that young men and women should be.

But rivalry is not confined to the peer group. At the same time as young people are finding their own sexual identity, their parents are conscious of imminent or present changes in themselves. Mother may be entering her menopause at the same time as the daughter achieves her menarche. Father may be aware of a spreading midriff and lack of muscular tone at the same time as his son is reaching the peak of fitness. He may also be experiencing some loss of sexual drive. It would be surprising if parents did not in some way feel jealous of their teenage children, aware of their own lost youth, and sometimes envious of freedoms which were less openly available to them when they were young, compared to their own children. Some parents have their own difficulties about sexuality and convey the impression that it is something to be ashamed of or guilty about — by what they say (including those who simultaneously stimulate and put off their children by making them their confidants in sexual matters [p. 96]); or by what they do — such as switching off the television whenever sexuality or nudity is shown. Some parents, again because of their own sexual problems, 'seduce' the young man or girl, while there are occasional substitute parent-figures who do the same [The seducing parent p. 100; Problems related to sexuality and rivalry p. 128].

> Dawn received such mixed messages from her home. Her mother confided in her that she found sex distasteful and painful; while her father, though not physically touching her, related so closely to her that Dawn herself normally avoided any young man who might present a sexual threat. Her closest friend was a young male homosexual, who represented for her a safe way of relating to a man without sexual threat. Only when she had drunk too much at parties did she become aware of any sexual desire for the opposite sex.

In most cases, of course, such obvious sexual stimulation as this is suppressed in the normal family, but a young person still has to struggle with the ambivalence he or she has to a parent, on the one hand as a love-object and a protective figure who is needed during a time of emotional turmoil; while on the other there is a wish to push a parent away, in order to find his or her own love-object, and his or her own confidence.

> Such push/pull feelings were clearly present in Ellen, who while at home was always arguing with her father, and pouring scorn on his ill-educated points of view; but away from home at college told her counsellor how much she adored her father, defended him against any

criticism, and even wrote letters back home to him telling him what a great father he was.

To love and yet to hate parents, who feel hurt (forgetting their own adolescence, or unaware of the adolescent's needs), is as difficult a conflict to contain as the earlier conflicts about loving and hating [p. 44]. If the strength of the anger felt seems surprising, Winnicott's words express its symbolic force — and he is writing of parents who try to understand: the feelings will be even more intense with parents who try to hang on to their 'children':

> If you do all you can to promote personal growth in your offspring you will need to be able to deal with startling results. If your children find themselves at all they will not be contented to find anything but the whole of themselves, and that will include the aggression and destructive elements in themselves as well as the elements that can be labelled loving. There will be this long tussle which you will need to survive.
>
> With some of your children you will be lucky if your ministrations quickly enable them to use symbols, to play, to dream, to be creative in satisfying ways, but even so the road to this point may be rocky. And in any case you will make mistakes and these mistakes will be seen and felt to be disastrous; and your children will try to make you feel responsible for setbacks even when you are not in fact responsible. Your children simply say: I never asked to be born.
>
> Your rewards come in the richness that may gradually appear in the personal potential of this or that boy or girl. And if you succeed you must be prepared to be jealous of your children who are getting better opportunities for personal development than you had yourselves. You will feel rewarded if one day your daughter asks you to do some baby-sitting for her, indicating thereby that she thinks you may be able to do this satisfactorily; of if your son wants to be like you in some way, or falls in love with a girl you would have liked yourself had you been younger. Rewards come *indirectly*. And of course you know you will not be thanked (1974 p. 168).

I have followed the themes of the G.S. from early to late adolescence. To take up A.S. themes when they become significant again, I return to mid-adolescence.

Middle adolescence: authority and independence

Winnicott's words above apply to the adolescent's wish to push away from parents, both as love-objects and as authority figures. Two further brief quotations from his paper on adolescence particularly apply to the middle period and relate to the A.S. A young person and his parents are often involved in boundary disputes: the adolescent wants independence, parents want to retain their sense of authority. Winnicott, again using the symbolism of phantasy, writes:

> If the child is to become an adult then this move is achieved over the dead body of an adult . . . where there is the challenge of the growing boy or girl, there let an adult meet the challenge. And it will not necessarily be nice.

He has omitted words in print which he used when he originally delivered his paper: 'It will not necessarily be nice . . . but it will be fun' (1974, pp. 170, 176).

The omission is unfortunate, although we can understand his wish to remove what appears to be a contradiction. The additional words express a sense of surviving, even of resurrection, which is equally important for the young person and for the parents. When an adolescent has been able to separate, then the relationship with parents does more than 'survive'. Erikson has said that in his early work he had to put it cautiously to young people that they might hate their parents. Later (when his ideas had caught on) he had to put it cautiously to them that they might *like* them!

Some of the depression prevalent in adolescence is due to this sense of loss of parents (again in phantasy). Death is certainly a preoccupation during certain periods of adolescence, and death of parents, relatives or of peers can have a great impact upon a young person. Where there is severe depression it may be because a parent has actually been lost, by death, or more commonly by separation and divorce, either of which can be as traumatic for the teenager as for a younger child [The eternal triangle p. 96]. The death of a parent (statistically more likely at this age than earlier in life) may enhance the phantasy of having killed a parent off, not allowing negative feelings to be worked through, as they are when the 'phantasy-killed' parent is seen to survive. A parent who is in ill health (physical or psychological) may be more difficult to challenge than one who is well, for fear that the challenge 'will kill him' [p. 48, 'Edward' p. 32].

> Ursula [p. 126] found it even more difficult to express her independence openly, not only because her father was strong-willed, but also because her mother had already suffered one severe heart attack. Open rebellion carried with it the fear that either her own action, or her father's reaction, might damage mother. The counsellor wondered at one point how Ursula had felt after she had criticized him; but Ursula said it was 'OK — you're paid to take it!' But some clients are equally concerned lest any criticism they make of their counsellor should cause damage and hurt.

Where parents do not get on well together, it may also be harder to separate from them, since the young person, though wishing to be independent, fears what will happen if he leaves them to fight it out with each other. Equally, the critical, hostile parent who does not permit any independence, and the over-indulgent parent who puts no boundaries on the teenager's rebellion, in their own ways prevent the adolescent achieving that maturity of judgement which embraces concern for others. Winnicott argues that a young person must be allowed to be immature, as long as adults do not abdicate responsibility (1974, p. 172).

As a society we are ambivalent about giving young people freedom. The legal age limits by which responsibility is defined vary: a young person can marry at sixteen, but not drink alcohol in a pub until eighteen. He can vote at eighteen, yet cannot be involved in a consenting homosexual relationship until twenty-one. Perhaps it is useful to allow such civil freedoms to be taken in stages, since the adolescent in the middle years is still tilting at windmills, knocking down rather than building up. This may remind us of the A.S., where at first knocking down bricks was more pleasurable than the constructive phase which followed. Such 'anarchism' is normal: only by knocking down first, and tearing the adult world apart in a somewhat hamfisted manner, does a young person become aware of the areas of concern which he addresses in his late adolescent ideologies.

This 'anarchic' kicking against authority in the home and in society takes many forms. Vandalism may be a sign of frustration, of a wish to test out destructive wishes, or the chaotic capabilities of any 'gang' of people. Obviously we do not include vandalism within the norm of adolescent anarchy, although some sections of the young population (students, for instance) are sometimes permitted to get away with 'high spirits', when others who are less privileged are seen as criminal and malevolent. Private rebellion against parental authority is seen not only in staying out late, promiscuity, and bouts of rage, but also more quietly in anorexia, suicide attempts or threats, or even in the wish to shock:

> Big gestures are sometimes necessary in order to assert independence. Frank's conventional family would be very shocked when he told them that he was a homosexual, but he smiled as he said it, as if it would give him considerable pleasure to see how disconcerted his father would be. The 'shock, horror' quality of his wish to come out was also apparent when his tutor rang the counsellor: 'I hear you've got something surprising to tell me about Frank.' The counsellor refused to be drawn into the game: 'If it's what I think it is he can tell you himself', taking this up with Frank when they next met.

Together with the need to achieve personal autonomy, there is also a strong wish for economic independence, which earning a wage can provide. The workplace provides a focus for some of the themes of the A.S. and of the latency stage. Young people who cannot find employment, together with students who remain financially dependent upon their parents, are often presented with the dilemma of needing parental support, and yet wanting to rebel against them; and with conflicts over how far they can exercise their freedom, especially where parents use their financial support as a threat or as moral blackmail. The choice of a career, or of training for a job, or higher education is another avenue for an adolescent's search for identity, although the reality of the national economic situation imposes severe restraints upon their freedom of choice.

Unless young people are pitched into parenthood when they are still young (which may be a way of avoiding a time of real independence [chapter 8]) much that goes on in this middle period prepares the ground for the stage of generativity, which follows young adulthood: assuming their own authority; being able to set their parents' authority in context; together with the desire of many young people to be better parents to their own children than they feel their own parents were to them. The movement for the more fortunate into the adult world of work prepares the way for the 'creativity' of that seventh stage, where work (as distinct from labour or toil) may be an expression of their personality.

We have already recognized in the A.S. that the counsellor can be seen as a parental figure, and is in any event something of an authority. In working with young people counsellors often find them anxious about needing adult help, and reluctant to accept it for any longer than is immediately necessary. 'I want to solve this myself' is commonly said, and is indeed a sign of a healthy wish to be independent. Acknowledging this wish (especially where there is no serious disturbance, but a more 'normal' crisis) is much more appropriate than it would be with adults in whom anxiety about being dependent leads to defensive independence. Young people are on the whole more adaptable, and often find quite brief counselling sufficient for the moment, preferring to arrange with the counsellor 'to come back if I need to' — thereby ensuring for themselves a safety net, which is seldom needed but which acts as a boost to their confidence.

Late adolescence: faith and responsibility

I use the word 'faith' instead of 'trust' to link the late period of adolescence to the first stage of life, because Erikson sees 'faith' — in its broadest sense, not simply religious faith — as one of the needs of any society, and as rooted in the mother–baby relationship. It was stated with reference to the O.S. that satisfactory development leads to belief in the basic goodness of the world. The young person may have much to criticize about the national and international scene, but such criticism ceases to be anarchic, and becomes constructive, demonstrating hope and idealism (here there are again links back to the O.S.), together with an optimism that things can be changed. Such a person does not give up on the world.

Early adolescence brought with it, apart from physiological changes, shifts in patterns of thinking from the concrete thought of latency to abstract, conceptual thinking. Such abstract thinking is now used not only in intellectual study, but in moral and ethical thinking. Hence the joy which some young people find in spending hours in discussion, working out their views of society, arguing about politics, religion, ethical matters and moral dilemmas. Such young people gain from articulating their ideas. They are not always those who have had the opportunity of further education; some students spend so much of their time getting their work done or catching up on personal relationships missed because of study, that they do not, as is popularly believed, set the world alight with their late-night arguments.

It is unlikely that such concerns will really arise until this later period of adolescence. Some, of course, seek to escape the problems of relationships and of the world by the use of drugs or alcohol (perhaps mistakenly thinking in the case of drugs that they do at least explore their inner world); but others are keen to join political groups, to espouse causes, and to work towards changing society. Students are privileged in being given what Erikson calls a 'psycho-social moratorium', in which they can be relatively free of the business of looking after themselves, and so can concentrate upon these wider issues. But Erikson's is a somewhat optimistic picture, more true of the affluent 1950s and 1960s than of the harsher economic climate of the 1980s, where working for a degree in order to get a job is likely to have a higher priority than joining pressure groups.

We do not have in Western industrial society a true equivalent of the initiation ceremonies in other cultures, through which the young person comes to adulthood. Confirmation or bar mitzvah are at the 'wrong' end of adolescence, appropriate in the days when young people started work at that age, but scarcely so apt in our own times. Yet late adolescence contains some of the elements of more primitive adolescent rites, being the time when young men and women learn and question society's law and lore, developing a sense of their own place in society and in the world. For the fast disappearing breed of apprentices, the transition to craftsman was often marked. Students have examinations or a degree which bears some relation to a *rite de passage*. For others perhaps marriage is seen as the achievement of adulthood — indeed some may marry too young in an attempt to show a maturity which sadly does not yet exist. The concerns of this period of adolescence point forward to the last stage of life, in which early optimism turns into realism, where the positive arrogance of young people becomes the tempered wisdom of experience, and where energetic faith in the life ahead of them changes to quiet satisfaction with the life which the old person has to leave behind. But this is not, of course, the whole picture: the opposite may be equally true, with the cynicism and disillusion of young people turning into the despair of the embittered older person.

Achieving identity

Some psychologists (e.g. Marcia 1975) have outlined types of adolescent identity, seen as the young person passes (at least in age) into young adulthood. Three of Marcia's four types approximate to descriptions typical of the earlier stages of childhood, though expressed in terms of themes reworked in adolescence:

(1) The identity confused or diffused adolescent

This describes the chaotic personality, or the playboy type who needs drugs, alcohol or sex to avoid confrontation and commitment. He resembles in some respects the narcissistic personality [p. 39, p. 137]. Such a person, when asked to complete the phrase 'I am . . . ' shows a negative view of self: 'I am nobody. I'm stupid. I'm confused.' He readily changes values, is vulnerable to feedback because of low self-esteem, and has difficulties in personal relationships.

(2) The foreclosed adolescent

Here there are links to A.S. difficulties about personal autonomy. The young person's identity is determined by parents or by peers. He does things because someone else says so, or because others do. He tends to be authoritarian, less able to evaluate critically, and can easily lose identity in the crowd and to the crowd. Black and white attitudes predominate. Religious faith may be used to foreclose the real questioning we would expect in late adolescence. Such people cannot allow themselves to experience 'the health of immaturity' (Winnicott 1974, p. 172). They complete 'I am . . . ' with such phrases as 'a daughter, a niece, my father's son, my neighbour's neighbour'. They have never really engaged in the tasks of middle adolescence.

> Gerald was actively searching for 'the meaning of life', but when he came to see a counsellor he was caught between the wish to belong to a dogmatic Christian group on the one hand, and to be 'one of the boys' who had a good time on the other. His parents were very protective: they did not let him stay out at night, and had always refused him a bicycle in case he hurt himself. Seeking counselling might have been a chance to work through wishes to belong to groups representing the first two types, and to move into the moratorium area below; but Gerald wanted the counsellor to tell him the answers, and was not yet mature enough to use the time to work things out for himself.

(3) The moratorium subject

Using Erikson's phrase, this describes the late adolescent type, one who expresses what adolescence is about, who is prepared to test out different roles, values and commitments, who experiments with relationships and ideas, but not in any callous way. Such a young person is prepared to challenge authority, and may be less immediately co-operative, but there is a positive ring to the self-description, 'I am searching, I am wondering, I am curious.' Such young people have much to gain from counselling if they seek it out, though their ability to cope with confusion may mean they do not require any extra outside help.

(4) The identity-achieved person

With the last 'type' we move into the young adulthood stage, although we need to recognize that even identity achieved at this stage is not necessarily identity for life. Adult development refines identity, and experience may well bring about significant changes; but the person who has reached this point will be able to tolerate better the confusion which inevitably accompanies changes in adult identity. So with such young identity-achieved people there is a sense of who they are, and of their role — sexual, vocational, and ideological. Decisions are made by considering alternatives. The irrational rebelliousness or the irrational need to conform have been left behind. The young man or woman is committed to work, has begun to form political, ethical and religious/philosophical views, and is able to engage in more intimate relationships. While not free from stress (indeed perhaps more prepared to face it), he is less vulnerable to it. Self-descriptions include phrases such as 'I am a teacher, a woman, a potential mother', or, most apt of all, 'I am me.'

The adolescent adult

Where adolescence has not been experienced to the full, or when growing older is obvious but feared, adults can regress to adolescence, in search of their lost youth [Narcissism and self-respect p. 39]. They seek out young people as sexual partners, in an attempt to prove themselves young and sexually active (when beneath they feel the effects of ageing and see the signs of it in themselves or their marital partner); or they have to have the sexual fling which they were unable to have when younger. While such adults who play at being young only arouse scorn in many adolescents, they are also liable to attract into a relationship young men or women who have not dissolved the oedipal tie to their parents and who therefore collude with the older person's wishes. When working with such adults, counsellors may want to look at the person's experience of adolescence (particularly inhibiting factors that meant he could not enjoy the freedom of that time); the relationship which is being avoided (i.e. with the partner of their own age); relationships with the person's adolescent children; or feelings about ageing (loss of physical strength and prowess, potency, attractiveness, etc.).

Adolescent turmoil or serious disturbance?

From all that we know and remember about adolescence, we expect it to be a turbulent period — indeed it is often the young person who seems 'old' and 'mature' during adolescence who is unusual. The virtue of this stage of life is its plasticity: young people are always on the move, changing, adapting, reworking their situations, striving towards identity. Even the young person whose childhood was relatively smooth and straightforward is unlikely to be spared encountering all the earlier issues in a stronger form. Counselling young people can bring rapid results, since they are less tied by conventions, permanent relationships and fixed attitudes.

The nature of adolescence therefore makes it difficult to distinguish between what lies within the norm, and what indicates more serious disturbance. Psychiatric illness is notoriously difficult to diagnose in persons of this age. What in the adult would be indications of the manic-depressive in the young person might be normal mood swings — right up, right down, at frequent intervals. What is felt to be deviant or outrageous behaviour in adults might be seen as more usual (if not always acceptable) in an adolescent, and may even be seen as high spirits. Dieting will be the concern of many a young woman, without it having to tip over into anorexia. Depression is common, without it being more than moodiness. Heavy drinking may even be only a feature of student life, part of the culture, and left behind when the young person graduates.

At the same time there are pointers to deeper disturbance, which might indicate the desirability of referral to more specialist resources. When anarchic words and phantasies are acted out in anarchic behaviour, a young person may become frightened of his destructiveness. Where work and relationships cease to matter or function, introversion is more extreme. Where a strong mood or behaviour pattern extends over a long period without showing signs of changing, there are indications of more serious problems. Where imagination runs riot and phantasies begin to feel too real, then psychotic features may be apparent. When unconventional dress and normal untidiness give way to a failure to look after himself, and the young person withdraws from human contact, psychiatric opinion may be indicated (see Ryle 1973, chapter 6). The following case illustrates such severe disturbance:

> Howard first presented with feelings of being isolated from people, but at the time appeared to be working fairly well, and in any case was

reluctant to see the counsellor a second time. When he returned a year later, with the same problem, he stayed in counselling, though more out of a sense of desperation than of hope. Let him speak for himself: 'I'm cut off from people . . . it's like going down a spiral staircase and passing people on their way up . . . I have no sense of time . . . I couldn't work out what was real at the theatre last evening, whether it was what was going on on stage or whether it was what was going on in me . . . I saw a dead cat yesterday lying in the road, and went up to it and felt nothing . . . going from one place to another is dangerous . . . I'm losing my marbles . . .'

Such condensing of some of his phrases in fact masks the erratic pattern of the sessions; some were clear, and others confused; in some the counsellor felt they were communicating (especially when he could draw upon the imagery of the O.S. to empathize with Howard), but in others he felt hopeless and helpless.

He only saw him while waiting for Howard to be offered a place in a therapeutic community. The psychiatrist who interviewed Howard confirmed the counsellor's opinion that Howard was schizoid [p. 37], but said that the disturbance was difficult to describe or to understand. He added, 'The problem about once-a-week psychotherapy is not so much that it is not enough, as that Howard has to be "open" at those times. A therapeutic community offers the advantage of any opening that occurs, no matter at what time.'

It is a problematic area, because writers on adolescence agree that young people, more than any other age group, react badly to being labelled, and that if they are labelled they are likely to carry it around with them for life, whether or not the original label was accurate. They may be suspicious of medical help (doctors being equated with parents), and afraid of psychiatrists (mental illness is even more terrifying to a young person than to most adults). Yet extreme episodes may be short-lived if dealt with speedily in the young person, leaving less of a mark than ongoing untreated borderline features. These are extremely sensitive areas for the counsellor, as much as they are for his clients. The counsellor has to make careful judgements, and will need to be constantly aware of the danger of being seen as the negative, critical bad-parent figure. He tries to ally himself with the young person's wish to find a self to be true to, so that if referral is ever necessary, it can be brought about more smoothly and positively.

References

Laufer M. (1974) *Adolescent Disturbance and Breakdown*, Penguin, Harmondsworth.
Marcia J.E. (1975) Development and Validation of Ego-Identity Status, in *Adolescent Behavior and Society*, R.W. Muuss (ed.), (2nd edn), Random House, New York.
Muuss R.W. (1968) *Theories of Adolescence* (2nd edn), Random House, New York.
Rayner E. (1978) *Human Development*, (2nd edn), George Allen and Unwin, London.
Ryle A. (1973) *Student Casualties*, Penguin, Harmondsworth.
Winnicott D.W. (1974) *Playing and Reality*, Penguin, Harmondsworth.

· 8 ·

PARADISE REGAINED?

The transition to adulthood

The Erikson model makes a clear-cut division between young, middle and late adulthood, each with its own tasks, and all culminating in the final stage of ego integrity in old age. It is a convenient model, but an arbitrary one, as all models must be. Adult life cannot be divided so neatly: work, for instance, which is included in Erikson's seventh stage, has clearly begun in young adulthood, if not before in adolescence. Questions of meaning (faith in the broadest sense) present themselves continuously from late adolescence. Intimacy is certainly not only relevant to young adulthood.

This is not to question the idea that with increasing chronological age there are new issues to be faced. In my own teaching, I use an exercise in which the class members divide into age bands, and list the satisfactions and frustrations of their own decade, memories of their last decade, and the fears and hopes of the next. Although it is rewarding to discover that every age group is glad to be the age it is, and does not regret having aged (this gives some hope to the younger members), it is also clear that certain issues are sharper in one age group than in another. For example, becoming thirty is dreaded by many of the younger women, whereas it is forty which is the more significant age for the men. People in their fifties appear to have more frustrations than those who are in their forties or sixties.

I believe it is more true to the spirit of the Erikson model — with its emphasis on reworking previous age issues in the present — to depart from a strictly chronological analysis of adulthood; and instead to divide adult life into four themes, relating them to the specific ages of the model, but not confining them to those ages. The sixth stage of 'intimacy versus isolation' therefore provides a starting point for looking at partnership on the one hand, and being single on the other. The seventh stage, generativity versus stagnation, provides the opportunity of looking at parents and children, and at issues about work, unemployment and retirement. The eighth stage, ego integrity versus despair, obviously deals with ageing and death, but also involves the search for meaning present throughout adult life. In each of the remaining chapter, while age-specific tasks are to the fore, I therefore extend the themes backwards and forwards over the whole life-span.

The single person

Before intimacy, says Erikson, there must be identity. Before entering a partnership, people need to have a period of being alone. Those who cannot tolerate being alone [Loneliness and being alone, p. 42] may seek to escape from inner loneliness through promiscuous sexual activity, or by moving from childhood dependency to marriage without a break — particularly in teenage marriage where adolescence is foreshortened. One of the causes of early pregnancy in adolescence may be to avoid loneliness, finding a solution by projecting dependent needs on to the baby. Likewise, early pregnancy in a new marriage can be a way of avoiding the intimacy of being just two people together.

> Ivor's eighteen-month-old relationship had just broken up. He was, of course, very upset, but perhaps as much because he was losing the promise of the home they were going to set up, as because his girlfriend had left him. They had lived together all that time and were creating a secure place in which he enjoyed doing things around the house. He was eighteen. He also spoke in the first session of his parents' separation, when his mother had walked out on him and his father — and went into a lot of detail about the domestic scene then. The counsellor observed that the present break was all the more painful because he and his girlfriend had been recreating what he had lost when he was eleven. Ivor agreed, but hastened to add (somewhat defensively?) that his girlfriend was not a mother-substitute. A few weeks later he moved in with an older separated woman.

> Judith became pregnant when she was seventeen. That may not appear significant, but the early age, and the fact she got pregnant without a steady relationship might be understood better in the light of her early experience. She was the apple of her family's eye when she

was a baby, and the only child. Two years later her brother arrived on the scene and (according to her mother) Judith's princess-like behaviour turned into tantrums. Judith remembered being depressed 'as long as I can remember'. She recalled dreams since the age of four, and still occurring now, which contained images of being locked out, left out, left behind, pushed out, etc. She described herself as 'like a leech', although her independence in actual life situations appeared to suggest that this was more a fear (wish) of what would happen if she allowed herself to become attached. So perhaps after all the baby, which she carried to full term before giving him away through adoption, was an attempt to recreate the intense early relationship with her mother from which her brother's arrival had been felt to separate her completely.

In any relationship (as we shall see at many points in adult life, e.g. dying) there needs to be an ebb and flow between closeness and solitude. Couples who are too closely bound up in each other appear to be afraid of separating out, which of course is necessary not only as a preparation for the time when death will surely separate them, but also in order to be able to work on their own individual agendas. Crises in life, although of course helped by having another with whom to share them, do not always coincide for both partners, and the individual in every partnership will need some space to work through his or her own particular concerns, alone as well as together.

The single person has more opportunity to work things out on his own. It may be one of the distinct advantages of being single, that there is ample opportunity to withdraw and (as one person put it) 'shut the front door on other people'. The single person need not be without companions and friends with whom to share concerns, although there will be times when not having a partner (or not having had children) will bring feelings of depression and loneliness of a different kind from inner loneliness.

But not all single people are so from their own choice. Some chose to look after a parent, and in doing so cut themselves off from an intimate relationship with a partner of their own age. While we cannot doubt that altruistic concern for a parent is one of the motives for such a decision, the counsellor will also wish to look for others: such as difficulties in breaking the parent/child tie sufficiently for each to be independent enough to face their own life issues. Such difficulties may stem from dependency needs or from oedipal ties, where the 'child' cannot permit herself (it is more commonly a woman) to leave the parent in order to find her own companion. Being single does not necessarily prevent people from developing the caring aspects of the seventh stage. Care, generativity and creativity may be present in the type of work they do. Nevertheless, living alone may indicate withdrawal from intimate relationships [Dependency and withdrawal, p. 35]. The depth of friendships and work relationships may help the counsellor assess how withdrawn a person is, and where there is general fear of closeness, it may indicate schizoid characteristics. But of course it has to be added that there are plenty of schizoid personalities who get married, and are withdrawn in relationships which would normally be expected to be close.

It is not always recognized how large is the number of adults who have single status in our society. Figures for 1978 put the figure as high as 29 per cent, with 7 per cent being single parents, and 15 per cent single people over the retirement age. With an increasing number of old people and of single parents, this figure is no doubt rising. The traditional nuclear family of two parents and two children is nowhere near the norm — only 33 per cent of households in Britain in 1978 (Study Commission on the Family 1980).

The adult living alone is therefore going to present with increasing frequency in clients coming for counselling. While some are alone by choice, and others are compelled by circumstances to live alone (the widowed, for instance), there will be instances where the counsellor looks to see if difficulties about initiating and maintaining intimate relationships can be identified.

Single people may find others threatening, but also find that they themselves can be seen as a threat to couples. The single woman, especially if divorced or a young to middle-aged widow, seems particularly prone to being viewed with suspicion by other women. Although this suspicion indicates that it is the other woman who has the problem with rivalry, and so is not the single person's fault, it is not easy to endure. We might also note (as yet something else for which the counsellor is on the look-out) that suicide rates are highest amongst single people — especially divorcees and elderly men living alone.

Ken and Linda shared their house with a single woman, Meg. Meg felt she was intrusive by being there, even though Linda had invited her — perhaps Meg had an underlying wish for a similar intimate relationship herself, with some feelings of her own for Ken. Yet Linda's subsequent sudden departure to live with another man (after Meg had found a place of her own) might also indicate that Linda had an unconscious wish to have Meg come between herself and Ken.

While the age of young adulthood starts with the majority of young adults in a single state, we should not forget, therefore, that becoming single again will be a common experience amongst adults in later stages of life, when they have to make the adjustment from intimacy and family life to being alone, at such points as separation, divorce, death of a partner, redundancy and retirement. The last two might be especially hard for single people whose life has been 'intimately' bound up with their work and who have found their main companionship through working with others [chapter 10: Work and no work; Bereavement, p. 199].

Choosing a partner

While social class, the example of the parental marriage, and similarity of interests and aspirations, together with sexual attraction, appear to play a large and obviously conscious part in selecting a partner, there are also unconscious factors. These factors include the influence of the relationship of a person to their parents, and the unconscious complementarity or similarity between two people, which helpers find significant in working with couples (see Dominian 1980, pp. 16–17, Cleese *et al.* 1983, pp. 14–18). The most obvious complement is being male and female, and Rayner makes much of the physical 'fit' between a man and a woman (1978, p. 133). Certainly we speak colloquially of 'the other half'. The personal characteristics of one partner (e.g. assertiveness) might be valued by the other (who may be shy, but shows the concern lacking in the first). There may be some kind of fit between strength in the one, and a wish in the other to be protected. Such partnerships, where neither changes or wishes to change, may work well enough even if the outsider would not find such a partnership to their own liking. Such choices can perhaps only be called 'neurotic' and 'collusive' when they break down.

> The partnership between Owen and Nicola started well enough. She was looking for a father figure who adored her, and he for a woman who would look after him as well as his own mother had done. So Nicola stayed at home, had babies, and pampered Owen's every need; in turn she received appreciation and doting love (but little help around the house!) When Nicola enrolled for evening classes she realized how much more she was capable of, and began to resent her self-imposed servile role. Owen felt threatened by a wife who had a mind of her own,

not because she was intelligent, but because it meant his own role came under challenge. The marriage entered a crisis where counselling became necessary to help each of them to try to adapt without tearing the other to pieces for failing to be 'the person I married'.

The attractions which hold two people together defy conclusive description. Complementarity seems to work better when one partner is able to respect the individuality of the other, and can enjoy the other having features (both physical/sexual and personal) which they do not themselves possess. The partner is then not someone to be feared, used or envied. He or she does not become an object upon whom the partner projects (and then criticizes or attacks) what is unacceptable in themselves, but rather is appreciated for providing those qualities the other does not have, or in whom some skills are not so proficient. Complementarity is the occasion for positive identification with a partner when it works well; but for jealousies and other negative feelings when it does not.

O.S. difficulties of intimacy

We have already seen two different ways in which dependency problems might affect a partnership, the first where a couple are so bound up with each other in a symbiotic relationship that they cannot be separated and cannot permit each other individuality; the second where one or both are withdrawn emotionally, and find difficulty in abandoning themselves to sexual and loving feelings, and therefore to each other. There can also be difficulties where one or both partners is so narcissistic that they are concerned only for their own needs, and have not developed sufficient awareness of the other's needs to accept differences in the other, or to tolerate frustration of their own wishes. It is as if the other exists like the early mother figure, simply to serve them. So one partner becomes demanding, while the other eventually struggles to meet those demands. In any intimate relationship there has to be shared caring (with each able to care for the other at different times), and therefore a balance between concern for the other and claiming some care for oneself.

The title of this chapter, 'Paradise Regained?', is of course meant to be ironical. As long as the romantic view of love dominates our culture — as it has for many centuries — it unfortunately reinforces the state of idealization which is but the first stage of most partnerships. The counsellor will work with clients who in later life still search for the ideal partner, who want to 'fall in love' again, and who seem not to have recognized that in most partnerships the symbiotic mother/baby phase is only one aspect of a total relationship. Couples grow together as they learn to embrace and value the ordinariness of life, as well as the high points, to work through differences as well as enjoy agreement. Satisfaction can be found in relationships in many more ways than through paradisal bliss alone [Idealization and splitting, p. 43]. Features of difficulties with intimacy are seen in this example.

> Polly was anxious about being 'sucked into' a relationship (her words), which was connected to her worry about how a partnership would work out when it entered a less idealized stage. She was very concerned about being attractive forever to any man she went out with (so much so that it went beyond the normal limits and showed O.S. narcissistic features). As soon as there was the slightest sign of lack of attention (e.g. a man not being as chatty as usual over dinner, or his failure to comment on how pretty she looked) she feared the worst, and began to withdraw; lest he be the one who broke the relationship off first. Not surprisingly she feared growing old and losing her physical attractiveness as much as she feared either herself or her partner becoming 'bored' with each other [see below, p. 162, for the way in which these concerns showed themselves also in the relationship with the counsellor].

A.S. difficulties of intimacy

Living together means learning to live with another's norms, values and 'rules'; often these are unwritten, and unexpressed verbally. Breaking such norms and rules, or not conforming to expected patterns of behaviour learned in the partner's family of origin, can lead to criticism, and to one person laying down 'orders' to the other. In the critical/submissive partnership, ways of living and making decisions are not openly questioned and shared. One partner becomes (or is felt to be) the authoritarian parent, while the other initially tries hard to please and conform, until he or she comes to the end of their tether and rebels. Decisions about money, about home-making, about management of the children and about the expectations of 'in-laws' can all become battlegrounds for two people who need to prove to each other their independence or dominance. Where A.S. problems interfere with a partnership, conflicts and disagreements become occasions for fighting old parent/child battles about freedom and autonomy. Even minor matters can become excuses for one partner to try to impress their authority on the other.

Sometimes difficulties arise from the fact that people are attracted by character traits in the other, which they do not themselves possess. The illustration [on p. 73] of Lionel's perfectionism, for instance, also contains an example of the effect that his obsession with tidiness had on his partner. She, in the end, could not stand it any longer and left him. But in the early stages of the relationship it is possible that she had expressed in her attitude the type of freedom which Lionel would himself have liked to possess.

Battles for supremacy reflect one side of A.S. problems in partnerships. Another side is the wish to please: one partner may always feel inadequate in the eyes of the other (because of their own expectations, not always because of the partner's), so having always to strain hard to feel good enough as a bread-winner, home-maker, as a parent of the other's children, or even as a lover. In the last-named instance, sex becomes both a demand and a performance, where results (the orgasm of the partner, for example) predominate over mutual enjoyment.

Another A.S. feature which may interfere with the intimacy of a couple is over-concentration upon work. [All work and no play, p. 74]: the husband or wife who lives for their career alone, or the partner who cannot relax at home and always has to be busy about the house. These different expressions of rigidity of attitude in one or both partners prevent a couple relaxing with each other, and using that important part of childhood and adolescent experience — the freedom to explore and experiment with each other discovering more about each other (not just sexually, but in the total relationship).

G.S. difficulties of intimacy

When the O.S. stage has not been negotiated satisfactorily, there may be difficulties and anxieties about engaging in a relationship which embraces sexuality, companionship and mutual caring — all of which go some way towards describing that elusive term 'love'. The temptation for a person who cannot enjoy such a partnership is to split off friendship and sexuality, or sexuality and care. The partner may therefore become the parent figure who is there to nurture and protect, but a sexual partner has to be sought outside the relationship. Some people can only be sexually active with a person to whom they are otherwise uncommitted [The eternal triangle, p. 96]. Sex within the partnership may become a way of trying to prove one's masculinity or femininity; or where there are anxieties about gender and role there may be competitiveness:

> Ralph had always been the major bread-winner in the family. When he was made redundant it was natural that he should have felt depressed. But his depression was made worse through having no income of his own and becoming dependent upon his wife's salary. He became increasingly chauvinistic, and in his counselling it was a long time before the woman counsellor was able to build up sufficient sense of equality between them for Ralph also to admit that much of his depression also came not just from feeling, but also being impotent.

Opting out of the shared tasks in the home may be the reaction of a man who finds it threatening to be 'maternal', and so avoids sharing in child-care and house-work. Worry about his masculinity may reinforce his A.S. wish to assert his authority, and so he does not discuss with his wife decisions which they as a couple should be making [Male and female, p. 86].

A person's parents (in his or her internal world) may intrude, sometimes in conscious phantasy: one man found it difficult to make love to his wife because he kept thinking she had turned into his mother. Since the parent–child relationship is inevitably carried over into the husband–wife relationship, the presence of negative features in the original relationship can seriously impede the present one. In some instances there may be even more obvious interference from parents (even when they have no wish to intrude), such as when a young couple have to live with one set of parents, or later in life when a widowed parent is brought into the family home. These are not easy situations, but they are even harder when oedipal ties have not been sufficiently broken. Children can likewise interfere with the intimacy of a partnership, particularly when a child is felt to be a strong rival for the partner's love and attention [Oedipus — myth and symbol p. 92]. Indeed, children cannot help but intrude upon the initial intimacy of a couple, and when they leave home there inevitably has to be renegotiation of intimacy, which in many ways is like the start of any relationship.

Changing patterns of intimacy

The intimacy of the couple has to be adapted to the changing circumstances which accompany the next stage of life — parenthood. But intimacy can never remain static, since each partner is always changing. The relationship has to be renewed and reworked at frequent intervals. There are always small, and sometimes large, changes of identity throughout life, and just as identity has to be achieved to allow intimacy in the first place, so the process will be repeated in miniature at other points. 'You're not the person I married' must be a common phrase. Although some changes may seem negative, many of them can become positive, as long as a partner is given the chance to adapt. Life would be very dull if changes did not occur.

The identity changes are numerous, and only a few can be mentioned here. In the early years of a partnership there are likely to be changes of home and of jobs. Some career changes will bring totally new identities with them for one partner. There may be geographical relocations which involve making new friends (more easily done when children are still young, and contact with other parents is encouraged through schools). It is not just in becoming a parent that identity changes, perhaps significantly, in one or both partners. It happens often when the 'children' leave home. Some couples speak of a 'second honeymoon' holiday at such times, the opportunity to explore each other again as on the first. Redundancy, and more especially retirement, cause partners to be together for much more of the time, and so necessitate a major readjustment. It is not surprising that divorce rates are at their highest at significant times: in the first two years (when it is discovered that intimacy does not work), seven to eleven years of marriage (when the children are at their most demanding); after 20 or so years (when the children have left home); and at retirement age.

The intimacy of the counselling relationship

It is sometimes suggested by counsellors that the helping relationship involves an intimacy which is almost on a par with the closest of human relationships. I have written about this elsewhere, observing the curious and one-sided nature of such a relationship (1982, pp. 44–6; see also Lowe 1972, pp. 220–1). It is important to draw a distinction between that type of intimacy which is present in the helping relationship and which has a unique quality to it, the intimacy that comes from a client who is more open to the counsellor than he or she would be to anyone else; and that wish for an intimate relationship which comes from transference or counter-transference feelings in the client or the counsellor, a wish that is in fact an illusion [The gender of the counsellor, p. 111].

Polly [p. 158] was indeed an attractive woman, and the counsellor felt this himself. He was aware as she described her feelings for him in the first six months of counselling that his counter-transference feelings matched hers. He was therefore cautious about taking up her feelings lest he was encouraging her for his own ends and not helping her to work through them. But he realized that when she talked of her need to make men admire her and pay her compliments that this was indeed what was happening to him. What he was experiencing was not simply his own wish to be admired, but the sort of flattery which Polly used to try and get back the compliments she so much needed.

He became less worried about letting her feelings for him be talked about; and helped her to begin to realize that she could be valued without having to dress up both herself and everything she said in the most attractive way. She found herself relating to him in a more ordinary fashion, and she started a new and better relationship with a man she had met. There her feelings of being boring and unattractive featured again although she could see what was happening to her.

One feature of every session was that Polly found it difficult to stay until the end: she wanted to leave about ten minutes before the end, and she acknowledged that this was because the counsellor calling a halt felt like a rejection of her for being dull.

Towards the end of the counselling contract she brought a long dream to one session. It was too detailed to include all her associations fully in this example, but two linked elements in it were a leopard which gently got hold of her arm but would not let her go, and a tussle over a coffin between herself and someone who reminded her of the counsellor; she was in this case reluctant herself to let the coffin go. The counsellor interpreted this feature of the dream as a possible indication of her feelings about ending. There was a part of her that wanted to leave and get away, but a part of her that wanted to stay. It was something like the end of each session when she described the tussle; she wanting to leave, he trying to help her to stay.

Polly agreed that this was a possibility but said that she did not feel the counsellor was trying to hang on to her. It was at this point that the session had to end and she got up to go, only to find that the latch on the door was down and she could not get out of the room! The counsellor, like many a psychodynamically-minded therapist, did not believe in sheer coincidence, and wondered whether he had 'inadvertently' slipped the catch when he had closed the door earlier. Perhaps his counter-transference feelings still needed some examination!

Because there is this curious intimacy between counsellor and client which others outside the sessions may find impossible to understand, it can be troublesome to the partner (including a counsellor's partner) who is not part of it. There are some partners, of course, who are content to let the client be identified as the one with the problem, since it lets them off the hook. They may support the client on the one hand, while undermining progress on the other by refusing to acknowledge any part in the problem. But other partners may be jealous of the closeness the client feels with the counsellor, and wonder what is being said about themselves — often feeling that they are being criticized. All these are difficult areas for the counsellor, who recognizes the value of a client having space and time (the separateness which is necessary in any partnership) and who therefore supports the privacy of the counselling. At the same time, she knows that much might be gained from the client sharing insights with the partner. The solution does not always lie in joint sessions, especially if the second partner is brought in after a long spell with the first — the second can feel that the counsellor has already taken the side of the first. Offering to see the second partner for an occasional session is not necessarily any more helpful. The offer of counselling with another helper might be considered with the chance of it leading to a 'foursome' later with both counsellors and both clients. But above all, the counsellor needs to be sensitive, and even more so when his client makes significant progress, to the accompanying changes in identity which mean the renegotiation of intimacy in the client's partnership. Counselling sometimes leads to the splitting of partnerships, but it would be sad if it so concentrated upon the one person that it did not also help the client to recognize the needs of his or her partner. If the partner is given the opportunity to adapt to the new identity emerging in the client, that partner may also change, with the result that genuine intimacy is for the first time discovered by both.

References

Cleese J. and Skynner R. (1983) *Families: and How to Survive Them*, Methuen, London.

Dominian J. (1980) *Marital Pathology*, Darton, Longman and Todd, London.

Jacobs M. (1982) *Still Small Voice*, S.P.C.K., London.

Lowe G. (1972) *The Growth of Personality*, Penguin, Harmondsworth.

Rayner E. (1978) *Human Development* (2nd edn), George Allen and Unwin, London.

Study Commission on the Family (1980), *Happy Families: a Discussion Document*.

· 9 ·

GENERATIVITY: PARENTS AND CHILDREN

Introduction

With the conception of the first child, the life cycle begins all over again. (It would not be inappropriate for the reader to go back and reread chapters 3 to 7 — but this time concentrating upon the references to parents rather than to children and adolescents.) As Rayner underlines, 'As a child grows, so it is necessary for a parent to change in emphatic (*sic* — although 'empathic' also applies — author) responsiveness to his/her child' (1978, p. 145). In this chapter, however, I will concentrate upon two aspects which do not appear in the earlier chapters: pregnancy and birth; and the child (now adult) in relationship to still older parents. This recapitulation of the early stages, although this time from the parent's viewpoint, I take as read, although it must be added that our memories of our parents influence our own parenthood. Sometimes this takes the rigid form of 'what was good for me will also be good for you'; sometimes the form is reactive: 'Look at the way I am treating you, not at all like my parents treated me'; sometimes (and most constructive) the experience is one of empathy: 'now I know what my parents had to go through with me.'

We live in a time when parenthood is a more positive choice than it has been before. It is a choice which recognizes commitment for some years ahead. Rayner calls this 'the keynote of adult maturity' (1978, p. 123). This is not to forget that there is an increasing number of single parents, who perhaps never intended to be so when they conceived their children [p. 155: 7 per cent of households in 1978 were single-parent]. Such men and women frequently have to combine two roles (nurturing and boundary-setting) at one and the same time, and they will experience less freedom and greater financial problems than two-parent families. These are extra burdens in addition to all the 'normal' emotional problems of bringing up children referred to in this and earlier chapters. Consequently, the single parent is under extra strain:

> Susan described what it had been like bringing up her two children single-handed for five years, and contrasted that period with the time since she had remarried. She said how difficult it had been to be both mother and father, and how even though sometimes now 'Daddy is the good guy and I'm seen as the bad guy when he comes home from work, that is far better than being the bad guy, and having no one to share your feelings with, or to discuss how to handle the kids.'

Pregnancy

Pregnancy is nowadays more often than not by choice; but even 'accidental' pregnancy may include some unconscious element of choice. Pregnancy may be desired (though in some people feared) as a way of recreating lost dependency, left behind in the process of growing up. Needs in a woman for more mothering can be projected on to the baby, and satisfied by keeping the baby dependent. Early pregnancy therefore may be a way of avoiding the state of being alone, which we have seen is one part of adolescent and adult experience, or may be a way of avoiding adult relationships [See example of 'Judith' on p. 153.] It can also be means of trying to prove adult status to oneself (this applies to young men and women) or to parents who tend to keep the young person as a child.

In counselling decisions about abortion, the urgency of the situation sometimes means that such possibilities are obscured. Yet where such unconscious motives exist, further unprotected intercourse may take place, with the possibility of yet another request for abortion. Lest it seems as if it is the woman alone who wants a child for unconscious motives, men too have their agenda. The wish to prove his fertility may be just as important to a man:

> Tony's casual relationship with a girl had led to her becoming pregnant. Tony was certainly not callous, but he was nonetheless all too efficient about helping to arrange an abortion for her. In truth, he seemed delighted to have fathered a child, even if it was now necessary to arrange the abortion; he was less concerned about the girl's feelings than his own. Tony's father had simply walked out on the family when

he was still tiny, and had never been heard of since; so perhaps Tony was trying to find the 'father' in himself, and that mattered more to him than any sense of inconvenience for the girl.

Despite these reservations, it is also part of normal experience for a pregnant woman to enjoy the interdependency of herself and her child, and to take legitimate pleasure from being turned in upon herself. Self-love and narcissistic needs interpenetrate her love for the baby and her concern for the baby's needs: the image which comes to mind is of a set of Russian dolls, with the baby inside the mother, but the mother also inside the baby. Winnicott's words, quoted earlier [p. 39], were written to young mothers. The phrase omitted on that page after 'Enjoy being turned in and almost in love with yourself', is 'the baby is so nearly part of you' (1964, p. 26). It is difficult to distinguish mother and baby in pregnancy. This may have repercussions for the father of the child, who not only feels pleased, but may also feel excluded, partly because intercourse might be more difficult during the pregnancy, but also because the baby may feel like a rival for his wife's care and attention. It is a time during which some men develop symptoms which seem to indicate a sympathetic pregnancy of their own; and during which some men look for a relationship outside the marriage.

When a baby is born, it matters to some parents greatly whether it is a boy or a girl. When the hoped-for boy turns out to be a girl, or vice versa, this may have subsequent repercussions for the identity given to the child:

> Vicky was the third girl, but her father desperately wanted her to be a boy. As she grew up, her father encouraged her (but not the other girls) to help him around the house; he took her to football matches; he discussed business matters with her. Vicky was happy enough to go along with this, because it meant that she was close to him, but she never felt close to him as a woman.
>
> Consequently, as an adult, she found it difficult to believe that anyone was genuine when they complimented her on 'feminine' aspects such as the clothes she wore, or her cooking; and she was diffident about her expectations of enjoying sex with her husband, who seemed to satisfy his own needs rather than hers.

Birth and loss

When pregnancy goes to full term, with a successful delivery, it is an occasion for both joy and sadness. The mother has gained a baby, although she has lost part of herself. The real baby replaces the phantasy baby whom she has thought about all during pregnancy. Reality, the demands of mothering, the sense of responsibility for one so fragile and helpless, feelings about the smallest abnormality in a baby, and anxiety about being a good mother can contribute to post-natal depression. But it is other conclusions to a pregnancy which are as likely to come to the counsellor's attention. Abortion, even if necessary, is also the loss of the opportunity to have a baby; feelings of grief may be less consciously acknowledged at the time, but may sometimes surface later. Guilt at giving expression to murderous phantasies is not uncommon: it may have been fed by the worst kind of anti-abortion publicity, but may not be solely caused by it. The counsellor will often find that this guilt can be lessened by helping the client to acknowledge any hints of such thoughts about 'murder' — this does not mean the counsellor believes that abortion is murder, but does accept that concern about life (however small) is appropriate, and that the murderous wishes in anyone can become inappropriately linked to real events.

> Zara was one of those gentle people who could never harm a fly. True, another side of her came out when she got drunk at a party and afterwards slept with a man whom she did not even know by name. But when she found she was pregnant she was very upset at the thought of an abortion, although she recognized that it was important to have one. Fortunately she saw a counsellor to clarify her decision, and he arranged for them to meet again afterwards. Zara went alone to the clinic in another city, and returned alone. On the train back, a goods train passed the other way, laden with military tanks, and that image stayed in her mind. She felt it applied to her, and though she knew rationally that what she had done was not murder, it nevertheless felt like a violation of life. Perhaps linked in with this feeling was one that linked the tanks with the man's violation of her own body, even if she had been a willing party. Whatever the meaning of the image (and no counsellor can ever be certain of the total meaning of any image), sharing it helped, and Zara was gradually able to work through her experience sufficiently to feel her old gentle self again.

It can be a surprise to a client that an abortion performed some years before still causes depression in the present. Anniversaries of an abortion, or of the time when a child might have been born had the pregnancy not been terminated, can be as significant as the anniversaries of other deaths:

Anna continually talked in her counselling sessions of pets and relatives dying, or of the fear of them dying. The counsellor did not wish to hazard a guess without more evidence, but being part of a general practice he had access to Anna's medical history. A glance at her notes confirmed his hunch that she had had an abortion some years before.

Guilt at having terminated a pregnancy can also lead to fears of being punished through being unable to conceive a second time. The warning which some doctors are obliged to give is often exaggerated in a patient's mind. This is yet another reason (in addition to dependency needs referred to above) why one abortion may be followed by further pregnancy and the request for a second abortion, proving fertility yet perpetuating a cycle of uncertainty. With some women it is only the birth of a replacement child that puts an abortion to rest.

There are two further outcomes to pregnancy which mean both a birth and a death at the same time. Stillbirth is clearly both, and giving a baby for adoption is a type of 'living death', which for the caring mother occasions a lifetime's concern about the child who was hers. In cases of stillbirth there is far greater need for professionals (doctors, nurses and clergy) to recognize its significance in the care which they give to the parents: allowing the dead baby to be seen and held, encouraging the death to be talked about at the time, arranging for proper recognition of the death through a religious or secular funeral (see Kirkley-Best et al. 1982; Case 1978). In all such instances of loss (abortion, stillbirth and adoption) there may be clues to the nature of the relationship and the degree of loss in the words used to describe the foetus/baby. 'Foetus' and 'it' are cold and more distancing terms. 'He', 'she' and 'the baby' may indicate recognition of, or the wish for, a human relationship and greater emotional involvement. 'The child' may refer to the unfulfilled phantasies of the child as he or she would have been in a few years time.

Just as the arrival of a new baby in the family can cause some difficulties for existing children, such as having to share mother's attention, so where there is a death at birth, or soon after it (as well as in later childhood) a child's phantasy wish to get rid of the new rival can mistakenly be felt to be the cause, leading to an understandable, yet unrealistic sense of guilt [Jealousy and competition, p. 112].

Parenthood as renunciation

The seventh stage of Erikson's model makes way for the final stage, which includes willingness to give up one's authority and claims over others. Parenthood also includes such renunciation, since it is a period of gradually letting go of the child through successive developmental stages. This is more acceptable when parents have themselves felt 'good enough' at each stage of their children's growth. A mother who has felt satisfaction in meeting the dependent needs of her baby will be ready to let him or her move into the stage of autonomy; a father who has felt the right balance between allowing freedom and exercising control will be more confident in allowing the adolescent to find his or her own way. The danger of all books on developmental psychology is their tendency to lay down what is right and wrong in child-rearing. This is not necessarily what the authors intend, but parents who want to do their job well tend to take what they read as gospel, and blame themselves rather than examine the complicated dynamics between parent and child. Winnicott is correct constantly to use the phrase 'good enough' of the task of parenting. As children grow away from them, parents who have done their job 'well enough' can more easily renounce their claims to be parental; often they will find outlets for their sense of responsibility, care and commitment in service to the wider community. Parents who do not feel satisfied can become self-centred:

> Individuals, then, often begin to indulge themselves as if they were their own — or one another's — one and only child (Erikson 1965, p. 259).

Parents and children: vice versa

One of the forebodings of adults in their forties (as their own children leave home) is the prospect of caring for their own elderly parents, and one of the difficulties of those who are in their fifties is that this prospect becomes a reality. Gratitude to parents can of course be repaid. One of the benefits of growing older is the ability to identify more with one's parents, when going through the different stages of parenting one's own children. But unless boundaries are made clear, caring for parents can be at the cost of the rediscovery of intimacy [p. 161] and the need that a couple has for space for themselves. Resentment at being burdened with parents can be reinforced and expressed in the opportunity to turn the tables on the older generation, the children becoming 'parents' to their own parents. The older generation are by then themselves entering their second 'childhood', inasmuch as increasing age and infirmity mean that at some stage many old people need help. Some continue to value their independence, others want to become dependent, and yet others resent being ordered around or any hint of belittlement even when it is not intended [Ageing, p. 186]. In this reversal of roles, ruthless games can be played, in which old people are infantilized more by the younger generation than they are by their natural physical weakness. It is at this point in family relationships that the real ability of parents and their children to relate adult to adult is exposed and tested. The infantilization of the old is still seen in too many institutions; while there may be some mirroring of this in even more frightening terms in the sadistic attacks which sometimes take place on the defenceless old person by the young. These are examples of acting-out the revenge which a younger generation might feel towards those who were once felt to be persecutory objects.

References

Case R. (1978) When birth is also a funeral, *Journal of Pastoral Care* (USA), Vol. XXXII: 1.

Erikson E. (1965) *Childhood and Society*, Penguin, Harmondsworth.

Kirkley-Best E. et al. (1982) On stillbirth: an open letter to the clergy, *Journal of Pastoral Care* (USA), Vol. XXXVI: 1.

Rayner E. (1978) *Human Development*, (2nd edn), George Allen and Unwin, London.

Winnicott D.W. (1964) *The Child, the Family and the Outside World*, Penguin, Harmondsworth.

· 10 ·

GENERATIVITY: WORK AND NO WORK

Introduction

Work and raising children (a job in itself) have always been the main preoccupations of adult life. Whether that work is outside or within the home, it takes up much of the waking day. Occupations are so varied that it is only of some jobs that we can say that work provides men and women with opportunities to exercise responsibility, to be creative, to be productive, to co-operate and to compete constructively with others, to earn money for more than basic necessities, and to make a positive contribution to the lives of others and to society as a whole. There is of course another side to all this: the punishment for Adam and Eve was expulsion from paradise, with the twin curses of the pain of childbirth and work as toil. So some work can also be monotonous, socially isolating, degrading or dangerous to health, poorly paid, or can encourage greed, cut-throat competition and sexual stereotyping. Despite such negative aspects, the vast majority of people prefer to work, even when their income is little more than meagre welfare benefits. Such is the 'work ethic' which is endemic in industrialized societies, and may be linked to 'anal' requirements to be productive.

Counsellors in the 1980s cannot but be aware of major problems in the area of work arising from unemployment, redundancy and early retirement. While not wishing to overlook the problems likely to be encountered by those clients who are in work (and related to their work), the following sections in other chapters cover many of the issues: anxieties about competence — Problems related to authority and control p. 125; guilt or anxiety in competitive situations — Jealousy and competition p. 112, 129; problems of accepting the authority structures in the work setting — The passive-aggressive personality p. 78; difficulties about working co-operatively — Jealousy and competition p. 112, p. 129; anxiety about being 'the boss' — Controlling others p. 80; the obsessional workaholic — All work and no play p. 74.

Rayner also suggests that some occupations require mastery of anxiety about the nature of the work involved, especially where that work involves coping with basic emotions (1978, p. 121). For instance, a doctor has to master anxieties about ill-health in order to be able to examine patients as a first step towards helping them back to health; just as a surgeon has to master anxieties about 'blood and guts'. Lionel [p. 73] showed a symptom of this type of difficulty, when he got depressed if a patient failed to respond to treatment.

Counsellors too have to master their anxieties (see Jacobs 1982, chapter 4) — particularly about the darker side of human nature such as aggression, or the 'seamier side' like sex. But perhaps the most difficult area for a counsellor to master is coping with helplessness, since it is axiomatic to his or her craft that clients are not, except in exceptional circumstances, given direct help or advice.

> Bernadette was in training, and therefore anxious to do well in order to pass her placement. But in addition, like many a learner, she took her work home with her, worrying about her clients' welfare between sessions, trying to plan ahead for all eventualities in her wish to help them in the time available to her. She was not helped by having parents who had expressed disappointment that she had not used her considerable intelligence and qualifications to go for a prestigious job, but had instead chosen a career which held little prospect of 'success' in terms of money or status.

I concentrate, in this chapter, mainly upon those people for whom the 'normal' working pattern has been disrupted: the unemployed; those who have been made redundant; those who have been compelled to take early retirement, or those who have accepted retirement at the normal age with reluctance. Some people of course welcome the freedom from full-time employment in order to pursue other interests, and their difficulties, if any, will be different — such as relating afresh to a partner [Changing patterns of intimacy, p. 161]. In the previous 'work-centred' age of latency, I referred to a mini-cycle of development [p. 122], and in looking at the issues which arise from havng no work, the Erikson cycle can again be related to the difficulties which might arise. (I draw in this chapter on material adapted from my paper 'Stuck' in *Work and No Work* 1981.)

No work — issues related to the O.S.

Being without work may seem a long way from issues concerning the dependency and trust of a baby upon mother. Yet the anxieties about being let down which are experienced by the baby might also be felt in the person who is axed from a job and unable to find alternative employment. It is not easy to feel valued in such circumstances. Trust has been placed in the promised goals of education and in contracts of employment; the breaking of that trust may lead to lack of faith in the powers that be or in society itself as not caring, and can spread to lack of faith in oneself. There is a basic split in society between those who have and those who have not, reminding us of the split in infancy between the hungry baby and the mother who appears to be withholding all the goodness she possesses. We might wonder how having a particular type of woman as prime minister (I write of the period 1979 onwards) affects people's views of society as mothering; were it not for her 'masculine' image she would perhaps be seen (as she was before the Falklands conflict) as the 'bad' mother. When those without work live in an economic world-order which appears to be breaking down, it is little wonder that those who are casualties of change also feel shattered, in the way we know babies can feel, without any sense of underlying order and unity. Hope is one of the basic strengths of this early stage; but hope for the unemployed is at the best temporarily and at the worst permanently destroyed. Drive, the other basic strength of this age, gives place to debilitating depression, withdrawal into a frightened and fractured self, and all the attendant difficulties of moving out of such a position.

Chris had been unemployed for three years. His main preoccupation was getting a job; and this had become so central for him that he could not hear what anyone else was saying to him, unless they were giving him an opening to express his feelings. His manner reminded the counsellor of a hungry baby, for whom nothing else matters than being fed. Chris had no space within himself for concern for others and their difficulties, even if they too were unemployed. Getting a job so dominated him that until that need was satisfied he could apparently not settle to any other activity, including relating to others on their terms and not just on his own. Chris's situation is probably not atypical of the effects of long-term unemployment. In fact he changed, at least partially, when he was helped to get involved as a voluntary helper in an unemployment centre. This 'job' gave him a sense of purpose which helped him to pay more attention to the needs of others outside himself.

It can be argued that politicians and society are not uncaring, and that welfare benefits cushion some of the effects of unemployment. Yet we already have evidence that some find it difficult to claim what is their due, because of the shame attached to feeling dependent. Work, even if it means being in some sense dependent upon an employer, at least enables a person to feel adult in earning what they receive. Living off benefits (apart from problems about the actual level of payment) may therefore reawaken dependency problems, encouraging some to sink into a dependency where they expect to be looked after, while others (their feelings reinforced by some political hyperbole) feel guilty at being dependent, and blame themselves. Unemployment may make people feel even more helpless and infantilized, so losing any hope of being able to make an impact on or contribution to society.

In the first stage of life, as we have seen , there is a close link between external circumstances and internal feelings. The boundaries between what happens to a person, and the way they feel about themselves, are blurred. We would then expect the most severe effects of unemployment (and unwelcome retirement) to be felt by those who are less adept at making distinctions between their circumstances and their view of self. The counsellor can therefore work towards helping such people understand (on a feeling level) that unemployment is not the result of lack of personal worth, but the result of economic policies and other external reality factors. If it can be demonstrated that these are not a personal attack upon the one individual, but an attack (some would say misguided) on the economic ills of society, then the feelings of personal worthlessness may be eased, making autonomy and initiative (the next two stages) more possible. That is not to deny that reality factors will be hard, but the person who finds, or recovers, a sense of their own inner value, like those who have 'faith' (of religious, political or moral kind), will be helped to endure much that life throws at them.

Regrettably, there are always those who in their rhetoric prefer to blame the people themselves, fastening upon one of the components of the O.S. — greed — as the cause of all the trouble. People are told that they have been too greedy for money and that is why they have lost their jobs. It is of course unfair because those who have lost their jobs are often those whose demands were more than justified. Such political arguments hook into that part of the unconscious which feels guilt at having been too demanding as children, perhaps making it more difficult to make demands that are in fact reasonable. Unemployment may be felt to be a just punishment of primitive wishes to have more. We certainly need to look for an explanation for so many unemployed appearing to take what happens to them lying down. Guilt and feelings of helplessness, reminiscent of this early stage of life, may provide part of the answer.

Employment enables most people to satisfy many of their needs, one of which may be particularly relevant to this stage, even if in some respects it is a negative solution to primitive problems in the large group. I refer to the splitting which we see in industrial relations, between 'bad' management and 'good' unions on the one side, or 'fair' bosses and 'awkward' shop stewards on the other, or the projection of blame on to the office staff, the workforce, the tools or the materials. These may not be healthy ways of relating, but we may wonder what happens when a person is out of work and these projections and this defence of splitting can no longer be used. The safety valve of industrial relations (however strained) is no longer there.

> Dave described with alarming frankness how he had taken his frustration out on his wife. When the bills came in, and anxieties about meeting such demands were too much, he would attack his wife if she too began to make unreasonable demands herself — demands which in better circumstances would have been reasonable, but were now impossible to meet. The marriage collapsed, although Dave was able to see the dangers of scapegoating those closest to him when he was denied any opportunity of voicing his real anger with distant powers-that-be. This recognition helped him become more understanding when he married again.

The more work has provided a channel for expression of negative feelings (on whatever side of industry), and the more aggression is deprived of an external target, the more may anger be turned back upon self and the family. Severe depression or suicidal feelings can also be expected to feature in such instances, unless a person is able to fight socially or politically for others who are similarly disadvantaged.

The counsellor is therefore in a difficult position, especially if he is envied for his ability to work, whether for a salary or voluntarily, or where he is seen as 'superior' for offering help from a comfortable life position. He tries to build or rebuild trust in himself as one who cares, while at the same time he may need to take some of the anger upon himself, and survive it, however unjustified it may appear to be. He will want to encourage expression of appropriate anger and of appropriate demands for change in basic living standards, at the same time knowing that it is not easy to see evidence of the positive outcome of constructive anger. Problems in the area of dependency may need to be explored before the unemployed person can move forward into autonomy and initiative. Distinguishing reality factors and intra-personal factors may be of the utmost importance where a person is severely and continuously depressed in the face of being without work.

Issues related to the A.S.

The person without work who regresses to this stage is more likely to see the world as unfair and unjust than as uncaring. There will not be the same strength of persecutory feeling, although self-blame and self-doubt may still be present. While there may be justified complaint about something being wrong with the system, any self-blame is more likely to be about being unable to do those things which others expect, or are felt to expect — such as being unable to provide for the family adequately, or being unable to get a job. Such a person, while not feeling as worthless as the devalued and depressed people of the first stage, can nonetheless feel incompetent in the sight of others: the family at home might be perceived as critical; while outside the home, it may be difficult to meet others, particularly those who are still in work, because of feelings of inferiority and 'loss of face'.

For both the unemployed and the unhappily retired there may also be difficulties arising from no longer being part of an authority structure, where (however lamentable it is) a person knows 'his place'. Being in work, or even being at school prior to going on the dole, a person can identify with the organization; in receiving orders and instructions, in giving them, in praise for good work, in criticism for slapdash work; the 'system' (whether fair or unfair) provides a sense of structure in which he feels secure enough to conform or to criticize. The counsellor has, of course, the opportunity to help a person find autonomy, and use what seems disaster as a point of growth. He may be able to observe how he is seen as the provider of control and structure, advice or orders [Passivity, p. 74], thus encouraging the client to take hold of the fears and opportunities of freedom; there may be some liberation in becoming his own boss, less answerable to others' good opinions; there may be some value in having his own time to structure. The passivity which accompanies being in work and out of work does not make this an easy task, and the counsellor will be tempted to assume the role of 'manager'. Being able to make decisions for themselves may be frightening and risky for some people, yet it is an adjustment which is necessary if the person out of work is to remain mentally and emotionally active, and to regain self-respect.

> Elisabeth had not sought work for over a year, since leaving university. She got depressed because of her inactivity; and the counsellor was tempted (like Elisabeth's mother) to drop hints about the value of getting something to do to occupy her. That would not have helped, as Elisabeth found it difficult to visit her mother because she felt she would only disappoint her, and her hints would begin to make her angry. Instead the counsellor took up Elisabeth's reluctance to seek work, which seemed based on her feeling that work meant becoming part of the system, and that she would only be an insignificant cog in a machine. Her father's legalistic attitude, schooling which had suppressed individual expression, and underlying anxiety that she was not up to competing with men combined to reinforce her inactivity. She said she preferred the freedom of not being in work, although it appeared that she was retreating from opportunities to use her own qualifications and eventual seniority to begin applying authority in a less restrictive way. One of the features of the relationship between the counsellor and Elisabeth was her constant attempt, despite being apparently anti-authority, to get the counsellor to give her answers.

Issues related to the G.S.

Large-scale unemployment means more intense competition for jobs. Those who have lost their jobs can sometimes fall hard, even believing that their 'fall from grace' is a just desert for over-reaching themselves. Contemplating application forms, interviews, and rejections in favour of others (younger, older, more qualified, less qualified) touches upon the whole phantasy area of rivalry. Even securing a job may mean overcoming guilt at succeeding at the cost of others who have not. Some people express considerable concern at meeting other applicants at interview and feeling the rivalry between them, and find it difficult to push themselves forward sufficiently for their own abilities to be recognized. There often appears a common feature in such people, which is the competitiveness felt in their own family against either parent or with siblings. Sportsmen (perhaps more than sportswomen) speak of the 'killer instinct' as a feature of the successful competitor, the ability when poised for victory, to drive the winning stroke home. A lack of drive on, say, the tennis court, may also prevail elsewhere:

> Freddie (though not a serious sportsman) described the difficulty he had over winning at tennis. He felt he gave up trying just at the point he could win a match, particularly when playing his father. Yet Freddie was the better player. So too in interviews for jobs: he felt so bad about doing the others in the waiting room out of a job that he fluffed every interview, until one day an interview was arranged where he did not meet the other candidates, and he was able to secure the position.

With scarcity of opportunities the person who is looking for work often has to lower his sights. Just as the child of this age learns to recognize limitations as well as strengths in the wishes for closeness with mother or father, and to recognize that he is not the only one, so in our own time limited career choice means that reality has to be faced. Childhood phantasies of 'what I'm going to be when I'm grown up' (pop star, astronaut — in fact boys' ideas are often more grandiose than those of girls) are by and large given up in adolescence, but in our present society there are even stricter limitations on what once might have been thought to be reasonable goals. Accepting lower status in a job may mean that the person who is capable of more has to limit his goals and even his standard of living: counselling takes place in society as it is, and although the counsellor may elsewhere work towards changing the system, in the individual sessions she has to help a person come to terms with reality, but without allowing that reality to do permanent or overall damage to his other aspirations (e.g. in relationships).

Because unemployment and retirement deprive a person of opportunities to participate in social relationships at work (particularly depriving young people of chances to identify with and learn from the social and work skills of adults), the counsellor may also have to assist the development of social skills, and help those whose life setting is less structured to initiate social relationships. There are also clearly needs, of which those involved in community work and action are already aware, for the provision of alternative social settings, which school or work had once given to young or retired people.

Issues related to latency and learning

Deprived of the opportunity to be productive, and to take pride in their work, it is little wonder that the unemployed and even the retired can feel inferior; those who adapt better are those who develop ways of expressing their need to be creative and productive outside work, or in alternatives to paid work. The more a person has invested in hard work as a way of proving worth or assuaging guilt, the harder it will be to preserve a sense of self-esteem when the chances of doing this are taken away (particularly for people like the workaholic, or the obsessional achiever).

Unemployment (and for some people, early retirement) may well mean having to retrain, or relearn, perhaps outside the setting of work. Obviously this will be constructive for many, who easily adapt to different working skills, and some even find satisfaction in working for themselves, and not for others. No work, or less work, gives people the chance to 'play' and use leisure time for more than resting. There will be those who look from their new position back at their previous full-time occupation, and see how much it depleted the rest of life, and how being a worker was to risk becoming over-conformist — they may see how easy it was to become, as Erikson puts it: 'a thoughtless slave of his [man's] technology and of those who are in a position to exploit it' (1965, p. 252).

Such reappraisal will be particularly valuable (but perhaps also particularly difficult) for those who have been influenced in family and school to over-achieve, and for whom work has been at the expense of 'play'. In their desire to please parents, teachers, supervisors and bosses they have been unable to find independent satisfaction for themselves. But there is another type of learner in family or school, whose efforts have been devalued or derided, for whom learning has become associated with demoralization, who has (as a consequence) defensively dismissed learning as irrelevant or impossible. Where school was little more than a legal or parental requirement, retraining or learning new skills, may seem like going back to school, and may be associated with unhappy or unfavourable experiences. Retraining cannot be considered positively, since it is associated too much with parent or teacher expectation; or with lack of interest from parents; or with feelings of inferiority towards those who learn more rapidly. Anything which smacks of education might therefore be resisted, or taken up only half-heartedly, when it might be that retraining or learning about new areas of life is not only essential, but rewarding. In working with the current situation, the counsellor will want to look into attitudes formed by previous learning settings.

Geoff's father was a semi-skilled worker who took great pride in the academic success and higher education of Geoff's two elder brothers. As neither of them showed much manual dexterity, Geoff, who did, became the son who could share his father's interest in rebuilding cars and other practical jobs. It was not that Geoff was unintelligent, but his father had often said to him, 'Of course you're like me, you won't go as far as they have, but you'll be good at my sort of work.' This identification with his father was satisfying enough at the time, but it also overshadowed Geoff in later life, when he discovered his own intellectual ability, and went to university by way of a college for mature students. Exams terrified him, because he could not get it out of his head that he was treading on territory that had been reserved for his brothers.

Issues related to adolescence and adulthood

The average person achieves some of his identity through employment in middle or late adolescence, so there may be difficulties for the young person without work when he reaches this point of the mini-cycle. Similarly a person's identity may need to be reshaped when changes in job occur or when there are changes from work to no work or retirement. Coming to terms with a new identity often means a period of mourning for the past before accepting the potentialities of the present.

Yet there is more to life than past and present experience. While we all look backwards, we also look forward. This ability to project oneself in hope and in imagination into the future is an important feature of making plans and taking decisions. It can be a spur to action, looking forward to a time when something will have been achieved. But it can also be a threat to action, when the barriers seem too large to surmount. Looking forward is therefore not always positive; it can also give rise to such thoughts as 'I'm afraid to take the next step' or even (and here the current situation may well engender such a phrase) 'What's the point?'

In short-term and long-term planning, the risk of unemployment, or the prospect of retirement, may raise such questions. The adolescent may be reluctant to risk becoming independent when employment prospects are bleak. It is safer to stay in the nest. Finding an identity will be even harder when identity through occupation ('What do you do?' is one of the most common opening gambits in meeting people for the first time) is either unavailable, or has been forced and not chosen. There may be in the young adult some concern about engaging in intimacy when there is little prospect of being able to support a home, or when there is no job to get away to. Most of us learn to live with our partners by being able to come and go from them to work — slowly becoming used to their ways, able to tolerate frustrations and argument by getting away from each other and cooling off, and able to meet others at work, at the shops, in pubs or clubs. Unemployment or retirement may therefore alter the patterns of intimate and family relationships [Changing patterns of intimacy, p. 161].

> Herbert, as his counsellor discovered after working with him for some time, was the sort of man you could only take in small doses. Given the chance he would become very clinging — it was, for instance, difficult to make a natural break with him at the end of sessions. This perception gave the counsellor some insight into the terrible situation which had first brought Herbert to him. He had retired from a life-time's loyal work in a factory. He was given his customary time-piece, and returned home, in some ways looking forward to his retirement. When he arrived he found his wife had committed suicide: the thought of having Herbert at home all day and every day was too much for her.

Those who are single and for whom work has been the sole expression of their natural wishes for generativity and creativity may find unemployment even harder to take. They have less opportunity for expressing their needs in the way that a family person can. Being 'wedded' to their work may mean that involuntary retirement or unemployment is for them like being left by a partner who no longer has need of them.

At any stage in adult life the person without work (or who is inactive through illness) may be involuntarily plunged into reflection and extended introspection — a state usually more reserved for old age. People who have opportunities (many of which come through having work and sufficient income) often look forward to a time when they will look back upon the achievement of their aspirations. They can afford the luxury of extended introspection. Their current plans are to some extent modified by thoughts such as: 'I wonder what I will feel about what I'm planning now when I come to look back on it', just as in moral decisions we sometimes think, 'if I do this now it will give me pleasure, but what will I feel tomorrow?'

I suggest that this same process (but from a very different base-line) also occurs in those who are without work. They too review forwards as well as back, and may look forward (or actually dread) a time when they will be looking back. We can therefore imagine the thoughts which different people may have: 'When I am old and weak, I will have the consolation of looking back with a sense of achievement' (positive), or 'If I remain without a job, and am unable to provide what I wish for my family, how will I feel about that when I am old and they have left home?' So redundancy may not just deprive a person of a job and of the wherewithal to buy a house, to give the children a good start, and to pay towards a pension, but also prevent a person looking forward with optimism to old age. Likewise, early retirement may deprive a person of pleasures accompanying seniority. Part of the satisfaction of old age is the contentment gained from having taught younger people the skills of the job, and from voluntarily handing over responsibility, knowing that one has helped others to take over.

Looking back in the last stage of life, and contemplation of what has gone before, goes on of course at other stages of life too, but nearly always then in the context of activity and change. Those who have no work may be forced to reflect for longer than they are ready for, and in a context where opportunities to change and rectify matters are limited. Reflection can of course be rewarding and constructive, but in younger active people too much of it can also be disabling.

> Ivy, having no family responsibilities, chose to leave her job when she was offered the opportunity of early retirement. She was able to indulge herself in the reading and thinking which she had always wanted. In many respects she seemed to have adjusted well to this way of life; but she nonetheless had an egocentricity about her which was not the same as the self-contentment often found in the older person. She did not show the same interest which older people often have in those who are younger than themselves. There seemed to those who knew her, a hollow ring to her constant recommendation of getting out of the rat-race, as being the best thing she had ever done.

Counselling provides an obvious setting for helping people to review not only their past and present, but also their future. Although I have dwelt in this chapter on the damage which can be done through being out of work, we should not forget that our future life-style is likely to provide much more time for reflection, and that it may provide more opportunities for personal and inter-personal growth, as long as opportunities exist to translate vision into action.

The generativity stage in the counsellor

It is the nature of the counsellor's work that it is generative both in the sense of work itself, and also in the sense of parenting. There are sometimes failures, and there is sometimes frustration, but on balance it is work which is sufficiently creative to give satisfaction to the counsellor as well as the client. One aspect of Erikson's term 'generativity' — work — has already been referred to in the section on the working alliance [p. 131]. The other aspect — parenting — has appeared in each of the chapters on the main themes, particularly in respect of the unhelpful temptation to 'parent' clients who wish the counsellor to look after them, nurture them, control them, or love them.

There is a danger implicit in Erikson's twinning of parenthood and work in the one stage of generativity and creativity. In the world of work, production and creation very often involve manipulation of animate and inanimate objects by the producer or creator. Even a work of art has a form and a framework whereby words, music, paint, etc., are handled, ordered and adjusted in an obviously active way by the artist. The work of being a parent or being a counsellor is not like that. Even the image of providing the right conditions for the tender plant to grow falls down, because a plant is passive and either responds or fails to respond to the right conditions, and its final form is predictable.

With children, and the 'child in the adult', the situation is different. Development and growth are interactional. For parents and counsellors there are temptations to mould the child or the client, to manipulate responses and patterns of behaviour, to order rather than provide the boundaries in which they may find their own ways of growing. Much of the generativity and creativity in counselling consists of containing the anxiety about growth and change, that through it there may be formed unique ways of being. The counsellor who is too caught up in the desire to be a 'successful parent' or a 'productive worker' is liable to produce clones, instead of allowing individuals the opportunity to create or re-create themselves (see Erikson's words, p. 8). Nowhere is this more true than in working with clients who feel helpless, whether because of unemployment or any other cause. Our solutions are not necessarily their solutions. Our patterns may not fit their situations. The comfortable, middle-class counsellor may in the end have more to learn from them about surviving than they from him.

References

Erikson E. (1965) *Childhood and Society*, Penguin, Harmondsworth.

Jacobs M. (1981) 'Stuck', in *Work and No Work,* British Association for Counselling, Rugby.

Jacobs M. (1982) *Still Small Voice*, S.P.C.K., London.

Rayner E. (1978) *Human Development* (2nd edn), George Allen and Unwin, London.

· 11 ·

FULL CIRCLE:

AGEING, INTEGRITY AND DEATH

Ageing

Ageing runs parallel with growth and development, but what makes ageing particularly significant is the psychological attitude of the person. On the whole children enjoy getting older, take pride in each new birthday, and look forward to becoming 'grown-ups'. Some young people pause at nineteen and temporarily dread the prospect of entering their twenties, before picking up once more their enthusiasm about maturing. Women are more conscious of their age in their twenties and thirties, probably because social conventions make some of them panic if they are not married by twenty-five, or pregnant by thirty. Unless the counsellor recognizes these pressures, including some medical opinion about late pregnancy, he is liable to misunderstand the young who feel they are getting too old too quickly.

With some minor hiccoughs, ageing up to the middle thirties presents no real threat. Maturing is welcomed. Until mid-point in the average life-span many people experience expansion of opportunity, of learning and of new skills, of family and of career achievement. Indeed it is not until the age of thirty that many begin to feel truly independent of parental expectations and more stable emotionally — although those in their twenties often see such stability as 'being conventional'.

The forties bring for many people an increasing sense of security and influence, although it is also the time when career development levels off, and retirement, or early retirement and redundancy begin to present a greater threat. Physical signs of ageing are more obvious, and are felt more within the body as well as showing up more in the mirror. The span of life ahead noticeably contracts, although increasing freedom with children becoming more independent still holds the prospect of further development of interests. Again it is women who experience ageing more patently with the menopause, but, as in so many situations involving some degree of loss, mental attitudes frequently govern physical responses to growing older (For a rare study of stages of adult life, and the different transitions for men and women, see Golan 1981.)

Letting go is present, as we have seen, from birth through to death, being less stressful when there has been sufficient fulfilment (both conscious and unconscious) of the specific needs of each age. Thus a baby who has experienced fulfilment of the need to be cared for can leave that all-enveloping care behind, because sufficient trust has been acquired; a child who has been allowed to be dependent is more ready to leave some of that dependency behind in the move into more autonomy. A child who can set hesitations about autonomy to rest is in a stronger position to take initiative; an adolescent who can challenge and yet still respect parents is better able to leave them; a young adult who has a secure enough identity can let go of his or her independence enough to enter an intimate relationship; parents who feel satisfied on balance with the way they have performed their parental tasks will be sad, but not depressed, as their adolescent children break away from them. In similar vein, it is Rayner's impression that women who have enjoyed bringing up children, and can then find a new identity, do not find the menopause particularly depressing. Those whose children have been their sole interest, or those who have not had children, tend to find the menopause more distressing (1978, p. 174). Men too can experience a psychological menopause, yet their concern about some diminution of sexual drive will not be of such great moment when they have experienced anxiety-free enjoyment and satisfaction in sexual relationships in previous years. The most anxious men are those who look back on their sexual relationships with regret and disappointment.

> John was fifty and in his second marriage, to a woman half his age. His first wife had had a series of affairs which John eventually discovered by chance. When he confronted her she walked out. He was taken by complete surprise, and was convinced that the reason for her behaviour must have been his sexual inadequacy. His counsellor felt there could well have been many other factors. John's second marriage was a constant anxiety to him: would he be sexually athletic enough to satisfy the younger woman? He was convinced, despite general factual evidence to the contrary of which he was aware, that he was rapidly losing his sex drive because of his age. He even moved around as if he were an old man.

In all growing and ageing, therefore, we may expect to find sadness as part of the natural response, but depression or despair more particularly when a person for some reason is unable to let go of the past; one of the reasons for such unwillingness is some remaining unfinished business which makes letting go too painful. We shall see this applies equally to attitudes to death, both in dying and in coping with bereavement. Resignation is seen by Erikson as a positive strength of old age, with despair being its opposite when resignation is not possible. Resignation starts, of course, earlier than old age itself.

> Kitty was an only child who had had to work very hard at school in order to satisfy her parents. She was not very clever, but she had been able to make up for the disappointment about her progress by working equally hard in her spare time to help her parents with their corner shop business. When she married and had children of her own she was determined not to put them through what she herself had experienced: they grew up as well adjusted children and normal teenagers. Yet when they left home she became very depressed. She could have been pleased that she had brought them up so free from pressure; but she failed to realize that in doing so she had all the time been 'working hard' to achieve this end, and that with their going she had suddenly not got them to work hard for — which was the only way she knew of feeling that she was acceptable.

Increasing age means accepting many more losses and limitations. By old age parents are probably already dead, and the death of friends and relatives (even perhaps of one's own children) becomes a part of life which features strongly; funerals and obituary columns become part of the staple diet of living — but not necessarily for morbid reasons. Hans Sachs, one of Freud's original colleagues, observes that in old age we forgive our friends for those things about them which have irritated us, because we triumph over them by outliving them (1948). Old age also brings limitations of physical strength and stamina. There are losses through retirement, such as the working role, and the structure of the working day. Reduced income means limitations and adjustments, at a time when even the most 'handy' of men and women are less able to save money by doing things for themselves. There will certainly be loss of independence in physical or mental infirmity. Such physical weaknesses may revive feelings of shame, difficulty in controlling the body or mind being linked to previous A.S. issues.

Yet this rather bleak picture neglects the advantages and new strengths which old age also brings to those who can accept the limitations. It can also be rewarding, to watch younger people whom one has trained and guided now taking over responsibilities, aware that one has helped them to learn and trusting that they will cope. (Here there are links to parenting, which apply also in the work setting.) Given sufficient financial security, there can be considerable relief at being able to let go of active responsibility. Where old people are respected for their experience, wisdom and judgement, there can be satisfaction at being in the background in a 'consultative' capacity, knowing that one's experience of life and work is valued by younger people — particularly by grandchildren. There is considerable pleasure in being with children again, but without the chores of actual parenthood; while for grandchildren there is the acceptance of the older generation's authority without too many feelings of being bound by it. Restructuring of time enables old and new interests to be pursued, and for the mind to be kept active — memory, for instance, appears to function better when there is continuing mental activity. Tolerance is frequently a quality which is acquired in old age, with older people often feeling less threatened by the young or by those who are different than, say, middle-aged people might feel. Aware too of the shortness of remaining life, it probably makes more sense to enjoy relationships while they last. Although coming to terms with intimacy in the partnership may be a problem upon retirement [Changing patterns of intimacy, p. 161], a partner can equally be even more appreciated for the loyalty and companionship of the past and present.

While an old person on retirement may still have 10 to 20 years of life to look forward to, and therefore in some ways still has opportunities to develop, the most significant feature of old age is the way in which 'the past in the present' comes into its own. It is a time when life as a whole is reviewed. Of course memory can play tricks, but it is often memories of the more distant past which are clearer than memory of more recent events or conversations. Perhaps the unconscious need not be feared so much, and what has been repressed comes through in a fine balance of positive and negative experiences — hardship in childhood, for instance, can be remembered for what it was, but with its positive qualities as well. Rayner speaks of the old person as a living historian to the young (1978, p. 181), but their history is just as important to themselves, and old people enjoy telling it — sometimes over and over again. In this telling of old stories there is a reworking of life, which Lowe (1972, p. 225) lists under the

Erikson stages: whom one has learned to trust (I); what to hold on to and what to let go (2); initiatives taken (3); practical and social skills (4); confirmation of identity (5); marriage (6); and work (7).

As I have already mentioned, issues of bodily control take an old person back to aspects of the A.S. and some mental infirmities reflect O.S. states. Senile dementia can give rise to fragmentation of thought, where phantasy appears to be as real as reality [Phantasy and reality, p. 55]. Rayner reminds us that even then the phantasy is symbolic and can best be understood when the symbols can be translated into present concerns — he provides some useful examples of this (1978, p. 185). If such fragmentation of thought does not unduly interfere with the task of ego integration, an old person's review of life has other more positive reminders of the resolution of the O.S. Ego integrity will include the acceptance of those things that have gone wrong, and the recognition that these cannot be changed (concern without overbearing guilt), and that on balance all the good things in life outweigh those experiences which have been bad [Transition, p. 59].

Some psychologists (e.g. Lowe 1972, p. 248) have suggested a number of psychological 'types' of old people, each one demonstrating a different resolution of this life review. Three of these types remind us of degrees of fixation in or regression to O.S. issues; one reminds us of features of the A.S.; and one only represents the psychological maturity of the person who has worked through the early childhood stages. The oral components can be seen in the self-hating old person, who is despairing and pessimistic, who turns anger into self-contempt, who has restricted interests, and who has such a negative view of the past that death is looked forward to as a merciful release. Such components are also seen in the hostile old person, whose anger is directed outwards, in criticism of others and in envy of younger people, but who is fearful of death. A rather different O.S. type is the dependent old person, who is passive and self-indulgent, comfort-loving and self-satisfied, although the narcissistic features of such a description bely other characteristics of this type, in whom there is not really a defensive reaction to old age and the prospect of death. Those who have uresolved narcissistic difficulties will be much more fearful of ageing and death [Narcissism and self-respect, p. 39]. In this third type, the wish is a rather more understandable one to end life in comfort and ease. The fourth type is the old person who is fearful of old age, retirement and infirmity, and who defensively remains or becomes compulsively active, rigidly self-sufficient and over-controlled, reminding us of the A.S. character. There is an anxiety about their activity which is different from the final type, the most psychologically mature old person, known as the 'constructive' type. This is a person who has high self-esteem and broad interests developed earlier in life, and who remains self-aware, enjoying the sense of responsibility which is appropriate to old age. He or she is eager to preserve personal integrity, and to enjoy a sense of tranquillity (like the dependent type), but (unlike the dependent type) remains aware of a sense of purpose and meaning in life, hoping for an even greater understanding of what life is all about.

The search for meaning

The importance of trust and faith was a major feature of our treatment of the O.S. In late adolescence too we saw the issue of finding some kind of faith as present in some young people, although if we broaden this concept to include purpose in living or a 'philosophy' (even if a home-spun one) by which people live, then most men and women have certain values or beliefs. These may not be expressed in metaphysical terms (indeed they may be largely materialistic), and they may not be as well-defined or even as altruistic as traditional faith is meant to be, but most people have at least a little of the philosopher, the person of faith (religious or humanist) and even the politician in them.

It is in this context that the search for meaning (or more commonly the wish to achieve certain objectives) continues throughout life, with an increasing wish to make sense of experience growing with age. Becker outlines four levels of meaning by which an individual can choose to live (1972, p. 185):

(1)   The basic level of the Personal — who one is, the 'true' self, what makes a person special, whom he feels the self to be deep down, 'the person he talks to when he is alone'.
(2)   The higher level of the Social — the extension of the self to include those with whom a person is close or intimate: partner, friends, children.
(3)   The next higher level of the Secular — symbols and allegiance at greater personal distance which are often of a compelling quality — the corporation, the party, the nation, knowledge (science and the human-ities), or humanity itself.
(4)   The highest level of the Sacred — 'the invisible and unknown level of power, the insides of nature, the source of creation, God'.

These levels of meaning are all to be found in the aspects of an old person's review of life as outlined by Lowe [p. 189], with the exception of the fourth level which has up to this point been omitted from our developmental model. Traditionally, psychoanalysis has appeared to be critical of, or even hostile towards religion, on the grounds that it represents a child's attempt to deal with fears of the external as well as the internal world, and with family relationships. Freud led the attack on religion and on some forms of political faith (notably bolshevism) in his essay on a *Weltanschauung* (a philosophy of life) in the *New Introductory Lectures* (1964). His example has been followed by Badcock (1980), who in a fascinating way (although with some glaring errors of fact) traces the development of civilization through types of religion (animism, totemism, etc.), until, in his view, man comes of age in psychoanalysis.

The problem with such interpretations is that they dwell exclusively on religion as a neurotic means of dealing with conflicts arising from the power of instinctual drives in both the individual and society, and so label all religion as a private or a collective neurosis. Not all analysts follow Freud's reasoning. Fromm (1967), for instance, distinguishes between positive and negative forms of religious belief and practice. If we are to take the search for meaning seriously, we cannot afford to dismiss it as simply the sign of a frightened child in the adult. We need to recognize that, in its more mature forms, religion (in the broadest sense) is supportive in crisis, and is a means of developing which is pertinent to the needs of the individual and of society. Becker concludes his book *The Birth and Death of Meaning* with these words:

> The ideal critique of a faith must always be whether it embodies within itself the fundamental contradictions of the human paradox and *yet is able to support them without fanaticism, sadism and narcissism, but with openness and trust.* Religion itself is an ideal of strength and of potential for growth, of what man might become by assuming the burden of his life, as well as by being partly relieved of it (1972, p. 196 — my italics).

Becker's words apply as much to faith in political ideologies and humanism as they do to faith in the supernatural.

The development of mature faith

Little study has been devoted to the development of trust in infancy and its relevance for the search for meaning in late adulthood, even though

Erikson's model provides us with the possibility of another 'mini-cycle' with which to examine such questions. One author who has combined the work of Erikson (1965), Piaget (on cognitive thinking, 1950), and Kohlberg (on the development of moral decision-making, 1963) is Fowler, who has conducted his own research (1981). The heart of his book is a description of seven stages of faith, which are not age-specific even though there are some links to chronological age (i.e. adults may be at any of these stages with the opportunity of still developing through to later stages). His numbering is different from Erikson's, and the stages are not parallel with all of Erikson's. Stage 0 is Erikson's oral stage, where trust, hope and mutuality are first formed. Stage 1 is intuitive and projective, where meaning is intuitively grasped. Stage 2 is literalism, where adults still at this point interpret stories and symbols literally. Stage 3 (where most adults are located) is the formulation of a personal view out of the complexity of relationships and values. It is a stage of faith which is still concerned with oneself. Stage 4 shifts the attention to tensions such as the individual versus the group, self-fulfilment versus service to others, relative and absolute values. Stage 5 (very rare prior to mid-life) is a period when the ironies and opposites of life can be brought together, when a person's past is reworked into the formation of a 'deeper self'. Being able to hold together life's paradoxes [see also Becker quotation p. 192, and reference to 'balance' p. 190] assists movement into the final Stage 6 (which few people reach) where life is experienced as being in tune with the transcendent. Fowler cites Gandhi and Martin Luther King as examples of those who have reached this stage.

Fowler also explores seven aspects of faith which in summarized form may provide a useful agenda for counselling those who are reviewing their life. Faith in his view consists of:

(1)   a form of logic — the capacity to reason;
(2)   perspective taking — moving from self-centredness to a perspective on the world;
(3)   a form of moral judgement — from the punishment–reward mode towards positive decision-making;
(4)   the provision of social awareness, identification with others (empathy);
(5)   the locus of authority, from attachment and dependency to personal decisions which are not confined to self-interest;
(6)   a form of world coherence — the patterns through which a person views the world;

(7) symbolic function — the content of images and metaphors together with their interpretation, from seeing symbols as magical to enabling them to find reality within the self.

The client's faith as an indication of maturity

With such a framework in mind, the counsellor can locate the expressions of faith presented by the client (faith, that is, not simply in God but in an ideology, or even in the counsellor himself) in the developmental stages to which we have referred throughout. For instance, in clients who in some way show O.S. difficulties, we might expect to find on the one hand hopeless pessimism or inability to trust anyone or any system (God, political change, the counsellor); or on the other, a primitive magical belief indicating total dependency on powers outside the self, who or which are expected to be favourable or rejecting, depending on the person's view of self. God may be seen as the universal provider, who, 'if only I wish hard enough or pray hard enough' will be influenced by thought. Faith at this stage is essentially narcissistic — concerned with self — although it may consist too of a projection of one's omnipotent phantasies on to another, or on to an ideology [Narcissism and self-respect, p. 39]. The wish for a perfect environment (the Garden of Eden; Utopia; or, in political terms, a Communist society, Victorian Britain, or any other 'golden age') suggests a view of society and the world as being presently evil, but in the future, after the Second Coming or the proletarian or monetarist revolution, a society which will be perfectly good. The primitive splitting of the good and the bad mother is seen in faith terms in the absolute dichotomy of God and the Devil, or of white and black magic, or of capitalism and Communism. In the counselling relationship, the helper is cast in the role of a magician who has only to speak the right word and all will be healed.

> Luke showed this primitive magical belief not only in his religious life, but also in his phantasy that a girl in his school must be in love with him. He looked for signs that God wanted her to marry him, such as clues in his bible reading, and glances which the girl in question shot in his direction. He did not worry that his preoccupation with her would interfere with his exams, since if God wanted him to pass, he would pass. He sent the girl presents of flowers and chocolates, and could not believe that it was her who rejected them: it must be her parents who were forcing her. He even ran naked in the rain one day because he felt that God wanted him to do this to prove his love for Him.

In his counselling sessions he talked non-stop, hardly listening to what his counsellor said. It was an opportunity for him to 'spout' about his beliefs, and to talk about his plans to become a politician; and perhaps he got from the counsellor the attention he seldom got from others — their reaction was probably to laugh at his eccentricities. It cannot be said that the counselling got very far except that Luke was able to express his grief for the girl who would not love him.

In connection with the A.S. we might expect to find beliefs in an authoritarian God or authoritarian ideology, rigidity of moral thinking and control, the expectation that if rules of faith are followed to the letter, guilt and the conscience will be wiped clean. This can be accompanied by severe criticism of others, even with sadistic punishment of them in word or action for their transgressions. The search is not so much for a perfect world as for a perfect self in whom there is no guilt. Ritualistic actions, mindless repetition of prayers, self-righteous and religious discipline of bible reading or attendance at Church services, absolute and often literal authority vested in the Word of God, the Church or the writings of political ideologists, fear of offending authorities, masochistic self-punishment (by a sadistic super-ego) — all these might point to fixation on problems of autonomy and control.

Miles was a devout Catholic, who intellectually put himself on the liberal wing of the church, but could not shake himself free from the legalistic religious discipline which his schooling had imparted to him. This education probably only confirmed the right-wing authoritarian views he got at home from his mother. Despite the forgiveness he received through confession, and the reassurance he was given by priests to whom he spoke, Miles worried inordinately about minor sins, which were scarcely sins at all, such as having one alcoholic drink as a nightcap. He could not receive communion when he felt so bad. Like other obsessional difficulties it was very difficult to shift this pattern of thinking. Miles knew he was worrying unnecessarily, but could not get beyond listing these worries in his counselling. It was as if 'free association' might give rise to thoughts and feelings which he would feel were even worse.

What of the oedipal stage? Becker writes of ideal faith as being 'without fanaticism, sadism and narcissism'. The last two express some A.S. and O.S. issues, so perhaps fanaticism expresses the negative aspects of the third stage of the development of faith? Badcock (1980) appears to view all religion (except psychoanalysis) as a primitive way of coping with oedipal conflicts, although he brings in earlier issues when it suits his argument. Although Badcock sees fanaticism as obsessional behaviour, there is an element present in most fanaticism that has oedipal undertones — the need to evangelize. In its worst form, this masks the wish to control others, to exert power over others, and to behave in an imperialistic manner. Badcock illustrates this in Egyptian monotheism, as well as in Christianity and Islam, but it also applies to other fanatical ideologies. The need to win others over to one's own faith at all costs, and the building of exclusive communities set apart by their religion from the 'rest' of mankind, is not at all like the true socialization which makes its appearance in the G.S. It has similarities to the wish to win over one parent, and the desire to have one parent belonging to oneself rather than to the other — indeed some fanatical religion splits families. Evangelism of this sort also often means proclaiming one's faith in an exhibitionist manner, which again is an oedipal feature, and is perhaps an indication of insecurity [Exhibitionism, p. 99]. The need to convince others seems to run parallel with the need continually to convince oneself, especially by getting others on one's side. Fanatical communities of faith also run the risk of becoming (metaphorically) incestuous.

The oedipal features, and identification of God with father, are seen in this example.

> Nina had a strong conviction that sexual intimacy before marriage was wrong. She cited God as her authority, since she knew this as an answer to prayer. In fact, as it later transpired, her father had also said that he wasn't going to have anyone messing around with his 'little girl' before marriage, so it is possible that her father's words were even more strongly imprinted upon her than her God's. Another reason seemed to be an incident a couple of years previously, when she had been intimate with a young man on holiday. At first she said that it was all his fault and that he had forced her, although she later said that she had gone back to see him a second time so it could happen again.
>
> Her strong conviction came under review when she fell in love with another member of her church; she then felt that there was nothing wrong in sex as long as it was the expression of a loving relationship. She had by then been able to distance herself, through her counselling, from the constant need to be the 'good girl' for her father. In this example, A.S. and G.S. factors interweave, and indeed rigid distinctions cannot be made in psychodynamic formulation if analytic thought itself is not to become another form of 'religion'.

Whatever the religious or political beliefs of the counsellor, they should not obscure the task of listening to, accepting as important, and working to understand the faith of the client. The imagery, the symbols and the language in which faith is expressed will illustrate, at least in some clients, how some of their beliefs and values run parallel with other difficulties; while in other clients their faith may indicate their aspirations to become a mature and integrated person: in working through their concerns they may be enabled to reach closer towards the legitimate and realistic hopes which in their faith they recognize, but through their emotional conflicts have found impossible to attain.

Dying

Care and counselling of the dying is a specialist area, in which there is an increasing interest and awareness and about which there is a rapidly growing body of literature; for example, Kübler-Ross (1969); Jackson (1972); Speck (1982). The emotional stages through which the dying person may pass are by now probably well known: denial, anger, bargaining, depression and acceptance.

Experience of the death of others, or closeness to death oneself, can have a major effect on attitudes to dying throughout life. For instance, a woman in her twenties was still dreaming different images of her own death years after a near-fatal car accident which happened when she was eight. In a society where death is so often institutionalized and locked away, facing the dying and facing death itself is not surprisingly overloaded with phantasies of the most negative kind. Even direct experience of another's death (and that is not as common as it once was) cannot adequately prepare a person for his own, since it is almost impossible to conceptualize it. Rayner suggests that recognition of being mortal and finite (which does not really occur in most people until middle age) is frightening, but that it is also a relief, because the denial of mortality can be shed. Any kind of denial engenders inner stress, and being able to throw off denial releases some of the tension (1978, p. 171).

It is often said that what accompanies death is more frightening and distressing than death itself. There is dread of pain, for instance, based upon the experience of earlier pain, although good terminal care can control pain; feelings of shame at being helpless and incontinent may be linked to early experiences in childhood; fears for those who will be left will depend upon the state of our relationships with them. No one can pretend that dying is easy, but it may be easier when those who are left behind (children, for instance) are seen to be able to cope for themselves; and when relationships have been sufficiently good it may be less difficult to let them go; anxieties about premature death may be more acute when there is still unfinished business, or there are open wounds, unrealized hopes, memories needing to be relived and reworked. Dying is a psychosomatic process as is shown by those whose failing bodies are able to cling to life because there are still emotional needs to be met.

> Olwen had an advanced cancer, and the doctors told her, when she asked, that she had only a few months at most to live. Despite being confined to her bed, Olwen worked from home to help other cancer victims whom she heard or read about, writing them letters of comfort. She herself received great support from her husband. Her one regret was that her eldest son would not visit her. He lived some distance away, but she felt that the real reason was that he could not face her in this condition. Despite requests from others he did not appear. Olwen was still alive, though less active, a year after the date which her doctors had given her. At last her son came to see her, and stayed a few hours. Within a week she had died. It appeared that she had waited until then, had been able to say her goodbye, and was then able to let herself go.

The commendatory rituals of religious practice actually give permission for the dying person to let go, for example 'Go forth upon your journey from this world . . .' (Church of England prayer). So too the family or the counsellor of the dying person may also wish to give their permission to him to let go of life, indicating thereby their acceptance of death. Where ego integrity has been achieved there will no doubt still be much sadness, but not despair.

Letting go is a two-way process, and requires also a letting-be. Attention has already been drawn to the continuous need throughout life for periods of withdrawal interspersed with longer periods of closeness with others. In dying, solitude also has its place, although this can sometimes be denied by shocked and distraught friends and relatives. Mitchell (1982) presents a case study of massive denial in the face of death:

> Valerie was a popular high-school girl who suddenly fell ill. It was difficult to diagnose her condition, but her doctors had little hope of saving her life. In desperation they gave her drugs which had very uncomfortable side-effects. The hospital chaplain who visited Valerie

found her mother and father in constant attendance, never leaving her side. The community in her home town were whipped up into a campaign of hope by the friends and local press, and her church congregation was praying for her recovery; they were convinced that if only they and she had enough faith she would come through. The pastor of her home church, despite his misgivings about the hysterical reaction, colluded with the community's wish for a vigil of prayer. Valerie's father also seemed to collude with his wife's need to maintain their watch over Valerie's bedside; while the doctors' use of drugs also seemed to be a denial, which father secretly regretted, seeing the discomfort his daughter was experiencing. It was not until the chaplain was able to visit Valerie alone (her parents being fast asleep in the room) that she was able to learn from Valerie that she felt she was having to put an act on for her parents and her community back home, and that she wished more often than she could admit that she would be left alone. Even after Valerie's death, her mother arranged a funeral that was more a celebration of resurrection than a true expression of the pain and grief which had been present but denied in the whole situation.

The case is a fascinating example of an immature religious faith in a whole community.

Because of their own personal distress at seeing others suffering and dying, helpers or relatives may find it difficult to hear what the dying person wishes to express or the questions they want to ask. The counselling method, of course, involves putting aside our own agenda in order to engage with the other's concerns. So the appropriateness of honesty about illness and death, and opportunities to take up issues about dying, depend upon sensitive awareness of the feelings and words of the dying person. The right moment will often present itself when the listener is sensitive to the person and to the issues; and it is far better to use that moment than to force the pace just because many of the books on the process of dying appear to suggest a need to pass through different stages — these books are in fact descriptive of various experiences and not prescriptions which helpers should follow to the letter (see also Johnstone 1982).

Bereavement

In coping with grief and loss we really do come full circle home, to the first stage of life. Grief, of course, applies to many other losses besides death: as a result of surgery (amputation, mastectomy, hysterectomy, vasectomy, etc), redundancy, divorce, abortion, geographical relocation, etc. Any bereavement can be a long process, to be measured in some cases in years rather than months. It has many stages, leading up to the final one during which the person who is lost, or that which is lost, is internalized, becoming more than a memory — almost an inner object — which is a reminder of the first stage of life.

The problem with a sudden loss, one which has not been anticipated and so cannot be thought through and planned for in the months or years preceding it, is the difficulty of making an internal adjustment that reflects the external circumstances. There are extra problems when a loss also means the cutting short of normal expectations. Thus the loss of a child, partner or even parent before the expected span of life, means that those who are left are likely to dwell on what 'could have been' for years to come. The same may also apply to loss of physical capabilities, even to voluntarily chosen losses such as male or female sterilization. Such may mean a premature rather than a natural end to the possibility of procreation, and so a premature adjustment to something which would have happened with and alongside the natural process of ageing.:

> After a vasectomy Paul began looking for other physical signs that he might be ageing before his time - although there was no reason why such signs should suddenly appear. He was convinced that he was losing handfuls of hair, even though his doctor could find nothing abnormal. There were of course links here with anxieties about potency; but physical signs which in later years might even be thought to be signs of 'maturity' were now being seen as signs of senility.

The stages of bereavement have been set out succinctly, with phrases to illustrate them, in a short book by Elizabeth Collick (1982), and I can do no better than to summarize them here. These stages are all possibilities, but it must again be said that they are descriptions, and not what everyone is bound to feel:

shock:	'I just went cold.'
numbness and unreality:	'This isn't me.'
disbelief:	'It can't be true.'
yearning:	'Come back.'
emptiness:	'An aching void.'
searching:	'He must be somewhere.'

anxiety:	'Must I sell the house?'
anger:	'He had no right to leave me like this.'
guilt:	'If only . . .'
remembering:	'I'm afraid of forgetting.'
depression:	'I'm too tired to bother.'
loss of identity and status:	'Who am I?'
stigma:	'I'm an embarrassment to others.'
sexual deprivation:	'To have a man's arms round me.'
loss of faith:	'Why?'
loneliness:	'I just dread weekends.'
acceptance:	'He'd have laughed about it.'
healing:	(See below.)

Anger is probably the most difficult of these feelings for a grieving person to acknowledge, either to self or to others — especially where the loss is through death (in divorce, of course anger may be the most obvious and some of the other feelings less permissible). Anger runs counter to the wish to hang on to love. The counsellor will hear that anger but often directed against others, such as the doctors or the hospital, the Church or God, and even other relatives. It is not uncommon for a funeral or the will to be the occasion of family splits and resurrected feuds, but hostile feelings are directed at one another rather than acknowledge anger with the one who has died. Idealizing the dead person may also be a way of unconsciously denying angry feelings (Murray Parkes 1978, chapter 6).

Where the anger persists and is unexpressed, the bereaved can turn it upon themselves, even suffering similar symptoms to those which were present in the deceased, symptoms which are physically real, but not of the same physical cause. The bereaved are then internalizing the 'bad' aspects of the one who has been lost. But where the negative emotions, such as those listed above, can be experienced, the way is opened for internalization of the whole person. C. S. Lewis describes such internalization well (without knowing the technical name for it) in his diary written after the death of his wife 'H':

Something quite unexpected has happened. It came this morning early. For various reasons, not in themselves at all mysterious, my heart was lighter than it had been for many weeks. For one thing I suppose I am recovering from a good deal of mere exhaustion, and after ten days of low hung grey skies and motionless warm dampness, the sun was shining and there was a light breeze. And suddenly, at the very moment when so far, I mourned H least, I remembered her best. Indeed it was something almost better than memory: an instantaneous unanswerable impression. To say it was like a meeting would go too far. Yet there was that in it which tempts one to use those words. It was as if the lifting of the sorrow removed a barrier. Why has no one told me these things? How easily I might have misjudged another man in the same situation. I might have said, 'He's got over it. He's forgotten his wife', when the truth was, 'He remembers her better because he has partly got over it' (1971).

The ability to carry on living, with confidence in oneself, after such a separation, depends upon a number of factors. Where a relationship has been brief and only touched the surface of oneself, separation may be felt as a simple memory — good, bad or indifferent. Where the relationship has been more extensive and has reached into deeper feelings, the situation is more complex. A relationship which has only hurt and damaged leaves a memory, pain and cautiousness about relating on the same level again. But most relationships of any depth contain good and bad feelings. What is perhaps most important is how we perceive the feelings which the one who has gone had towards us. Yet even that perception may be influenced by our view of ourselves — if we have underlying uncertainties about ourselves carried over from early experience, we may feel the other did not care, when in fact he or she did. Any anger we then feel, however unjustified, makes the process of internalization difficult. We go on feeling uncared for, unloved.

But where the relationship has been felt, overall, to be a good, caring and loving one, then of course that person will be missed; but the pervading feeling and memory will be a pleasure to recall, and will bring sustenance and strength to the self. There will be no need to cling, no need to rail. Instead there is quiet contentment, a feeling of good fortune, a deep sense of having been added to; and we can say with conviction, 'I'm glad we knew each other.'

Coda

Full circle? How can birth be like death? It is because in the experience of being born and of breaking the ties with the mother a process is begun, which is only in one sense completed by the end of the first stage of development. In every other sense it is a process which is never completed, but is repeated in many forms and at different ages: in learning autonomy; in learning to let go of aspirations for the parent of the opposite sex; in identifying with the parent of the same sex; in learning at school; in training and in counselling in relation to teachers or therapist. The pattern recurs too through adolescence, intimacy, in becoming a parent, in work, at retirement and in death and bereavement. It is a process not only of relating to others, but of internalizing them in the building up of the self. The continually developing self in turn relates anew to others and becomes, at least in part, something of them.

Karl Abraham's words (1927), about the early stage of infancy, apply as much to death in the future, and all present stages in between:

> The loved object is not gone, for now I carry it within myself and can never lose it.

They are appropriate too at the ending of a good counselling relationship, and at a somewhat different level, one might hope that they apply also to the closing of a book by a reader.

References

Abraham K. (1927) *Selected Papers,* Hogarth Press, London.

Badcock C.R. (1980) *The Psychoanalysis of Culture,* Basil Blackwell, Oxford.

Becker E. (1972) *The Birth and Death of Meaning,* Penguin, Harmondsworth.

Collick E. (1982) *Through Grief: the Experience of Bereavement,* Mirfield Publications, Mirfield, Yorks.

Erikson E. (1965) *Childhood and Society,* Penguin, Harmondsworth.

Fowler J. W. (1981) *Stages of Faith: the Psychology of Human Development and the Quest for Meaning,* Harper and Row, New York.

Freud S. (1964) *New Introductory Lectures on Psychoanalysis,* Hogarth Press, London

Fromm E. (1967) *Psychoanalysis and Religion,* Bantam Books, New York.

Golan N. (1981) *Passing Through Transitions,* Collier Macmillan, London.

Jackson E. (ed.) (1982) *Counselling the Dying,* S.C.M. Press, London.

Johnstone C.B. (1982) On asking the right question, *Journal of Pastoral Care* (USA), Vol. XXXVI: 1.

Kohlberg L. (1963) Moral development and identification, in *Child Psychology* H. W. Stevenson (ed.), University of Chicago Press.

Kübler-Ross E. (1969) *On Death and Dying,* Tavistock Publications, London.

Lewis C. S. (1971) *A Grief Observed,* Faber Paperbacks, London.

Lowe G. (1972) *The Growth of Personality,* Penguin, Harmondsworth.

Mitchell K. (1982) A death and a community, *Journal of Pastoral Care* (USA) Vol. XXXVI:1.

Murray Parkes C. (1978) *Bereavement — Studies of Grief in Adult Life,* Penguin, Harmondsworth.

Piaget J. (1950) *The Psychology of Intelligence,* Routledge & Kegan Paul, London.

Rayner E. (1978) *Human Development* (2nd edn.), George Allen and Unwin, London.

Sachs H. (1948) *Masks of Love and Life,* Sci-Art Publishers, Cambridge, Mass.

Speck P. and Ainsworth-Smith I. (1982) *Letting Go: Caring for the Dying and Bereaved,* S.P.C.K., London.

APPENDIX

Summaries of the three sets of major themes

(1) The Oral/Dependency/Trust Stage (O.S.)

(2) The Anal/Authority/Autonomy Stage (A.S.)

(3) The Genital/Oedipal/Rivalry/Social Stage (G.S.)

(1) The Oral/Dependency/Trust Stage (O.S.)

	Main references
Indications of satisfactory development and possible aims in counselling	
Basic sense of trust and faith in others, the environment and the self; basic sense of the 'world' as good.	33, 145, 191
Ability to contain and work through bad experiences and feelings, without being overwhelmed by them in long-term.	33, 177
Healthy self-respect and self-regard, while still able to accept shortcomings, own mortality, and weaknesses; the integration of 'good' and 'bad' in relation to self and in relation to others.	33, 39, 44 189, 197
Recognition of boundaries between self and others, self and the world; presence of and distinction between subjective and objective thinking and experience.	30, 123, 175

	Main references
Having separate identity — able to own thoughts and feelings, without projection or introjection. At same time able to identify through empathy and with concern for and with others — recognition of others' separateness.	32, 54, 157
Ability to trust and depend appropriately upon others, to engage in intimacy while still retaining sense of self.	32, chapter 8
Ability to move between caring for others and receiving care from others.	54, 157
Ability to be alone when necessary — inner harmony and self-esteem.	42, 153
Ability to put experiences in perspective, retaining a sense of hope even in adversity.	43, 189
Tolerance of frustration; ability to defer immediate gratification when necessary, or to be able to make appropriate substitutions.	39, 58, 123
Ability to express appropriate anger or assertiveness when frustrated or discontented, without fear of being destructive.	12, 50
Creative use of phantasy and imagination, and of identification, without it becoming a substitute for real relationships or achievements.	55
The internalization of good aspects of others, particularly after loss or bereavement.	201

Difficulties associated with O.S. themes

Confusion of self and not-self. Confused time and space boundaries; confused body/mind imagery, thoughts or perceptions. Cognitive disturbance, bizarre	30, 49, 55, 150, 190

Main
references

thoughts or behaviour. Long-standing feelings of chaos,
or being 'in pieces'.

Delusions or hallucinations.   31, 55

Paranoid feelings from self-hate to paranoid   46, 190
schizophrenia. Intense prejudice or feelings of being
discriminated against without basis in reality.

Living in phantasy, especially the psychotic or near-   55
psychotic personality.

Over-dependent, clinging, demanding person; the   34, 43
over-possessive person.   157, 190

Addictions — drugs, drink, food; problems with   12, 31, 35
deferring gratification, over-eating or reaction against   138, 145,
food in anorexia. Acting as if limitless supplies   147
available — including over-spending. Difficulties
accepting limits.

Guilt about making demands.   12, 37, 175

Fears of being abandoned, rejected, being left alone.   36, 41

Persistent anger as a result of bereavement.   201

The withdrawn person, schizoid personality; inability to   36, 124, 155
trust, fears of being swallowed up by others or of
draining others with demands.

Narcissistic person, always concerned about self,   39, 137, 157
wanting everything own way; manipulative; magical   190, 194,
beliefs and thinking, grandiose thinking.

Intense anger or rage as reaction to frustration.   39, 48

Manic-depressive swings from omnipotent feelings to   135, 149
self-loathing and worthlessness.

The over-humble person, unable to accept self as   41
having any worth.

	Main references
Idealization of significant others, including the counsellor.	45, 57, 157
Splitting — idealizing some, denigrating others, problems with ambivalence.	45, 176, 194
Destructive anger, especially where acted out, or so afraid anger will prove destructive that cannot express it.	46, 52, 171
Anxiety or guilt over destructive wishes having severely damaged others.	47, 142, 168
Envy, perhaps with destructive wishes attached.	51
Chronic hopelessness, despair and pessimism.	175, 194
Use of others (e.g. children or clients) to project own wishes to be mothered or cared for — over-concern for others.	42, 43, 153
Some pregnancies (especially in adolescence) as ways of avoiding breaking dependent ties.	153, 166
Narcissistic hypochondriacal symptoms.	40
Learning difficulties arising from lack of trust.	123
The difficulties assessing levels of disturbance in adolescents.	149
Seeking idealized relationships and their impact on marital problems.	157
Fear of being engulfed or overwhelmed by the other in sexual relationships.	104

The relationship style in the counsellor-client interaction (O.S.).

Difficulty in forming and sustaining the relationship.   34, 36, 41
The client who withdraws through fear of dependency.

Client unable to swallow anything counsellor   38
says — but not in argumentative way as in A.S.
Suspicious, not trusting the counsellor — fear that
counsellor will reject or turn hostile.

Over-dependent and over reliant on counsellor — as a   33, 35, 37
lifeline (rather than as advice-giver in A.S.). Wholesale
swallowing of what counsellor says. Difficulties giving
counsellor up at breaks and ends of sessions.

Idealizing or worshipping counsellor, perhaps   45
denigrating self as well, or running down other helpers.

Wish to be the only one in counsellor's life — or the   39, 41
opposite, unable to claim time and attention.

Magical expectations of the counsellor — difficulty   123, 194
accepting own responsibility for change.

Intolerance to frustration of solutions taking time.   34

Hostility to counsellor when he appears uncaring by   49
setting limits, or not obviously helping.

Demanding of more time and attention, perhaps also   37, 45
of physical affection (being held rather than sex).

Putting the counsellor (male or female) into a maternal   59
role, with the implication being: '*hold* me', '*feed* me',
'*touch* me' — conveyed in tone and manner even if
not in words.

Unable to relate to counsellor because caught up in   55, 150
inner phantasy world — bizarre thoughts and
associations which are hardly responsive to counsellor's

interventions. (Probably indicates serious disturbance
and need for referral.)

The counsellor's task, as related to O.S. Themes

Reliability and consistency; keeping to time, not outwardly panicking when client feels overwhelmed, but not acceding to demands for more except in special circumstances. Careful and sensitive setting of limits.	34, 37
Creation of climate of trust, where client does not fear rejection for what they feel or say; where client does not have to fear damaging counsellor by being open about demands or anger.	34, 49
Help clients distinguish what lies in them and what lies in others — observe projections and negative internalization.	31, 32, 46
Refusal to collude with splitting of helpers — not allowing self to be set up as 'good parent' while others seen as bad. Encouragement of positive and negative feelings towards the same 'object'.	45
Help dependent clients to find their own self-esteem, so that they might become less dependent on supplies of love from the counselling.	37
Especially towards the close of counselling dependent clients, encourage the positive signs of independence.	38
Attempt to tie in previous difficulties of trusting so that difficulty in trusting counsellor can be understood.	34
Allow frustration and anger with counsellor to be voiced, especially at failure to supply all client's needs.	34, 38, 49

Main
references

Distinguish between appropriate and inappropriate   50
guilt, and help client understand that the strength of
feelings can be related to the 'helplessness' of the
frightened child within.

With seriously disturbed clients: Support all positive   55
indications of positive thinking, wishes or action, and
support all realistic perceptions of situations.

Try to remain a good enough figure for any   46
suggestion of referral to be seen as caring, not
rejecting. Encourage client's wish for more specialist
help where this is expressed.

Keep clear of interpretations, unless able to discuss
the client first with someone experienced in working
with the more disturbed.

Little and often may be more appropriate than
longer weekly sessions, especially at the height of a
crisis.

Attempt to find out about any psychiatric history,   35, 45, 81
suicide attempts, and about previous episodes of similar
disturbance — all this will assist a supervisor to assess
the risk, and plan most appropriate help.

(2) The Anal/Authority/Autonomy Stage (A.S.)

*Indications of satisfactory development and possible aims in
counselling*

Self-esteem, competence, trust in one's capabilities.   121, 125,
                                                           180

Sense of order, justice and fairness — the 'world' felt to   83, 177
be basically fair.

Confident self-control without being over-controlled. Sense of 'will-power' and ability to sustain effort.	63
Ability to let go feelings in appropriate ways.	63
Ability to take measured risks.	74, 75
Ability to make judgements of right and wrong in an informed way, and for oneself.	59, 144
Acceptance of the authority of self and others, but also able to question and confront authority figures when necessary. Acceptance of personal responsibility.	76, 80, 126
Balance between work, play and relaxation. Able to give expression to artistic and/or physical side.	73
Sense of inner order, but also capable of adaptation and change. Tolerance of temporary disorder or uncertainty.	126
Acceptance and enjoyment of the whole body — especially those parts colloquially known as 'nasty/dirty'.	137
Sense of co-ordination — being able to do things without fearing mistakes (i.e. able to make mistakes).	61
Sharing of authority and decision-making in marital or other (e.g. working) partnerships.	158
Ability to relinquish authority over children as they mature.	142, 170
Ability to let go of obvious authority and active responsibility with increasing age, so that others can take over.	183, 188

Main
references

Difficulties associated with A.S. themes

Perfectionism — over-tidy and over-organized — *or*   13, 71, 126,
disorganization (i.e. of external affairs, not the internal   195
disintegration more typical of the O.S.)

Obsessional rituals/thoughts; checking.   71, 195

Rigid self-control, unable to let go, emotional   63, 74
constipation.

Intellectualization, fear of feelings spoiling sense of   63
order or control.

Fear of soiling or spoiling, especially of anger spoiling.   68, 77

Unable to take risks, requiring certainty. Panic about   72, 75, 178
conflicts because of the need for all to be clear.   195
Obsessional moving from one side of a situation to the
other in trying to make a decision, therefore not
making it for fear of getting it wrong.

Rigid control of others. Law-and-order types,   80, 147
sometimes with strict religious moralizing.   158, 195

Wanting rules, advice, orders.   75, 195

Over-critical of self and others — masochistic.   65, 81, 195

Over-protective of self and others.   76

Afraid of getting hands dirty (literally or   188, 197
metaphorically). Shame at lack of bodily control.

Need to achieve over-stressed in self or others   170
(especially children as symbols of parent's need to
achieve).

Workaholic — inability to play, or relax in
play; — inability to relax and let go in old age; *or*   67, 73, 126
inability to work because it is seen as conformist, or   159, 191

through fear of criticism of work and consequent loss of
self-esteem.

Resentful submission to authority figures.   75

Unable to be critical of others, especially authorities.   75, 195

Rejection of authority just because it is authority.   78

Inability to be an authority figure, to manage others   80
and set limits.

Over-conformity to peer group, society or authority   147, 177
figures; needing structures.

Foreclosed adolescent type.   147.

Shame and doubt.   68

Need to 'confess' in order to feel 'clean' without wish to   195
look at underlying difficulties.

Feeling loved only if able to meet other's or own   70, 159
'conditions' — conditional love.

Uncontrolled letting go of feelings — impulsive.   63

Soiling or spoiling others (sadistic) or self (masochistic).   81
Sex used to spoil or control others.

Explosive anger as a result of bottling it up and letting   77
go too forcefully.

Learning difficulties associated with perfectionism, fear   125, 180
of criticism, authority problems.

Sexual performance more important than mutual   159
enjoyment.

Parenting of children overinfluenced by wish to be   63, 73, 175
perfect parent (perhaps using books as providing 'rules'
of child-rearing).

Turning the tables on old people by becoming the   170
authoritarian 'parent' to them.

Main
references

The relationship style in the counsellor–client interaction (A.S.)

Holding back or holding in feelings.   63, 77

Withholding of anger because of fear of its   78
explosiveness or fear of it spoiling.

Keeping exciting feelings at a distance — through   64
intellectualizing, vagueness, lot of detail, trivia,
precision, or through boring and monotonous talk and
delivery.

Difficulty acting upon counselling insights because of   72
obsessional ruminations; listening but unable to make
decisions for fear of getting them wrong.

Shame — head bowed, eyes averted; weight of guilt;   69
shifting blame at times on to others, denying own
responsibility.

Difficulty revealing thoughts and feelings through   69
shame.

Imagery of soiling, disgust, mess, 'dirty', 'foul', etc.

Inability to accept what counsellor says because   68, 102
makes him into an authority figure. 'Yes . . . but'   138, 78
remarks. Might be accompanied by sullenness, constant
complaining.

Hesitancy about, or fear of counsellor taking   14, 78
control; not wishing to feel tied down; might result in
feelings in each of struggling to control other, or
arguments.

Fear of criticism and judgement from the   65, 127
counsellor — client perhaps also over-critical of self.

Critical of the counsellor, hair-splitting; or splitting   78, 79
different helpers so that one 'authority' set against
another, one played off against the other.

Main
references

Wanting rules and advice from the counsellor.   75, 80

Seeing the helper in a paternal (authority) role,   76, 177
whatever the gender of the counsellor, or of the
dominant authority figure in the family of origin: '*make
me, tell me, do it for me,* approve of my actions . . .
etc,'

The counsellor's task, as related to A.S. themes

Avoid actually becoming an authority figure — i.e.   76, 177
avoid laying down rules or giving advice (unless a
person is very disturbed and management is
appropriate.)

Observe to the client the wish to make the counsellor   68, 75, 127
more authoritarian or expert than he can be — point
out occasions when the client appears to be giving
away own authority to the counsellor. Help client to
become own authority in a positive (not punitive) way.

Link the wish for, or fear of, counsellor as authority   75
figure, to the way client felt about parental authority.

Watch for client's fear of counsellor being critical,   65, 78, 127
thereby making it more difficult for some things to be
said.

Bring out feelings/excitement hidden behind   64, 78
monotony, intellectualization, etc, — remembering that
client is also afraid to own such feelings, feels 'bad'
about them.

Help client distinguish between appropriate and   50, 68
inappropriate guilt and/or shame.

Locate client's fear of judgement or criticism, where   66
projected on to others, as in fact within self.

*Main
references*

The Genital/Oedipal/Rivalry/Social Stage (G.S)

*Indications of satisfactory development and possible aims in
counselling*

Detachment from parents to be able to make independent choice of sexual partner, not too influenced by relationship with parents (especially by negative factors).	92, 98, 115 156, 159
Internalization of positive qualities of parents and significant others — the formation of positive ego-ideal, positive aims and aspirations in relationships.	93, 115
Firm foundation of sexual identity, both in respect of predominant gender orientation, but also able to accept homosexual aspects of self, which can be sublimated in relationships.	86, 139 167
Acceptance of physical differences between the sexes without fear or envy.	89
Acceptance of sexual feelings as wholesome, but also able to sublimate (and inhibit direct expression of sexuality) in the majority of human relationships.	97, 115
Ability to engage in whole relationship with a sexual partner, in which the sexual, affectionate, caring and other feelings can come together.	103, 115, 159
As parents to be able to accept the child's sexuality and love, neither crushing it, nor colluding wth the child against the partner.	93, 100
Ability to share and co-operate with others, in the family, peer group, in mixed gender groups, etc.	112, 157

Ability to compete in genuinely competitive situations,   112, 178
without guilt at succeeding or anger/shame/depression
at not succeeding.

Difficulties associated with G.S. themes

Triangular situations: splitting of sex/affection/care on
                    to two or more persons;   103, 159

                    parents using children as allies   93, 160, 167
                    against each other, or as
                    replacements for partner; children
                    coming between parents;

                    'eternal triangles':   96
                    two men/one woman
                    two women/one man.

Over-competitive: seeing situations as competitive   112, 129
when they are not.

Jealousy.   112, 139

Fear of rivalry/competition, either of losing out or of   112, 129,
winning.   178

Inhibition of sexuality through guilt or fear of rejection.   97, 102

Sex seen as threatening because too associated with   103, 159
oedipal ties.

Rejection of child's love by parents, *or* over-closeness   97
permitted or actively encouraged.

Inhibition of curiosity, initiative and adventure, in   102, 103,
sexual matters, but in other matters too.   130

Exhibitionism or furtive sexuality (voyeurism) and   99, 104, 129
implied doubts about sexuality in such behaviour.   196

Main
references

Histrionic/hysteric/Don Juan/sexual tease.   105

Feeling inferior to peers, especially members of own   89, 103, 139
sex.

Difficulties identifying with parent of same   103, 115
sex — internalizing their negative rather than their
positive qualities.

Ability to relate to opposite sex only as long as they are   95, 99, 103,
'safe' and unattainable — that is not sexually arousing,   140
'safely' married or engaged, untouchable, distant
figures.

Feelings of inadequacy as a man or woman.   89, 187

Sexual relations which show need for a partner who is   103
'inferior' or submissive, who does not present too great
a threat, for example paedophilia (attraction to
children), *or* attacks on women because they represent
a threat.

Chauvinism and extremist feminism such as attacks   87, 104
(physical and verbal) on the opposite sex. Denigration
of the opposite sex.

Confusion of sexual identity: fears of showing   86, 107,
'masculine' or 'feminine' characteristics.   160, 167

Anxieties about homosexuality.   66, 76, 88,
                                                              103, 107

Learning difficulties associated with inhibitions,   128
competitiveness, or highly charged emotions towards
teachers.

The relationship style in the counsellor–client interaction (G.S.)

Difficulty talking about sex, as being 'naughty but nice'   99, 102, 111
for example, sex seen as threat because too exciting
(unlike A.S., where sex seen as dirty, disgusting).

Use of stimulating intimate talk to excite the counsellor: 105, 144,
seduction and perhaps rejection of helper through talk.   162
Counter-transference feelings of excitement in
counsellor *may* be an indication of this.

Wish for counsellor to be friend/partner or lover.   99, 161, 163

Attempts to make 'alliance' with counsellor against
another helper, or against client's partner: in the case
of two helpers, especially when one is male and other
female.

Jealousy of others seen by the counsellor, or of his   114
outside relationships. Wanting to be special: *primus
inter pares*, not the only one as in O.S.

Comparison of self with others seen by counsellor,   114
perhaps disguising wish to be special.

Curiosity about others seen by counsellor, or about   114
counsellor's private life.

Gender of counsellor may be important — fears of the   111
opposite sex; or of homosexual anxiety. May be seen
in definite request to see a male or a female counsellor.

Difficulty for client to accept what counsellor says   77
because seems submissive, especially difficult if
opposite sex or same sex seen as a threat.

*Main
references*

The counsellor's task, as related to G.S. themes

Enable clients to talk about their own sexuality, their   99
feelings towards others, their views of their own
attractiveness.

Look for difficulties (e.g. previous experiences) which   98, 101
lead them to doubt themselves as sexually attractive (or
as too sexually attractive).

Help clients to feel appreciated by the counsellor,   99
without this becoming seductive, nor holding out the
promise of a special relationship.

Accept the sexual feelings in the counselling   99, 102, 131
relationship (in client or in self), without deliberately   162
encouraging them, nor playing on them.

Allow anger/frustration to be expressed that the   99
counsellor cannot be a friend/special person; link in
perhaps with the unattainable parent figure.

Avoid being caught by splitting, becoming an ally for   96
the client against another helper or member of the
family.

Watch for rivalry between client/counsellor, especially   111, 114
where both of same gender; or when working with   131, 160
client who sees counsellor of opposite sex as a
threatening representative of that sex; or watch for
feelings of inferiority in the client when comparing self
to the 'image' client has of the counsellor's gender.

Question assumptions that personal qualities are in   88
themselves signs of 'masculinity' or 'femininity'.

BIBLIOGRAPHY

Abraham, K. (1927) *Selected Papers,* Hogarth Press, London

Alexander, F. and French, T. M. (1946) *Psychoanalytic Therapy,* Ronald Press, New York.

Anzieu, D. (1984) *The Group and the Unconscious,* Routledge & Kegan Paul, London.

Badcock, C. R. (1980) *The Psychoanalysis of Culture,* Basil Blackwell, Oxford.

Becker, E. (1972) *The Birth and Death of Meaning,* Penguin, Harmondsworth.

Belotti, E. (1975) *Little Girls,* Writers and Readers Publishing Co-operative, London.

Berne, E. (1968) *Games People Play,* Penguin, Harmondsworth.

Bettelheim, B. (1983) *Freud and Man's Soul,* Chatto and Windus/Hogarth Press, London.

Case, R. (1978) When birth is also a funeral, *Journal of Pastoral Care* (USA), Vol. XXXII, 1.

Chodorow, N. (1978) *The Reproduction of Mothering,* University of California.

Cleese, J. and Skynner, R. (1983) *Families: and How to Survive Them,* Methuen, London.

Collick, E. (1982) *Through Grief: the Experience of Bereavement,* Mirfield Publications, Mirfield, Yorks.

Dinnerstein, D. (1978) *The Rocking of the Cradle and the Ruling of the World,* Souvenir Press, London.

Dominian, J. (1980) *Marital Pathology,* Darton Longman and Todd, London.

Dunne, J. S. (1979) *Time and Myth,* S.C.M. Press, London.

Erikson, E. (1965) *Childhood and Society,* Penguin, Harmondsworth.

Erikson, E. (1978) *Toys and Reasons,* Marion Boyars, London.

Fairbairn, W. R. D. (1952) *Psychoanalytic Studies of the Personality,* Tavistock Publications, London.

Fenichel, O. (1946) *The Psychoanalytical Theory of Neurosis,* Routledge & Kegan Paul, London.

Fowler, J. W. (1981) *Stages of Faith: the Psychology of Human Development and the Quest for Meaning,* Harper and Row, New York.

Freud, A. (1973) *Normality and Pathology in Childhood,* Penguin, Harmondsworth.

Freud, S. (1963) *Introductory Lectures on Psychoanalysis,* Hogarth Press, London.

Freud, S. (1964) *New Introductory Lectures on Psychoanalysis,* Hogarth Press, London.

Fromm, E. (1967) *Psychoanalysis and Religion,* Bantam Books, New York.

Golan, N. (1981) *Passing Through Transitions,* Collier Macmillan, London.

Guntrip, H. (1961) *Personality Structure and Human Interaction,* Hogarth Press, London.

Guntrip, H. (1968) *Schizoid Phenomena, Object Relations and the Self,* Hogarth Press, London.

Haines, D. G. (1978) Paths and companions, *Journal of Pastoral Care* (USA), Vol. XXXII, 1.

Hartung, B. (1979) The capacity to enter latency in learning pastoral psychotherapy, *Journal of Supervision and Training in Ministry,* Vol. 2 (Chicago, Illinois).

Jackson, E. (ed.) (1982) *Counselling the Dying,* S.C.M. Press, London.

Jacobs M. (1976) Naming and labelling, *Contact: Journal of Pastoral Studies,* 1976, 3.

Jacobs M. (1981) Stuck, in *Work and No Work,* British Association for Counselling, Rugby.

Jacobs M. (1982) *Still Small Voice,* S.P.C.K., London.

Jacobs M. (1985) *Swift to Hear,* S.P.C.K., London.

Johnstone, C. B. (1982) On asking the right question *Journal of Pastoral Care* (USA), Vol. XXXVI, 1.

Jung, C. G. (1953) *Two Essays on Analytical Psychology,* Routledge & Kegan Paul, London.

Kirkley-Best, E. et al. (1982) On stillbirth: an open letter to the clergy, *Journal of Pastoral Care* (USA), Vol. XXXVI, 1.

Kohlberg, L. (1963) *Moral Development and Identification* in *Child Psychology,* H. W. Stevenson (ed.), University of Chicago.

Kübler-Ross, E. (1969) *On Death and Dying,* Tavistock Publications, London.

Laufer, M. (1974) *Adolescent Disturbance and Breakdown,* Penguin, Harmondsworth.

Le Carré, J. (1974) *Tinker, Tailor, Soldier, Spy,* Hodder and Stoughton, London.

Le Guin, U. (1971) *A Wizard of Earthsea,* Puffin Books (Penguin), Harmondsworth.

Lewis, C. S. (1971) *A Grief Observed,* Faber Paperbacks, London.

Lowe, G. (1972) *The Growth of Personality,* Penguin, Harmondsworth.

Macquarrie, J. (1966) *Principles of Christian Theology,* S.C.M. Press, London.

Malan, D. H. (1976) *Toward the Validation of Dynamic Psychotherapy,* Plenum Medical Book Co., New York.

Malan, D. H. (1979) *Individual Psychotherapy and the Science of Psychodynamics,* Butterworth, London.

Marcia, J.E. (1975) Development and Validation of Ego-Identity Status, in *Adolescent Behaviour and Society,* R.W. Muuss (ed.) (2nd edn), Random House, New York.

Masson, J. M. (1984) *The Assault on Truth: Freud's Suppression of the Seduction Theory,* Faber, London.

Miller, A. (1979) Depression and grandiosity as related forms of narcissistic disturbances, *International Review of Psychoanalysis,* 1979, 6:72.

Mitchell, K. (1982) A death and a community, *Journal of Pastoral Care* (USA), Vol. XXXVI, 1.

Murray Parkes, C. (1978) *Bereavement — Studies of Grief in Adult Life,* Penguin, Harmondsworth.

Muuss, R. W. (1968) *Theories of Adolescence* (2nd edn.), Random House, New York.

Piaget, J. (1950) *The Psychology of Intelligence,* Routledge & Kegan Paul, London.

Prins, H. A. (1975) A danger to themselves and others (social workers and potentially dangerous clients), *British Journal of Social Work,* 5, pp. 297–309.

Prins, H. A. (1980) *Offenders, Deviants or Patients,* Tavistock Publications, London.

Rayner, E. (1978) *Human Development* (2nd edn), George Allen and Unwin, London.

Rubins, J. L. (1978) *Karen Horney,* Weidenfeld and Nicolson, London.

Rycroft, C. (1972) *A Critical Dictionary of Psychoanalysis,* Penguin, Harmondsworth.

Ryle, A. (1973) *Student Casualties,* Penguin, Harmondsworth.

Sachs, H. (1948) *Masks of Love and Life,* Sci-Art Publishers, Cambridge, Mass.

Segal, H. (1973) *Introduction to the Work of Melanie Klein* (enlarged edn), Hogarth Press, London.

Sendak, M. (1970) *Where the Wild Things Are,* Puffin Books (Penguin), Harmondsworth.

Speck, P. and Ainsworth-Smith, I. (1982) *Letting Go: Caring for the Dying and Bereaved,* S.P.C.K., London.

Storr, A. (1979) *The Art of Psychotherapy,* Secker and Warburg, London.

Study Commission on the Family (1980) *Happy Families: a Discussion Document.*

Thomas, D. M. (1981) *The White Hotel,* Penguin, Harmondsworth.

Thompson, F. (1973) *Lark Rise to Candleford,* Penguin, Harmondsworth.

Thurber, J. (1962) *The Thirteen Clocks,* Puffin Books (Penguin), Harmondsworth.

Weatherhead, L. (1963) *Psychology, Religion and Healing* (2nd edn revised), Hodder and Stoughton, London.

Winnicott, D. W. (1964) *The Child, the Family and the Outside World,* Penguin, Harmondsworth.

Winnicott, D. W. (1965a) *The Family and Individual Development,* Tavistock Publications, London.

Winnicott, D. W. (1965b) *The Maturational Processes and the Facilitating Environment,* Hogarth Press, London.

Winnicott, D. W. (1974) *Playing and Reality,* Penguin, Harmondsworth.

INDEX

(see also Appendix for references to main themes)

co-operation with others,   129, 172
co-ordination, physical,   13, 61, 63, 74,
  83
counselling: as encouraging
  introversion,   42;
  as teaching,   124;
  ending of,   203;
  humour in,   74–75;
  intimacy of,   161–163;
  latency aspects of,   131–133;
  of partners,   163;
counsellor: anxiety of,   173;
  as advantaged,   176, 184;
  as authority-figure,   80, 131, 144,
    177–178, 184;
  as super-ego projection,   67, 111,
    127, 151;
  as unobtainable,   99, 161–163;
  beliefs of,   197;
  gender of,   111–112;
  generativity stage in,   184;
  idealization of,   45
counter-transference,   13, 132,
  162–163
Country Wife, The,   126
creativity,   172, 182, 184
crisis,   4, 7, 34, 121, 154
critical parent,   7, 67, 102–103,
  125–126
criticism, openness to,   54
cruelty,   77, 81–83, 135
crushes,   98, 121, 135
curiosity,   135:
  infantile sexual,   11, 85, 87, 90

dance and drama,   130
damaged: fear of having,   47;
  by sex,   110
day-dreams,   55, 56, 123
death,   8, 30, 31, 40–41, 48, 94, 128,
  136, 142, 153, 156, 169, 187, 190,
  197–203:
  as psychosomatic,   198;
  effect on marriage of parent's,   97;
  — wishes,   48, 94, 113, 142, 168,
    169
defecation,   61, 121
defences,   11, 41, 45, 46, 68, 78, 123,
  176
delusions,   21

demands, making,   12–13, 37, 38–39,
  47
dementia, senile,   190
denial,   42, 46, 197, 198–199, 200,
  201:
  of death,   197;
  of own strengths,   45
denigration,   45, 91–92:
  of women,   82
dependency,   12–13, 20, 29–30, 32,
  35–39, 43, 58, 99, 123–125, 154,
  157–158, 166, 170, 171, 174–177,
  187, 190, 193
dependability,   33–35, 38
depression,   50, 78, 109, 114, 135,
  142, 149, 154, 168, 176, 197, 201
desire to know,   11
despair,   34, 146
destructive anger,   49–50, 52, 53, 66,
  77–78, 142, 143
destructiveness, self-,   49
detachment from parents,   94–96
detailed speaking,   65
developmental psychology,   4
devil,   69, 194
diagnosis,   21, 23–24
dinosaurs, as persecutory
  objects,   51–52, 54
disappointment,   68
disbelief,   200
discipline,   78
disgust,   34, 102, 138
distancing in relationships,   34, 99
  (*see also* withdrawal, emotional)
disturbance, serious,   22, 30, 46, 89,
  106, 149–151
divorce,   142, 156, 161, 200
doctors,   56, 72–73, 75–76, 101, 151,
  169, 173, 201
Dominian, J.,   156
Don Juan,   105–106
doubt,   33, 61
drained, feeling,   37
dreams,   8, 16–17, 52–53, 54, 94, 154
drive, lack of,   174–177
drugs,   21, 31–32, 35, 56–57, 145,
  147
dualism,   45
dummy,   37
Dunne, J.,   43